KODANSHA INTERNATIONAL
Tokyo • New York • London

KABUKI

Masakatsu Gunji

Photographs by **Chiaki Yoshida**

Introduction by **Donald Keene**

Pls. 1–9. *Sukeroku Yukari no Edo-zakura*

Pls. 1–8. One of the "Eighteen Favorite Kabuki Plays," this piece presents its hero in the double identity of Sukeroku and Soga no Gorō. Seeking a sword that has been stolen from his family, Sukeroku comes to the Yoshiwara gay quarters, where he deliberately picks quarrels and makes others draw their swords so that he may have a chance to inspect them. In the course of doing so, he comes across his rival, Ikyū. (*Sukeroku*, Ichikawa Danjūrō; *Agemaki*, Nakamura Utaemon; *Ikyū*, Kataoka Nizaemon; *Shiratama*, Nakamura Shikan)

Pl. 1. (*Overleaf*) Arriving at the gay quarters, Sukeroku opens his umbrella, holds it up high and tilted to one side in his right hand, while his left hand, slightly clenched, appears from inside the front of his kimono. Facing the audience, he stands with legs together and to the sound of the clappers, strikes a *mie*. This marks the end of his grand entrance.

Pl. 2. (*Title page*) In front of the brothel Miura-ya in the main thoroughfare of the gay quarters, courtesans are lined up in brilliant array.

Pls. 3–8. Sukeroku appears for the first time on the *hanamichi*. Preserving the Edo period style of entry, he approaches wearing a purple band around his head and carrying an umbrella in his hand, an idealization of the style affected by dashing young men-about-Edo of the day. Sukeroku's entrance is accompanied by the sound of *katōbushi* music, the use of which is reserved for the role of Sukeroku alone.

Pl. 9. As the story develops, Suke-roku· realizes that the sword drawn by Ikyū is Tomokirimaru, the one he has been looking for. He draws closer to Ikyū, but Ikyū hides the sword behind him. Agemaki comes between the two and prevents a fight. In the second scene, the three actors change costumes, Agemaki's, inspired by the Tanabata Festival, features a white outer robe, and an *obi* with a poetry card (*tanzaku*) and colored-paper pattern; Ikyū's, taken from Peking opera, bears a design suggesting an emperor. Sukeroku changes into a *kamiko* (literally, "paper robe"), indicating that he has fallen on hard times.

Distributed in the United States by Kodansha America, Inc., 114 Fifth Avenue, New York, N.Y. 10011, and in the United Kingdom and continental Europe by Kodansha Europe Ltd., 95 Aldwych, London WC2B 4JF.
Published by Kodansha International Ltd., 17-14, Otowa 1-chome, Bunkyo-ku, Tokyo 112, and Kodansha America, Inc.
Copyright © 1985 by Kodansha International Ltd. All rights reserved. Printed in Japan.

First edition, 1985
    96 10 9 8 7 6

Original edition translated by John Bester. Revised and new material for this edition translated by Janet Goff. Photo credit: Fig. 303, Keizo Kaneko.

Editor's Note: Japanese proper names are treated in Japanese style: family name first and given name second. Actors no longer living as of June 1985, are indicated by generation numbers appearing in conjunction with their names. Certain plays are illustrated with photographs taken from more than one performance and may thus feature different actors.

Library of Congress Cataloging in Publication Data

Gunji, Masakatsu, 1913–
    Kabuki.

    Bibliography: p.
    Includes indexes.
    1. Kabuki.   I. Yoshida, Chiaki, 1918–
II. Title.
PN2924.5.K3G7813   1985   792'.0952   85–5197
ISBN 4–7700–1232–2 (in Japan)
ISBN 0–87011–732–7 (U.S.)

CONTENTS

INTRODUCTION

I T EMBARRASSES me now to mention it, but I wrote my first comments on kabuki long before I ever witnessed a performance. On the basis of some readings in the texts of kabuki plays I opined that kabuki was "a modernized, expanded, and rather debased form of the Nō." It was certainly audacious, if not irresponsible, to have characterized with such confidence a form of theater that I knew only from books, yet if I may say a word in my defense, other scholars have not hesitated to analyze and evaluate ancient Greek drama (though no one can be sure what a performance was like), and a Shakespearean expert would not refuse to include in his discussion such works as *King John* or *Pericles*, simply because he had never had the chance to see them. The tradition of considering a play as a special kind of literary work, rather than as an element in a theatrical performance, is obviously deep-rooted in the West, as these instances suggest. The illiterate question that still is asked of foreign visitors: "Who is the Shakespeare of your country?" is indicative of the basic assumption that in all parts of the world—and not only where English is spoken—the supreme works of literature must be in the form of drama. In the case of Nō and Bunraku, two Japanese theatrical arts I have described elsewhere, it is indeed possible to judge whether a play is good or bad by reading it, and the presentation alone cannot make a bad play into a good one. But in the case of kabuki any such judgments as those I expressed years ago, based exclusively on a reading knowledge of the plays, are doomed inevitably to miss the mark.

Kabuki as a theater is above all theatrical. Such literary merits as the texts possess are of no greater importance than the many other elements contributing to the success of the whole, especially the dance, costuming, and stage effects. A knowledge of the text alone gives one no more idea of the total impression of a kabuki play than, say, a knowledge of the libretto gives of *Il Trovatore*. Every element involved is exploited to yield the most intense possible dramatic effect, with such success indeed that, having started with my initial prejudices against kabuki, I am now convinced that it truly provides one of the supreme theatrical experiences of the world.

Of the different varieties of Japanese theater—Nō, Bunraku, kabuki, and modern drama—kabuki is the easiest for a foreigner to enjoy. The moment the curtain is pulled aside to reveal the magnificent spectacle on the great stage, even the most blasé theatergoer feels a unique excitement. Kabuki unashamedly makes use of even the crudest devices (as well as the subtlest) to achieve its ends. The Japanese are known for their fondness for suggestion and understatement, revealed in their landscape gardening, the tea ceremony, or the Nō theater, but kabuki delights in the wildest exaggeration. As the play *Shibaraku* starts, the curtain is drawn back to reveal a display of warriors, court ladies, priests, and strongmen arrayed across the immensely wide stage. To emphasize the ferocity of the strongmen, their heavily padded bodies are painted brick red, and their faces are boldly decorated. They speak with contemptuous sneers and fierce rolling of the eyes. But at a cry from the *hanamichi*, the passageway through the audience, the whole company quakes with fear; even the strongmen who seemed a moment ago to be ready to defy heaven itself now cringe in dismay. What manner of creature could have so terrorized them, we wonder, only for the hero to enter, wearing a preposterously long sword and dressed in a costume with hanging sleeves almost as big as himself. What more dramatic entrance for an actor exists? Yet anyone reading the text of *Shibaraku* could only suppose the play was absurd, childish fantasy. Seen in the kabuki theater it is nothing short of thrilling.

Unlike the Nō theater in which the actors efface their own personalities, sometimes behind masks, and any attempt of an actor to call attention to his particular talents would be in grossly bad taste, kabuki gives full play to the individuality of each performer and even exaggerates it. The actor is always acting, and the audience, far from desiring the illusion that it is watching reality, delights in the knowledge that it is in the theater. Nobody takes it amiss even if in the middle of a dramatic scene an actor steps out of his role to present to the audience his son or protégé and request its kind patronage. If an actor is asked in the course of a play who is his favorite performer he unhesitatingly names himself, to the amusement of the spectators. Audiences go to kabuki above all to see the great actors. Of course there are favorites among the works performed, and the real aficionados may know by heart whole sections of dialogue, but the chief interest of a given day's performance consists in observing how particular actors respond to the demands of their parts and modify them. As for the dramatists—the putative "Shakespeares of Japan"—they are of hardly any interest except to the scholars. Most spectators are unaware who wrote even their favorite plays, and the programs sold in the theater, though devoting much space to gossip about the actors and painstakingly listing every last musician in the company, often fail to mention the names of the dramatists. Surely no more striking evidence could be found for the supremacy of the actors in this theater.

Kabuki, unlike the aristocratic Nō, began and developed as a popular theater. Today, as the result of the competition from other varieties of entertainment, the movies and television especially, the appeal of kabuki for the general public has undoubtedly been seriously weakened. The actors still retain their followings, but where formerly there were strongholds of kabuki all over the country, today the actors are almost all included in a few companies of star performers, based in Tokyo, who make only occasional visits elsewhere. Inevitably this has deprived kabuki of its original basis of support in the common people, and the traditional cries from the audience, greeting actors on their appearances or praising their skill, no longer explode like firecrackers throughout the theater, but have a hollow, cultivated ring. Kabuki is still as brilliant a spectacle as ever, but it has become well-mannered. Instead of a raucous audience in the theater for a day of fun and feasting, it now plays increasingly before audiences as severely attentive as those at the Comédie Française. There is no danger that kabuki will disappear: the government has conspicuously extended its protection, notably in the form of the splendid new National Theater. More plays than ever, especially those from the half-forgotten repertoire, are being presented. But kabuki is changing rapidly, despite the faithful adherence to traditions, as the old audiences of plebeian lovers of kabuki dwindled, intimidated perhaps by the elegant surroundings or by the elevated prices of the tickets.

Without its accustomed audience of connoisseurs able to detect the slightest variation from the normal manner of delivering a line and moving the body or to evaluate unerringly the abilities of actors of roughly equal standing, kabuki must inevitably change, for it cannot count on the give-and-take between actors and spectators that was so important in the creation of the art. At this pivotal moment in the history of kabuki nothing could be more desired than an authoritative statement on what kabuki is and what it has meant to the Japanese people since its inception, and no one is better qualified than Professor Gunji to make it. His scholarly researches have yielded many important discoveries about kabuki, especially in its formative period, and he has traced in the dances and playlets performed at religious festivals all over Japan today many elements submerged or even lost in kabuki, suggesting how intimately kabuki has been associated with every aspect of Japanese life. Professor Gunji is a true connoisseur, whose knowledge of kabuki has been formed not only through his extensive study of the written materials but through innumerable experiences in the theater. Every student of kabuki, whether in Japan or the West, is indebted to him for his many publications, and it is an occasion for celebration that the present synthesis of his researches should appear in a worthy form, accompanied by splendid photographs that transmit to the reader the visual beauty of a performance. We can only hope that kabuki will continue for many years to come to dazzle audiences with its magnificent theatricality, but if by some misfortune the art should falter, Professor Gunji's book will serve as an invaluable record of this most important branch of the theatrical heritage of the Japanese.

DONALD KEENE

REMINISCENCES

I N THE days when I was at university, it was considered unhealthy for a student to show too avid an enthusiasm for kabuki, and one went to the theater with a certain inescapable sense of guilt. The air of ill-repute that traditionally surrounded the act of theatergoing seems, in fact, to have persisted right up until the time of World War II.

Cramming my student's cap into my pocket, I would run up the stairs to the gallery, and worm my way through the standing throngs to the very front. It was only then, when my hands finally grasped the rail at the front of the gallery, that I relaxed: at last, I had only to wait for the magic world of kabuki to unfold itself before me.

From the gallery of the Kabuki-za, one gazed down into a deep chasm. An actor making his appearance along the *hanamachi* was completely invisible until he had reached the point where the *hanamichi* joined the stage. In the same way, whenever an actor standing on a high dais placed on the stage stood up, his head vanished from sight behind the top of the proscenium arch. Yet, on the other hand, there was no place like the gallery for savoring the stirring calls from audience to actor that burst out at moments of high excitement. With their split-second timing, they brought the stage scene suddenly and excitingly to life. More than any book could hope to do, they conveyed something of the essential nature of kabuki as a dramatic art.

It was at the Kabuki-za that I was first exposed to the art of Nakamura Utaemon V—that brilliant, magnificent art that combined the steadiness of a mighty rock with the grace of a heron in flight. By my time, his legs were uncertain, and his entrances were all made on the revolving stage, yet such was the impression he made on me that I can still see him vividly in my mind's eye as the heroine Yodogimi, or Miyagino, or as the Taira hero Kiyomori. To an astonishing degree, his presence seemed to fill, to dominate, the whole stage.

I remember, too, the incomparable youth and freshness of Ichimura Uzaemon XV in such "young man" roles as Miuranosuke or Gompachi; the wonderful profile—like a face out of an *ukiyo-e* print—of Sawamura Sōjūrō in the role of Karukaya; the way the acting of Sawamura Gennosuke seemed momentarily to bring the whole of old Edo to life again; and the inimitably Kyoto-Osaka style of Enjaku. Compared with these men of an older generation, actors such as Onoe Kikugorō VI—so well known that people referred to him simply as "The Sixth"— Nakamura Kichiemon, and Ichikawa Sadanji had a different, more contemporary air, close to our own generation. In a sense, one felt more personally in touch with them, but they failed to strike one with awe.

Even so, my first experience of kabuki after the war, when shortly after the close of hostilities, I went to see the venerable Nakamura Baigyoku, then on a visit from Osaka at the Tokyo Theater, was an overwhelmingly moving experience. Together with a feeling that the war was really over at last, the occasion inspired an immense thankfulness for the mere fact of being still alive; I had never realized until then just how strong was the impression of sheer life that the kabuki can convey.

Through these varied experiences, I made the acquaintance of a world of beauty and of life that I could never have known through literature, or indeed any other art. Dramatically, kabuki is by no means so well tailored as either modern Japanese drama or the drama of the West. There are not a few times when one is bored—or repelled, even, by the suffocating world of feudal morality. Yet these things do not matter: what matters is the blazing moments of beauty, of unquenchable life, that make up for everything else.

For me at least, those moments were enough to set my heart pounding, to make me forget all the patches of tedium, and to summon once again from the penitential fires of boredom the phoenix of artistic illusion. The effect was unexpected, overwhelming. "Art" in kabuki is something more than mere techniques of acting. It is the summation of a way of life; it is the distillation of a long tradition and the sensibility of a nation.

There are times when art occurs without relation to the original nature or literal theme of drama—when, for example, it crops up improbably in the most unabashedly erotic love scene or the most bloodthirsty murder scene. Yet, wherever it occurs, it brings with it something that one is forced to recognize as fundamental to the eternal human values.

Kabuki is innocent of the ritual qualities, the religious meanings with which *bugaku* and Nō are imbued. If it is, in any sense, a "Way" as those other arts are, then that "Way" takes the form of a hidden path through the dense forest of human nature. Indeed, might not that very fact account for the increasing interest that kabuki is attracting throughout the world today? Might not its appeal be due precisely to those universally artistic and human qualities that triumph over all its apparent exoticism?

THE SPIRIT OF KABUKI

FOUR CLASSICAL performing arts survive in Japan today: the court dances known as *bugaku*; the Nō theater; Bunraku, the puppet theater; and kabuki. Each of them has achieved its own individual type of beauty. In the case of *bugaku* that beauty might be described as stately and elegant, while in the Nō it is remote, subtle, faintly mysterious. These two types of beauty, in Japanese *yūga* and *yūgen* respectively, also represented the generally accepted aesthetic ideals of the ages in which they evolved. The beauty of both Bunraku and kabuki, however, is too complex and comprises too many different elements to be so easily summarized.

Bunraku and kabuki both came into existence around the same time; they grew side by side, and each exerted a considerable influence on the other's development. It is natural, therefore, that their ideals of beauty should have much in common. These ideals are difficult to define in words, but perhaps one might say that both Bunraku and kabuki sought to give expression, through all the varied aesthetic forms at their command, to the joys and sorrows of the common people living in a feudal society. In a sense, the beauty of the Bunraku puppet theater is aesthetically more "pure" than that of kabuki. On the other hand, it lacks the vivid sense of humanity and vitality that only flesh-and-blood actors can convey to an audience.

The art of *bugaku* was nurtured by the imperial courts of ancient times, while the Nō theater developed under the protection of the medieval shogun. Both forms are accordingly characterized by a certain aristocratic grace and economy. Bunraku and kabuki, on the other hand, were an integral part of the lives of the ordinary people during the premodern Edo period. They were dependent on the patronage of the masses, and were often forced to pander to their likes and dislikes in order to maintain their own economic independence—with the result that they contain undeniable elements of banality and vulgarity. What is remarkable, however, is the degree to which those who were responsible for creating the kabuki drama refused to let it degenerate into a purely popular form appealing to the lowest common denominator in public taste, but used finely developed techniques to create a high degree of formal beauty. Equally remarkable, too, is the innate sense of beauty displayed by the ordinary people, who constantly criticized what they were offered, until there finally emerged a stage art unlike any other the world has known. More remarkable still is that all this took place under the restraints imposed by a feudal society and within the confines of an island country that, for the greater part of kabuki's period of development, was almost entirely isolated from the rest of the world.

Since it was a product of an age when Japanese society was already highly developed, with many modern aspects to its economic structure, kabuki could hardly remain uninfluenced by the aesthetic ideals that governed the other arts of its day, both fine and decorative. Thus its ties were particularly close with the *ukiyo-e* woodblock print and shamisen music. There was a considerable exchange between kabuki and the *ukiyo-e* in both subject matter and use of color; and it was in the kabuki and Bunraku theaters that shamisen music underwent its greatest development. On the other hand, acting and production methods came to be determined to a great extent by the nature of the music used.

The musical element and the pictorial element form, in fact, the two great mainstays of kabuki. The sensitive feeling shown for pictorial beauty largely derives from the necessity to transmute the common people's taste for the grotesque and the erotic into something on a higher aesthetic plane. Even so, it is undeniable that both color and movement are less restrained in kabuki than in the *ukiyo-e* print, a sign of a greater need to pander to the public. Shamisen music, in the same way, was condemned by officials and scholars of the Edo period as licentious. It is certain that it can be sensual and suggestive in a way unknown to the music of Nō, for example, yet that is not to deny that in kabuki it achieves a very great artistic refinement.

In kabuki, tragedy and comedy, realism and romanticism go hand in hand. Elements of the musical and of the realistic drama exist side by side within one and the same play, creating a rich and varied beauty. There is one aesthetic concept, however, that runs throughout the whole, giving it consistency. This is the concept of *yatsushi*.

The idea of *yatsushi*, which has much in common with the spirit of *haikai* (in the *haiku* style, that is, abbreviated and evocative) that established itself in the Edo period, is basically the attempt to modernize everything, to translate it into terms of contemporary society, to parody the old (though not necessarily in the grosser sense) by recreating it in terms of the present and familiar. This means, for instance, that the characters appearing in a play must adopt dual identities; they will appear, perhaps, in contemporary guise, but will make it clear that "in fact" they are well-known characters from the past, and there will be constant crossreferences between the two sets of characters and settings. Kabuki itself, indeed, is no more than a *yatsushi* of Nō and Kyōgen, in the same way that *haiku* is a *yatsushi* of the classical *waka* verse form

Unlike Nō, which was the object of official protection, kabuki was subject to constant oppression by the Tokugawa shogunate—the samurai, in fact, were in theory forbidden even to go to see it. Kabuki lay under a constant shadow of official disapproval, and was not allowed to deal with certain historical facts or with certain subjects of contemporary gossip. Under such circumstances, it naturally tended to present everything "in disguise," and in this sense *yatsushi* was a clever means of presenting actuality in the guise of fiction.

Long years of peace and seclusion from the outside world had left energies that in a large city such as Edo found little other outlet than in devising new and ever more ingenious manners of amusement within the restricted sphere available. A typical example of this was an extension of the idea of *yatsushi* known as *mitate*, a kind of intellectual game in which famous characters or episodes from the classics and history would be updated and appear in—sometimes rather outrageous— contemporary grab and situations. A good example is seen in the "Seven Sages of the Bamboo Grove," familiar figures in Chinese literature as well as in Chinese and Japanese art, who reappear in Edo times as the "Seven Courtesans of the Bamboo Grove." (Typically, there is a pun involved too: the "Seven Courtesans" is written with Chinese characters having the same pronunciation as "Seven Sages.")

The type of "dual identity-double meaning" game represented by *yatsushi* and *mitate*, with all their elaborate ramifications, is one of the most characteristic features of the kabuki. Sukeroku, the dashing hero of the celebrated play *Sukeroku Yukari no Edo-zakura*, comes swaggering into the gay quarters of Yoshiwara in a dual role: he is himself, the dandy of the day who is in love with the courtesan Agemaki; and at the same time he is the medieval figure Soga no Gorō, come to take revenge on the villain who has murdered his father. In the same way, Yaoya Oshichi, daughter of a merchant class family and heroine of a famous Edo period love story, is identified in another play with the Heian period poetess Ono no Komachi. The more eccentric the identification and the more opportunities for ingenuity it offered, the more highly it was appreciated. By ignoring distinctions of historical period and bringing the great figures of history and literature down to the level of the contemporary society, *mitate* won the hearts of the populace of Edo.

Opportunities for *mitate* were constantly being found in the production also, and combined with emphasis on stylized, pictorial beauty in delighting the eyes of the audience. A good example occurs in the play *Soga no Taimen* when, at the end of an act, the four main characters—Kudō, Asaina, and the two Soga brothers—take up predetermined positions on the stage and strike a *mie*, one of the exaggeratedly theatrical poses that are used to mark moments of emotional climax. The effect is striking enough in itself, but audiences of the Edo period knew that it was also intended to represent a crane—symbol of long life and prosperity— flying over the summit of Mt. Fuji. Kudō, who stands on a dais to the right of the stage with a closed fan held upside down in front of his chest, is the crane. The fan represents the bird's beak, while the sword that he holds in his left hand is traditionally supposed to suggest its open wings. Gorō, one of the brothers, who stands in the center of the stage, is the peak of the mountain, while his brother Jūrō and Asaina, who crouch down in front of him on the left of the stage, represent the long slopes that sweep down from it on either side. The plays dealing with the Soga brothers' revenge are considered to be auspicious pieces, and are traditionally performed at the New Year, which is why this particular *mitate* is introduced here. The swordfights that frequently occur in kabuki, despite their apparent bloodthirstiness, also contain many examples of *mitate*, and the various formations into which the participants are arranged in the course of a fight are intended to suggest all kinds of customs and natural phenomena. It is the inventiveness shown in this respect that accounts for much of the interest of such scenes.

Although one speaks of inventiveness, inventiveness alone of course is not enough, and it was the task of *mitate* not only to provide scope for it, but also to impose certain rules that govern it and give it artistic value. And it was the translation of *mitate* into terms as close as possible to the life of the common people, with all the elements of exaggeration and humor it involved, that constituted *yatsushi*.

The beauty of kabuki derives in large measure from this playful, fanciful, elaborately involved attitude, and the four hundred year history of kabuki aesthetics is the history of efforts to use this attitude as a vehicle for serious artistic expression as well as to perfect a set of highly developed acting techniques.

While acting techniques must depend, of course, on individual actors to give them life, kabuki is characterized by certain styles or patterns of acting, known in Japanese as *kata*. The mastery of these requires a great deal of training, and they are handed down in families of actors from generation to generation.

Zeami, the man who brought the Nō theater to maturity, declared in his writings that "the family is continuity." A family tradition of acting may depend on blood relationships, or merely on artistic kinship; in the latter case, ability is the criterion by which a good artist chooses his successor. Generally speaking, this type of system is characteristic of all classical performing arts of Japan; in this one respect, *bugaku*, Nō, Bunraku, and kabuki are all alike. With Bunraku and kabuki however, the strict system whereby a man passes his experience on to a single successor has come to lay emphasis on the technical aspects of an actor's ability rather than on close spiritual contact with his predecessor. The ceremony at which an actor takes over the name of an illustrious elder is primarily a sign that he is carrying on the acting traditions of that family; it is the family, in short, that is important rather than the individual. For this same reason, there has always been a strong code of ethics among actors (as among other Japanese artists), that governs their behavior as artists and their obligations to the family or school to which they belong. To succeed an actor means to take over his art in the name of the family, the sign of the true tradition being the *kata* that the younger actor inherits from him.

Since kabuki makes comparatively little use of dramatic opposition and conflict, the plots tend to consist of the relation of a succession of events, and the acting to be a string of different *kata* arranged so as to show all the different facets of the actor's ability. It is for reasons such as these that kabuki acting techniques place great emphasis on *ma*—the slight dramatic pause left between a particular moment in the narrative as expressed in the music or dialogue, and the bodily movements and facial expressions that correspond to that moment in the acting.

In kabuki, the relationship between acts and scenes is not so taut as in the Western drama, and the formal construction of a kabuki play tends to be weak. The development is reminiscent, rather, of a picture scroll that displays one scene after another as one unrolls it, or of the Japanese *renga*, a long poem consisting of any number of short verses linked together. Each scene, moreover, has extremely well-defined situations, and often constitutes a unit that can exist independently of the rest. It is because so many kabuki plays are not so much organic wholes as a collection of semi-independent parts that it is possible nowadays—when the average theatergoer's stamina is not what it once was—to perform in isolation a single act or two from a long kabuki play. Another factor contributing to the lack of formal coherence is the fact that a play was as often as not a kind of omnibus, with a number of different playwrights assuming responsibility for different parts of the play as vehicles for displaying their own prowess.

This does not mean that the construction of a kabuki play was entirely haphazard; there naturally evolved certain rules of dramaturgy, a kind of *kata* for a play as a whole. This is particularly true of the later stages of kabuki's development, when it was common to use a theme that had often been used before, rewriting it so as to show off the actors' art. Yet the fact remains that careful, compact construction is not kabuki's forte. Indeed, the chief thing that distinguishes kabuki from the drama of the West may be the fact that the play and the acting do not form an integral whole with the play dominant, but move along parallel courses, so that either may take precedence over the other as the case requires.

HISTORY

KABUKI HAD its origins in the "kabuki dance" (*kabuki odori*) that Okuni, a shrine maiden at the Grand Shrine of Izumo, is said to have started in the latter half of the sixteenth century. The first mention of *kabuki odori* in written records occurs in 1603 (the eighth year of the Keichō era). By that time, however, it already seems to have acquired a certain celebrity, and in practice it almost certainly dates from a somewhat earlier period.

In the latter half of the sixteenth century the word *kabuki*, which today refers exclusively to the classical stage entertainment, was in common use in everyday conversation. It derived from the verb *kabuku*, whose basic meaning was to tilt forward—as does an object whose center of gravity undergoes forward displacement—but in popular speech was extended metaphorically to signify customs or behavior that departed from the traditional or conventional norm or were likely to draw attention. As such, the word came to carry a distinct flavor of disapproval when used by moralists and educators. In Saikaku's *The Diary of a Woman Who Loved Love*, for instance, one character complains that the people of Osaka had an outlook that was more "*kabuki*" than he had expected. In another contemporary work, someone else complains that a man's face is so "out of kilter" that "a mere touch would send him over." The *Butoku Hennen Shūsei* (an Edo period record of samurai words and deeds) says, "In his licentiousness he equalled the very worst of the *kabukimono* of the day." The extent to which the word—and the attitudes it described—became prevalent can be surmised from the fact that in 1650 the shogunate itself issued an edict declaring that "members of the merchant class shall refrain from outlandish (*kabukitaru*) behavior." It requires little effort today, in the latter half of the twentieth century, to imagine the ways in which the word was used, and the kind of people and behavior to which it referred. And it seems most likely that the word *kabuki odori* as used of the dance started by Okuni conveyed, in the early days at least, a definite tinge of popular disapproval.

The first type of dance performed by Okuni was a *nembutsu odori*, a type of religious dance accompanied by invocations of Amida that Saint Kūya is said to have devised in the tenth century as a means of drawing the common people into the Buddhist fold. In medieval times, when the rule of the aristocracy was replaced by a warrior class government and an age of strife and uncertainty gave rise to new and more popular forms of religion, the dance was revived with great success by Saint Ippen, and people began to perform the *nembutsu odori* at the annual Festival of the Dead (*Bon*) as a means of praying for the souls of those who had died in the civil wars. The dance survives today, and as *bon odori* still forms one of the favorite rituals of the year, especially in the country calendar.

The transitional period between the medieval age and the establishment of a strict feudal system under the Tokugawa saw a great deal of social unrest and bloodshed. It was Oda Nobunaga who first succeeded in unifying the country, but he was soon succeeded by Toyotomi Hideyoshi, who gave way in turn to Tokugawa Ieyasu. Once the firm hand of the Tokugawa imposed peace on a nation so long torn by civil strife, the *nembutsu odori* became more popular than ever. At first, one of the chief purposes was, as before, to pray for the repose of those who had fallen in battle, but as life established a more settled pattern and the common people began to enjoy, if not affluence, at least a slight easing of hardship, all kinds of embellishments were added to the dance, and it increasingly came to acquire the nature of a popular entertainment. Lavish costumes began to be used, including fancy dress, and various decorations and props made their appearance on the platforms on which the dance was performed.

This new type of *nembutsu odori* came to be known as *furyū* ("embellished dance") *nembutsu*, or sometimes simply as *furyū*. A contemporary record describes how the great Oda Nobunaga himself participated in a *bon* dance dressed up as a female angel. For a man with the highest rank in the land to prance amidst the common people in the guise of a woman would surely have qualified, in contemporary parlance, to be described as rather *kabuki*.

The *nembutsu odori* of this period seems to have been lively, to say the least, since a contemporary record relates how on one occasion young and old, men and women, and monks with them, gathered and danced in an *odori-dō* ("dance hall") till they went through the floor. It seems probable that the *nembutsu odori* that Okuni danced was also no sedate, pious affair, but the so-called *furyū nembutsu*. This surmise is borne out by an illustrated scroll called *Kabuki Zōshi*, believed to date from around the end of the Keichō era (1596–1615), in which she is shown in the act of dancing the *nembutsu odori*. She is dressed in the latest fashion, wearing the trousers recently introduced into Japan by the Portuguese and a type of lacquered "coolie hat" (*kasa*) called "southern-barbarian (that is, foreign-style) *kasa*," and with a gong dangling on her breast or in her hands. Other pictures show her attired in men's clothes with a Christian cross hanging at her neck. It is most unlikely, of course, that Okuni was a Christian; the cross was probably worn simply as an accessory for the sake of its exotic novelty. The country had not yet been shut off from the outside world; the missionaries of Holland, Spain, and Portugal were bringing aspects of the culture of their countries to Japan, and mingling with the audiences shown watching Okuni dance there are foreign sea captains and merchants.

Although Okuni is usually referred to as a "shrine maiden of the Grand Shrine of Izumo," it should be remembered that popular religious beliefs in her day did not trouble themselves with fine distinctions between Shintoism and Buddhism, and were quite ready even to dabble in a little Christianity. It was not at all odd that Okuni should embody aspects of all those religions, or that a shrine maiden at one of the great strongholds of Shintoism should dance a Buddhist dance with a Christian cross swinging before her breast. She lived during that brief period when Japanese culture began to acquire a cosmopolitan flavor before entering into its long centuries of isolationism, and quite probably her willingness to incorporate the latest fads into her *nembutsu odori* was precisely what gave her popularity with the masses.

The *furyū nembutsu* in vogue at the time also made free use of popular songs and dances. Okuni herself interspersed her *nembutsu odori* with popular folk dance favorites such as *yayako odori* and *kaka odori*, and before long she was also mimicking the appearance and behavior of the *kabukimono* of her day. The result—the entertainment referred to as *kabuki odori*—was a kind of "musical" derived from all these varied elements. The *Kabuki Zōshi* describes one of her performances. First she would dance the *nembutsu odori*, then a certain Nagoya Sanza would come up onto the stage from among the audience. The real Nagoya Sanza was a samurai famed as one of the most extravagantly *kabuki* men of his day. He had been killed in a quarrel in 1602, however, and it seems that Okuni was merely following the example of the Nō theater in bringing onstage some well-known figure from the past and having him describe episodes from his life—the difference being that, since this was a popular entertainment, the elegant poets and heroic warriors of the Nō stage were replaced by a popular figure of foppishness who had died only a short while before. It seems certain that the Nagoya Sanza who appears in the *Kabuki Zōshi* was not the real man, but an actor playing the part; dramatically speaking, the early kabuki was simply borrowing the construction of the earlier Nō play.

This Nagoya Sanza would appear onstage accompanied by a clown-type companion known as *saruwaka* and, hand in hand with Okuni, would perform a dance recalling the more *kabuki* aspects of his days on earth. These aspects were summed up in two principal scenes: a scene of dalliance with the proprietress of a teahouse, and a scene in a public bathhouse.

The popular aspect of tea drinking in Japan—as opposed to its more aesthetic treatment as seen in the tea ceremony—was represented by the teahouses that sprang up along the streets of the cities and on the highways between them. In the sixteenth and seventeenth centuries, each teahouse commonly employed an attractive mistress whose presence served to draw in large numbers of local dandies. In her stage representation Okuni would dress herself up as a man and, with the comic *saruwaka* acting as a kind of intermediary, make advances to the teahouse madam, the whole scene being rounded off with a dance performed hand in hand by the two lovers.

To end the performance, there was a bathhouse scene. The public bathhouses, which first came into being in the Muromachi period, were steam baths, and they too employed girls to attract the young blades. It was because it showed scenes such as this, together with scenes in teahouses of the kind just mentioned, all enacted in song and dance, that Okuni's entertainment was generally known as *kabuki odori*. Its popularity gave rise to many imitations, most of them by groups of performing prostitutes. Before long, similar troupes of women were performing *kabuki odori* all over the country, and kabuki at this stage in its history is known accordingly as "prostitute kabuki" (*yūjo kabuki*) or "woman kabuki" (*onna kabuki*). It was at this stage that the shamisen, the three-stringed, plucked instrument so closely associated with the kabuki today, made its first appearance on the stage. The instrument, originally Chinese, had first made its way to the Ryūkyūs, then around 1560 had been introduced into Japan. It was with this instrument that the prostitutes who performed the early kabuki chose to accompany their performances, and it has continued as the mainstay of kabuki music to this day.

In "woman kabuki" the star of a troupe would occupy the center of the stage, seated on an imported Chinese chair decorated with peacock feathers, tiger or leopard skins, and the like, and would play the shamisen while her companions danced around her. Celebrated courtesans whose names are known to us today include Sadoshima Shōkichi, Dekishima Hayato, Murayama Sakon, and Ikushima Tango no Kami. The daimyo of the day vied with each other in becoming the patrons of these celebrated prostitutes. Lord Mizuno of Hyūga is said to have paid thirty pieces of silver for the services of Dekishima Hayato, and in 1608 had her perform in Kyoto under his patronage. The celebrated general Asano Yoshinaga (1516–1613) bought the services of a courtesan called Katsuragi. In 1610 Katō Kiyomasa summoned the *onna kabuki* to Nagoya to celebrate the building of Nagoya Castle, and Date Masamune summoned a troupe of courtesans all the way to his fief at Sendai, in the north of Honshu, to perform for him there.

In time, the decadent behavior of the daimyo could be overlooked no longer, and in 1629 the shogunate prohibited women from appearing on the stage altogether.

WAKASHU KABUKI AND *YARŌ* KABUKI

With the prohibition of *onna kabuki*, its place was taken by a type of *kabuki odori* performed by troupes of youths (*wakashu*) and known as *wakashu kabuki*. These troupes were not organized especially to replace *onna kabuki*, but had been performing alongside the women's troupes since around the Keichō era; the suppression of *onna kabuki* merely served to bring them into sudden prominence.

Troupes of boy entertainers had, in fact, existed for a long time for the purpose of performing *kōwakamai* (medieval dances), *hōka* (acrobatics), or Nō theater. Under the influence of Okuni's *kabuki odori*, they had incorporated elements from *kabuki odori* into their own performances, or in some cases had switched over to performing *kabuki odori* exclusively.

Although there were, naturally, differences between the ''woman kabuki'' and the ''boy kabuki,'' they were basically similar in nature, since in both cases art was a secondary consideration to the troupes' fundamental purpose, which was prostitution. Where the differences were concerned, perhaps the greatest distinguishing characteristic of the ''boy kabuki'' was its introduction of the type of acrobatics known as *hōka*.

Hōka (literally, ''throwing'') had derived from traditional skills such as *katanadama* and *shinadama* (types of juggling with swords, balls, etc.) dating back to the *sangaku* of ancient times, a circus-like entertainment imported from China. In medieval times, men known as *tsuji hōka* or *hōkashi* would drift about the country in the garb of monks, earning a living by means of such skills. Around the late sixteenth century, new acrobatic skills such as those known as *makurakaeshi* (''wooden pillow juggling'') and *kagonuke* (''squeezing out of a basket,'' an escape art in which the performers' hands were tied) came into Japan from China via Nagasaki, and were taken over by the *wakashu*. When these troupes of youths switched to kabuki, these skills were taken over by kabuki in its turn, and provided the basis for the semi-acrobatic swordfights and other displays of acrobatic skill still to be seen in kabuki today.

The tightrope walking and sliding, balancing, and other acrobatic skills that were worked into kabuki plays later during the Genroku era (1688–1704), can be said to have derived from the troupes performing *hōka* and *kumomai*. The latter, performed by a type of acrobatic troupe specializing in tightrope walking, was itself derived from the *hōka*. The well-known Muromachi screen paintings showing scenes on the banks of the river at Shijō in Kyoto and scenes ''Within and Without the Capital'' include pictures of this *kumomai*.

Two further innovations were provided by the troupes of performers specializing in *kōwakamai*, a medieval dance performed exclusively by young men, who brought to kabuki both elements from their dances and the dramatic stories that they illustrated. In the same way, the troupes of youths specializing in Nō brought in elements from the Nō drama and the Kyōgen farces that are always performed with it. In this way, kabuki acquired the Nō-derived type of dance known as *komai*, which differed from the dances proper to *kabuki odori*. The *komai jūrokuban* of later times, a set of sixteen short dance pieces, can be seen as derived from these *komai*.

It was in 1624, during the period of *wakashu kabuki*, that the Saruwaka-za, the ancestor of the Nakamura-za, the foremost of the three officially licensed troupes of later days, was founded. This troupe, whose leader was traditionally known as Saruwaka Kanzaburō, specialized in the clownish antics known as *saruwaka*, and it was for this reason that this type of clowning and mime came to occupy such an important place in kabuki.

The heyday of the *wakashu kabuki* corresponded with the rule of the third Tokugawa Shogun, Iemitsu. Iemitsu frequently summoned Saruwaka Kanzaburō's troupe to Edo Castle to perform for him, while the daimyo would recruit troupes of entertainers from among their own pages and have them perform *wakashu* dances as a way of keeping the shogun in a good temper. In 1635, for example, such powerful and famous lords as the Dainagon of Kii, Ōi Toshikatsu, and Matsudaira Nobutsuna all provided dances performed by youths for their master's pleasure. Thanks to the special proclivities of the ruler of the day, *wakashu kabuki* flourished greatly, but no sooner was Iemitsu dead than this form of kabuki was officially proscribed, just as the *onna kabuki* had been before it. The date was 1652; the period of *wakashu kabuki* had lasted twenty-four years.

In the Edo period, a man was considered to have reached maturity, and shaved off his front hair as a sign of it, at the age of twenty. The boys who performed kabuki were accordingly forced to "mature" before their time by having their front hair shaved off, and thanks to this transparent ruse it proved possible to continue kabuki performances once more. This renewed *wakashu kabuki* is referred to as *yarō kabuki*, *yarō* being a term for an adult male.

Still more important, it was decided at the same time to drop the term *kabuki*, which had come to acquire overtones of the forbidden, and to make a fresh start under the name *monomane kyōgen zukushi*. This new "official" name did not succeed in supplanting the word kabuki in the popular parlance, where it has remained firmly fixed to the present day, but the change of name was accompanied by a conscious effort to change the content also, and this is extremely important. In fact, the history of kabuki as a dramatic art in the sense in which it is familiar to us today can be considered to have begun with the *monomane kyōgen zukushi*, which must be seen as differing quite clearly in its nature from the *onna kabuki* and *wakashu kabuki* that preceded it.

MONOMANE KYŌGEN ZUKUSHI AND THE EMERGENCE OF THE *ONNAGATA*

The word *monomane* here means something like "imitation" or "mime," and as such hints at a course of development different from the pure dance of *kabuki odori*, while *kyōgen* signifies a spoken drama in the manner of Nō and Kyōgen. The change of name, in short, was a declaration that henceforth the form was to be basically a dialogue drama relying on mime for many of its effects, a kind of up-to-date version of Nō and Kyōgen. What was happening in practice was that the Nō and Kyōgen plays that had been perfected in the previous age were being made over into kabuki, and this process inevitably meant great strides forward for kabuki as drama.

As kabuki thus grew to maturity in its dramatic aspects, the need to fill all kinds of different feminine roles grew more and more pressing, and, in the enforced absence of the genuine thing, men were increasingly obliged to take over specifically feminine roles. As a result, there emerged the type of female impersonator unique to kabuki known as *onnagata*. At the same time, in order to reassure officialdom that the "women" who appeared on the stage were not real, it was necessary to register in advance the actors who were to play such parts. Troupes began to register certain actors with the local magistrate as *onnagata* to distinguish them from the *otokogata*, who played exclusively male roles. The characteristic division of kabuki actors into types specializing in particular kinds of roles can be said to have begun with the registration of the *onnagata*.

The most popular of all the *onnagata* at the time was an actor called Ukon Genzaemon, and the chief reason for his popularity was the *komai* type of dances that he performed. The dance elements of kabuki were henceforth gradually taken over by *onnagata*; the specialization in dancing that is a feature of the *onnagata*'s art to this day can be traced back to the very beginnings of *onnagata* as such. One of the pieces for which Ukon Genzaemon was especially famous was called *Kaidō-kudari*, and was a kabuki version of the Kyōgen dance of the same name; here too, one can see how techniques from Nō and Kyōgen were being added to those of the original *kabuki odori* during this period.

At the same time, the Nō and Kyōgen actors from non-official troupes who came into kabuki at this stage played a great part in developing its techniques and the basic structure of its plays. Their contribution consisted, essentially, in modernizing and adapting for the kabuki stage what were originally Nō and Kyōgen pieces.

It was along these lines, thus, that the new *monomane kyōgen zukushi* developed. Nevertheless, a constant feature of kabuki ever since the days of Okuni, a feature that distinguished it clearly from Nō, had been that it portrayed the contemporary world. The kabuki and the gay quarters, the two most up-to-date and glamorous sources of inspiration for the culture of the common people in the Edo period, had been in close rapport from the very beginning, and although *yūjo kabuki* as such had disappeared, the tradition of having *onnagata* portray courtesans on the stage was to persist throughout the history of kabuki.

The pattern set by Okuni when she showed a young fop of the day dallying with a teahouse madam was carried on during this period by the type of play known as *Shimabara kyōgen*. Shimabara was the name of the gay quarters of Kyoto, and the plays consisted of scenes involving the courtesans of the quarter and their patrons (in the case of Yoshiwara, the most celebrated gay quarters of Edo, the name *Yoshiwara asobi kyōgen* was used). Such was the popularity of these pieces that around the middle of the seventeenth century the term *Shimabara kyōgen* was almost synonymous with kabuki. Before long, the authorities decided that this was not good for public morals, and the name was banned. Despite this, however, the same type of theme was carried on in what came to be known as *keisei kai no kyōgen* ("buying-a-courtesan plays," see p. 38). They were to provide one of the most important patterns for plays during the golden age of the succeeding Genroku era.

This period also saw further development of the *yakugara* (see p. 38) system, whereby each actor specialized in one particular kind of role. Thus the courtesan in such plays would be played by a type of actor that came to be known as *waka-oyama* (young *onnagata*), while her patron was played by a *tachiyaku* (actor specializing in male roles), the master of the brothel by a *dōkeyaku* (comic role), the man's companion by a *yakkogata* (servant role), and so on. In the Empō era (1673–81), with the development of the social and historical dramas, the plays began to deal in conflicts between good and evil, and new types of actors known as *akumingata* ("bad guy role") or *katakiyaku* ("enemy role") began to specialize in villain roles.

GENROKU KABUKI

The Genroku era, culturally speaking one of the most brilliant epochs of the whole Edo period, saw the emergence of popular arts of a remarkably high level in the fields of literature, painting (the print), and the decorative arts. Kabuki and puppet drama likewise reached a kind of peak, and a special term, "Genroku kabuki," is given to kabuki of this era. Its chief characteristic is an extremely well-balanced overall development in which the plays themselves, acting and production techniques, and dramatic criticism all made great strides hand in hand. Where the plays themselves are concerned, the most important step forward was the emergence of the first true dramatists. In 1680, Tominaga Heibei was officially listed as "playwright" in a theater program, thereby proclaiming the existence of the dramatist as a profession in its own right. He was followed by Chikamatsu Monzaemon, the first dramatist who was not also an actor himself. Although Chikamatsu is known primarily as a writer of plays for the puppet theater (many of them subsequently adapted for kabuki), he also, during his earlier years, produced a number of works for the kabuki stage. Unfortunately, these works have not survived as integral libretti but only as plot outlines; thus we are familiar with their structure—the skeletons, as it were—but not with the living flesh of their language. Even here, moreover, it is not possible to attribute everything with certainty to Chikamatsu himself, since it was the custom of the day for actors to amend and improvise freely. We know the names of various other playwrights besides Chikamatsu—Kaneko Kichizaemon and Mimasuya Hyōgo among them—but in most cases they were actors who wrote plays in their spare time. Thus Kaneko was a *dōkeyaku* in the Osaka-Kyoto area, while Mimasuya was the pen name of the Edo actor Ichikawa Danjūrō I.

In their themes, the libretti of the plays of the Genroku era were virtually all *o-ie sōdō*, plays based on some dispute or other within a high-ranking family; and their principal scenes derived from the "gay quarters" type of play of the preceding age, with plenty of scope for the conceit of *yatsushi* (p. 16). This *yatsushi* usually involved some character of high rank—most often a daimyo or a samurai—who was reduced in circumstances on account of an *o-ie sōdō* and went to the gay quarters in humble garb (*yatsushi* originally meant "disguise") to call on a courtesan whose patron he had once been. This, of course, gave great scope for a sentimental and amorous scene between the two. The style of acting called for in the latter type of scene was known either as *yatsushigoto* or *wagoto*, the *wagoto* meaning something like "soft stuff" or "gentle stuff"—"romantic stuff," in short.

An actor celebrated for his *wagoto* was Sakata Tōjūrō, and the *wagoto* that he perfected has survived to the present day as one of the standard techniques of kabuki acting. The play *Yoshidaya*, for example, which is still performed, is considered as preserving the style of acting originally developed by Tōjūrō. During his lifetime Tōjūrō is said to have taken the part of Izaemon (the hero in plays such as *Yoshidaya* and centered around the courtesan Yūgiri) more than eighteen times, winning great acclaim. The play *Yoshidaya* tells how Izaemon, who has fallen in love with a courtesan called Yūgiri, uses all his money without a thought for his family. As a result, he is cast off by his parents. He comes to visit Yūgiri in humble dress and a celebrated love scene follows.

The *wagoto* style of acting flourished particularly in the Kyoto-Osaka area. Edo, on the other hand, was known for its *aragoto*, of which the most renowned exponent was Ichikawa Danjūrō I. *Aragoto*, or "rough stuff," usually involved a tremendous amount of swaggering about by some superhuman hero; his face was usually painted bright red, or done in the traditional style of makeup known as *kumadori* (see p. 50), and he made a great display of dispatching villains with the utmost ease. Compared with the Kyoto-Osaka region, Edo was still a "frontier area," and its population—since the city was the headquarters of the shogunate—naturally contained a high proportion of samurai. The outlook of the populace as a whole, therefore, was rougher and more bellicose than that of Kyoto or Osaka, and this, it seems, was reflected in its dramatic tastes.

Kabuki performances in this era were often timed to coincide with the *kaichō* of shrines and temples—when a shrine or temple in the provinces would bring its images to the cities to show them to the faithful and to solicit funds—and references to the virtues of the gods and Buddhas were often worked into the libretti. Sometimes the finale would even include an appearance onstage by the deity in question, or a dance of homage to him. Many celebrated plays, including Chikamatsu's *Keisei Hotoke no Hara* and *Keisei Mibu Dai-nembutsu*, were written along these lines.

Other celebrated actors of the Genroku era beside those already mentioned included Yoshizawa Ayame and Mizuki Tatsunosuke, who were leading *onnagata* in the Osaka area, and, in Edo, Nakamura Shichisaburō, who was famous for his *wagoto*. During this period, there was as yet no system whereby names were handed down through generations of actors—which is, in itself, a sign of the vigor and freedom of this formative period of kabuki acting.

Particularly popular in this early period were the dances performed by the *onnagata*, carrying on the traditions of the preceding age. There was a great vogue, for instance, for what was known as *onryōgoto* ("resentful spirit stuff"), in which the *onnagata* previously shown in *wagoto* scenes with the hero is thrown over for another, or betrayed or murdered, and appears as a vengeful ghost unable to find rest in the next world. Mizuki Tatsunosuke, one of the actors already mentioned above, was noted for a dance known as "seven changes" (*nanabake*) because in it the spirit of the woman he was portraying appeared in seven different forms; this was to constitute the basis of what was later known as *shichihenge* ("seven transformations"), a kind of quick-change technique in which the actor appeared in many different costumes, or different roles, in rapid succession. This spectacular kind of technique was balanced, on the other hand, by the more realistic type of acting expounded by Yoshizawa Ayame; known as *jigei* ("ground technique"), it underwent considerable development at this stage in the growth of kabuki.

It was the latter, more realistic tradition of acting, that was to give rise to the type of kabuki play known as *sewamono*, roughly translatable as "social drama." This type of play usually consisted of a dramatization of actual incidents that had occurred in the society of the day, especially the more sensational type of incident involving murder or love-suicide. Apart from the purely sensational appeal of their themes, however, these social dramas also reflected popular religious beliefs to a certain extent, insofar as their performance was looked on as a means of praying for the peace of the souls of those who had died unhappy deaths in the incidents portrayed. In the case of the courtesan Yūgiri, for example, plays based on the incident in which she died were repeated periodically, the title being prefixed with "On the First Anniversary of Yūgiri's Demise," "On the Third Anniversary of Yūgiri's Demise," and so on, in accordance with the Buddhist custom of holding services for the deceased at fixed intervals after their death.

At this early stage of the kabuki, these *sewamono* plays were known as *kiri-kyōgen* or "final plays" because they were performed at the very end of a day's performance as a kind of appendix. In their content, they were at first little more than a kind of dramatic reportage; however, as they grew in popularity and their dramatic and artistic content developed, they came to acquire a status comparable to that of the older kabuki plays. Thus the former came to be known as *jidaimono* ("period pieces") or *ichibanmemono* ("first pieces"), while the *sewamono* came to be known as *nibanmemono* ("second pieces"), and the day's programs came to consist, typically, of two long plays—one *jidaimono* and one *sewamono*. With time, moreover, playwrights began to combine the content of both types of plays into one, and to produce long, omnibus-type plays that lasted all day, with the first half portraying principally the world of the samurai and the second half the world of the merchants.

A further noteworthy feature of this period is the establishment of the authority of dramatic criticism. Criticism of a kind had been in existence for some time already, in the form of *yarō hyōbanki* ("actors' reputation reports"). These however, had been based on *yūjo hyōbanki*, and for the most part merely did for actors what the latter had done for the popular courtesans of the day, that is, provide a kind of illustrated booklet extolling the virtues of the subject for the benefit of his or her fans. However, a work entitled *Yakusha Kuchi Jamisen*, published in 1699, marked an enormous stride forward, as it contained what can be classified as genuine dramatic criticism. It consisted of three volumes, one devoted to each of the great cities of the day—Kyoto, Osaka, and Edo—and marked the first issue of what was to become an annual publication devoted to criticism of plays and acting. This annual, which continued to appear right up until the early years of the Meiji era (1868–1911), a period of nearly three centuries, can have had few parallels in the history of drama anywhere in the world.

Yakusha Kuchi Jamisen represented an advance over anything that had gone before in the severity of its judgments and, in a sense, its comprehensiveness. The chief emphasis, however, was on the techniques of the actors concerned. Somewhat later, a work called *Yakusha Rongo* ("Actors' Analects") was published, devoted to the words and deeds of such famous actors of the day as Tōjūrō and Ayame. It gives a very good picture of trends in the theater during the Genroku era, as well as of theory and practice in the actor's art of the day; indeed, in the latter respect, no better work was to be produced throughout the Edo period.

THE CONFLUENCE OF BUNRAKU AND KABUKI

During the first half of the eighteenth century, kabuki changed its course of development and began to show signs of having reached a point of rest. It is largely due to developments during these years that it came to exhibit the type of stylized beauty that is so characteristic of it today.

The changes were in part the result of misfortune. In 1704, the Edo actor Ichikawa Danjūrō I was killed onstage by a fellow actor. In 1708, Nakamura Shichisaburō died, and the following year the Osaka actor Sakata Tōjūrō also died. Kabuki had thus lost some of its leading actors. On top of this, a clandestine relationship involving a maid in the shogun's private quarters called Ejima and a kabuki actor called Ikushima Shingorō was brought to light in 1714, and consequently the theater at which the offending actor played—the Yamamura-za, one of the four licensed theaters in Edo—was ordered pulled down. From then on until the Meiji Restoration, kabuki in Edo was carried on by three theaters only—the Nakamura-za, Ichimura-za, and Morita-za, controlled by hereditary managements and subject to constant restrictions from above.

Partly as a result of these events, kabuki began to develop certain signs of rigidity that ultimately were bound up with the perfection of the feudal system under the rule of the Tokugawa. Following the death of several of its best actors, members of the "second generation" carried on the techniques that they had developed, and the tendency for acting to settle into fixed patterns began. As a result of the Ejima-Ikushima affair, troublesome restrictions were imposed on both theaters and performances. The shogunate even began to interfere with the content of the plays themselves, and it became impossible to present plays dealing with many contemporary themes.

Another sign of a new formalism gradually creeping over kabuki was the fact that certain themes came to be associated with particular periods of the year, certain plays tending to become almost yearly rituals. For example, the New Year's program in Osaka came always to include a play set in the gay quarters, with the word *keisei* (the title of a high-ranking courtesan) prefixed to its title. Likewise, at the New Year in 1709, the year in which Tōjūrō died, all four of the theaters in Edo put on plays dealing with the Soga brothers, one of the most popular themes in Japanese theater, and all four were great hits. From that time on, a play on the same theme became an indispensable part of the program every New Year.

The Soga plays of Edo are all based on the well-known Kamakura period story of two brothers who took revenge on the man who murdered their father. The story's special popularity in Edo was partly due to three factors: first, the fact that the story takes place in Izu and Hakone, both of them districts close to Edo and thus familiar to Edo audiences; second, the fondness of Edo's samurai-dominated society for tales emphasizing the martial virtues; and third, popular belief in the god Kōjin, of whom the two brothers were believed to be an incarnation. The brothers in the tale succeed in killing their enemy, but the elder brother Jūrō is killed in the fight, while the younger brother Gorō is captured and beheaded. The Japanese public had always sympathized with the two, and it had long been the custom to represent their deeds on the stage at the time of the summer *Bon* festival. Now, with the development of kabuki, the representations at the New Year came to take the place of this as an annual ritual performed in their memory. The general pattern of the Soga plays also became fixed—naturally enough, since they were all based on the same story. Thus the scene known today as "The Soga Confrontation," in which the brothers come face to face with their foe, Kudō Suketsune, became an indispensable part of the ritual, and it became something of an annual test of a playwright's skill to devise fresh methods and new settings for bringing the two sides together.

As we have seen, a new genre known as *sewamono* developed during the Genroku era, but in 1722 the form was dealt a severe blow in the form of a ban on plays dealing with love-suicide. The decree banning them, an outcome of the Kyōhō Reforms initiated by the eighth Tokugawa Shogun, Yoshimune, during the Kyōhō era, also stipulated that the word hitherto used for "double suicide," *shinjū*, which had considerable romantic overtones, should be replaced by the prosaic word *aitaijini* (something like "dual death") and decreed that couples who had attempted double suicide should be reduced to the level of outcasts and put on public show at the end of a bridge in some public place. Thus not only was one of the principal themes of *sewamono* officially banned, but the theme itself was deprived of much of its romantic appeal of the public. This had a great effect in undermining kabuki's foothold in actuality, and that foothold was still further weakened by the enormous influence exerted on kabuki by the puppet theater.

The puppet theater was enjoying a great vogue at the time; one writer of the day even declared that it had become so popular that "kabuki might as well not exist." The puppet theater is, by its very nature, artificial and indirect compared with kabuki. Kabuki relied for much of its effect on human movement, posture, and speech, and it seems likely that the restrictions placed on the immediacy and topicality that had been one of kabuki's strongest points helped divert public interest towards the more artistic—or at least, artificial—puppet theater. During the Genroku era, the *sewamono*, and especially the love-suicide pieces, written for the puppet theater by Chikamatsu Monzaemon had succeeded in creating a modern drama out of what had been a medieval art, but these ultra-realistic and sensational pieces had, like the kabuki *sewamono*, been subject to official repression in the Kyōhō era. In their place, a type of play developed that placed more emphasis on musical and structural elements; the result was a type of piece less realistic, but more integrated and abstract.

One of the chief works of Chikamatsu's last years, *Kokusenya Kassen*, written in 1716, is a large-scale period play for puppets set in both China and Japan. It enjoyed enormous popularity, running for seventeen months, and overshadowed kabuki so completely that it was finally adapted and kabuki versions were presented in Kyoto, Osaka, and Edo. Some kabuki actors and authors, deploring this new tendency, declared that to imitate the style of puppets would only hasten kabuki's own decline, but in practice *Kokusenya Kassen* marked the beginning of a great flood of adaptations from the puppet theater. Works such as *Sugawara Denju Tenarai Kagami*, *Yoshitsune Sembonzakura*, and *Kanadehon Chūshingura*—known as the three masterpieces of the *jōruri* theater—had been transferred to the kabuki stage within a month of their first performances. When *Yoshitsune Sembonzakura* was presented as kabuki at the Nakamura-za in Edo, it ran for more than seventy days. The dependence of kabuki on the puppet theater had become complete.

It inevitably followed that kabuki itself underwent drastic changes. For the performances of *Yoshitsune Sembonzakura*, the theater went so far as to hire puppeteers and musicians from the Takemoto-za, the home of the puppet theater in Osaka, to assist at rehearsals. The natural result was that large importations were made from the puppet theater into kabuki; these affected production, acting, and even things such as stage machinery. The greatest and most essential influence, however, was the wholesale taking over by kabuki of the type of music known as *gidayū bushi*, developed by Takemoto Gidayū; and since the motions of the actors were to a large extent controlled by the music, these in their turn were affected by the movements of the dolls for which the music was originally intended. The influence has persisted in kabuki ever since, and a large number of kabuki plays given today are in fact adaptations from the puppet theater.

Today, the *gidayū bushi* found in kabuki is popularly known as *chobo*, and the plays themselves as *gidayū kyōgen*, *dendenmono*, or *maruhonmono* (see p. 42). The actors of the Osaka area—the original home of Bunraku—are still reputed to retain an inimitable flavor of their own in such pieces taken over from the puppet theater.

In time, the custom developed of including *gidayū* music even in plays that were originally written for kabuki. This practice was begun in Osaka by the playwright Namiki Shōzō (1730–73), and by the end of the Edo period such plays were being written in Edo by Kawatake Mokuami (1861–93) for performance by Ichikawa Kodanji IV, an actor who had gone to Edo from Osaka.

The great influence from the puppet theater that was such a marked characteristic of this period served to emphasize still further the nature of kabuki as a kind of music-drama, which in turn encouraged the tendency to stylize kabuki in all its aspects. A conspicuous example of this tendency is to be found in the development of stage machinery. Here too, the influence of the puppet theater was very great, but more than this even, it was the invention of the revolving stage that, together with the already existing *hanamichi* ("flower way," see p. 54), played a particularly large part in developing kabuki's spectacular side and nurturing its own peculiar methods of production. The revolving stage was first invented in 1758 by the Osaka playwright Namiki Shōzō mentioned above. Originally a writer of puppet plays who switched to kabuki in mid-career, his works owed a great deal to Bunraku in their dramaturgy and use of the stage.

THE GOLDEN AGE OF EDO KABUKI

Until the middle of the eighteenth century, the development of kabuki took place in Kyoto and Osaka rather than Edo, but in the Meiwa, An'ei, and Temmei eras (from 1751 to 1788) the characteristic culture of Edo began its own unique flowering, in which kabuki was to play a prominent part.

Long years of freedom from civil strife had turned the samurai's thoughts away from war, and by this time even those who were direct retainers of the shogun had developed a taste for the theater. Samurai were known to play the shamisen in broad daylight—sometimes even frequenting the kabuki theater, where they would play among the musicians out of sight in the box on the left of the stage. At the same time, the wealthy merchants of the Kuramae area of Asakusa, who earned a living by converting the samurai's rice stipends into money or lending money to the daimyo, were taking the lead in developing a true Edo culture. Music in Edo was particularly encouraged by a society of eighteen cultured men known as *jūhachi daitsū* (the "Eighteen Great Connoisseurs"), and the technical and spiritual deepening of voice-and-shamisen music led in turn to the golden age of kabuki as music-drama. The hero of *Sukeroku Yukari no Edo-zakura*, today listed among the "Eighteen Favorite Plays" of the Kabuki repertoire, is said to have been modeled on one of the members of *jūhachi daitsū*. The character Sukeroku was originally a stereotype of the dandy of the Kyoto-Osaka area, and various earlier plays had dealt with him and his mistress, the courtesan Agemaki. But for *Sukeroku* the hero was remodeled so as to suggest one of the *jūhachi daitsū*, and the whole was worked up into a play expressly designed to show a typical dandy of Edo. More important still, the type of music used to accompany the play, a type of *jōruri* known as *katō bushi*, had come into being under the patronage of the wealthy merchants of the city.

The character Sukeroku, a symbol of the smart, stylish man-about-Edo proved enormously popular. In a sense, he was the merchant class's reply to the samurai. The play itself represented the development in Edo of a type of drama making much use of popular speech and the bandying of insults was not known in the Kyoto-Osaka area. Similarly, the *katō bushi* that accompanies Sukeroku as he makes his entry along the *hanamichi* is a type of music that was established as an independent school in 1717 by a man called Katō Masumi, a pupil of Handayū of Edo, and is a typical product of the culture of the great money-lending merchants of that city.

This was the age in which voice-and-shamisen music made its greatest strides and reached the very peak of its popularity. One of the leading styles of performance was known as *bungo bushi* since it was originated by a man called Bungo no Jō. A development from a style of shamisen playing popular in the Kyoto-Osaka area, known as *itchū bushi*, it had a reputation for the delicacy of its effects and also for its eroticism. A popular song of the day compared the various styles of shamisen music with various styles of dress, ranging from the formal *kamishimo* and *hakama* (see p. 49) to the tight drawers worn by the workman. *Bungo bushi* came last on the list, and the song's comment was "how cute—birthday suit!" As we have already seen, however, in 1736 the shogunate banned plays dealing with love-suicides, and at the same time there was a ban on the performance of *bungo bushi* in Edo. Bungo no Jō was banished from the city, and is said to have returned to the Kyoto area. Nevertheless, the tradition of *bungo bushi* persisted in the city, and gave rise to various other schools of shamisen music such as the Tomimoto, Tokiwazu, and Kiyomoto schools. The *tokiwazu* and *kiyomoto* music that is still popular today is a direct descendant of these.

The chief characteristic of this *jōruri* music that henceforth played such a prominent part in kabuki is that it developed in the kabuki theater in Edo rather than the puppet theater in Osaka. At the same time, the various other types of ballads (*nagauta*) that had been used in the theater since earlier times came under the influence of these types of *jōruri*, and such popular forms as *ogie bushi*, a reserved, quiet variety of song accompanied only by shamisen, and *meriyasu*, a melancholy type of song, came into being as a result.

Under the stimulus of the great strides made in theater music in Edo, the type of dance-drama known as *shosagoto* (see p. 42) was brought to perfection in this period, and a number of men such as Horikoshi Nisōji and Sakurada Jisuke made their names writing the books (see p. 40) for them. From this time on, it became the custom to include one or two of these dance numbers in each day's performance. Moreover, while it had previously been a kind of unwritten agreement that they should be performed by *onnagata*, Nakamura Nakazō I showed that dances could also be performed by men specializing in male roles, thereby paving the way for future development along the same lines. Such typical *shosagoto* of the Temmei era as *Futaomote, Seki no To, Modorikago,* and *Shitadashi Sambasō*—all of them still popular today—were first performed by Nakazō.

THE HIGH NOON OF EDO KABUKI

In 1790, Namiki Gohei, a pupil of the Osaka playwright Namiki Shōzō, came to Edo. He is credited with having instilled the dramaturgy of Edo kabuki with the more rationalistic outlook of the Kyoto-Osaka playwrights. In Edo, it was the custom to give one title to the whole of a day's performances, but to divide the actual content into two, a "first piece" and a "second piece." The first of these would be a period piece and the second a contemporary piece, but elaborate parallels would be drawn between the characters in the two plays, who were supposed to be the same persons appearing in different ages and under different guises. For example, Soga no Gorō in the first piece, a personage from the Kamakura period, would be identified with Sukeroku, a contemporary figure, in the second piece.

It was Gohei's achievement to do away with this fanciful Edo method of presentation and present the two worlds—the historical and the contemporary—as entirely separate entities. His play *Godairiki Koi no Fūjime* is psychological and rational in its approach to a degree quite unknown in the plays of the Edo dramatists. All the Edo *sewamono* from this time on were influenced by it to a greater or lesser degree, and in that sense it was a forerunner of the *kizewa* ("straight *sewa*") plays developed by Tsuruya Namboku during the following period.

Tsuruya Namboku (1755–1829) is considered to have been not only the leading dramatist of the Bunka and Bunsei eras (1804–30), but also one of the greatest that kabuki has ever produced. In its realistic techniques and its inventiveness, his work outstrips that of any of his rivals. A typical Edoite, he was influenced in some respects by Gohei, but showed a more fanciful bent than his predecessor. For example, he brought together the "first piece" and "second piece" once again, but, as he used it, this less "rational" method enabled him in practice, in individual sections of the play, to portray more frankly than would otherwise have been possible the wretched lives led by the lower classes of the day, as well as the world of crime. The shogunate at the time did not permit the use in the theater of subjects that would afford obvious grounds for criticism of the government of the day.

In his best-known work, *Tōkaidō Yotsuya Kaidan*, Namboku blends the supernatural and actual worlds to produce what is generally acknowledged as a masterpiece, in which he succeeds in portraying the corruption of samurai society, the world of petty villainy, and the wretched lot of women in a feudal society.

Namboku's portrayal of the villains and streetwalkers of low-class society produced a whole new category of plays on the same lines, which were known as *kizewa*. The generally decadent atmosphere of the late Edo period gave rise, in kabuki, to a definite taste for sentimental scenes, scenes of killing and torture, and for the grotesque and supernatural. The popular novels of the day were also heavily influenced by kabuki. Their content often consisted of a reworking of well-known plays; their illustrations were based directly on scenes from the theater; and even the faces of the characters in the illustrations were likenesses of popular actors. Kabuki in its turn often drew its material from these "theatrical" novels, and a lively exchange took place between the two. There was also a remarkable increase in the number of wood-block prints portraying actors or scenes from the theater. And the same period saw an astonishing spread in the popularity of kabuki, extending from the great cities to smaller towns and even into the country. Troupes would go touring in the provinces; plays would be performed in stalls erected in the grounds of temples and shrines; and in the country the farmers would perform plays known as *ji kyōgen* or *ji shibai* ("local theater") for their own amusement.

Before long, however, the social, moral, and economic impasse into which the country was drifting prompted the government to attempt widespread reforms. These, known as the Tempō Reforms (1841–43) and undertaken under the administration of Lord Mizuno of Echizen, were an attempt to return to the healthier, more austere regime of the early feudal period. In line with this aim, they at first set out to eradicate the kabuki theater, potentially the most influential of all the amusements of the common people. In practice, the attempt was abandoned (on the recommendation of one Tōyama Kinshirō, a town magistrate at the time who was well acquainted with the feelings of the masses and knew the effect on them that such a ban would have), yet even so the theaters were driven from their home near Nihombashi, in the center of Edo, and reestablished themselves on a new site at Saruwaka-chō, on the northern edge of the city near Yoshiwara. There they flourished until the early years of the Meiji era.

THE LAST YEARS OF EDO KABUKI

The three theaters newly built at Saruwaka-chō consisted of the same officially licensed theaters as before—Nakamura-za, Ichimura-za, and Morita-za—together with two theaters for the performance of Bunraku. The drama in the Kyoto-Osaka area during these years was in a decline compared with its counterpart in Edo; there were two theaters in Kyoto and two in Osaka, but most of the new plays were written by Edo playwrights such as Segawa Jokō and Kawatake Mokuami. The work of the latter can be seen as a final summing-up of kabuki in Edo.

The Tempō Reforms soon petered out, and the inevitable reaction against them actually encouraged the tendency towards overripeness and decadence. Eventually, new pressures both in and outside of Japan were to bring about the gradual collapse of the shogunate, and at the same time kabuki itself began to show signs of a tendency towards diffusion, rather than integration as before.

Kabuki, child of the three largest cities in the nation—Kyoto, Osaka, and Edo— had hitherto been characterized by a high degree of urbanity and sophistication. Now, however, it began to be affected by a new and more provincial flavor. In *ukiyo-e*, Hokusai and Hiroshige had expressed, in series of prints such as the "Fifty-three Stations on the Tōkaidō Highway," a new interest in the provinces and in travel. In literature, comic travelogues such as Jippensha Ikku's *Tōkaidōchū Hizakurige* were becoming popular. And in the kabuki theater of these late years, an increasing number of plays came to deal with country people and farmers.

The play *Higashiyama Sakura Sōshi*, which was written by Segawa Jokō, a pupil of Tsuruya Namboku, and performed for the first time in 1851, is notable as the only play in the history of kabuki that deals with the peasant risings of the Edo period. Plays with country folk as their leading characters had begun with Gohei's *Godairiki*, in which he dealt with a country samurai in Kyushu. Mokuami's work included *Chijimiya Shinsuke*, in which he draws a contrast between a city geisha and the hero Shinsuke, a silk crepe merchant of simple heart who has come to the great city from the province of Echigo. In another play, *Kagotsurube*, Mokuami shows how the very sincerity of his hero, a physically ill-favored country man called Sano Jirōzaemon, finally drives him to commit murder.

At the same time, Mokuami and other playwrights produced a large number of plays about thieves, a class of plays known collectively as *shiranamimono* (*shiranami* was a popular term for a thief). *Nezumi Kozō*, *Sannin Kichiza*, *Benten Kozō*, *Kamiyui Shinza*, and many others all dealt with a particular class of minor wrongdoer in the towns. These heroes were objects of great admiration among the common people on account of their "Robin Hood" qualities; the robber Nezumi Kozō, for instance, steals money from the mansion of a great lord in order to give it to the poor. A focal point in this type of play was provided by the *yusuriba* ("extortion scene"), in which a variety of rascals would call on a daimyo, a wealthy merchant, or some other rich man and take advantage of some weakness in his position in order to extract money from him. The scene in which the hero made his entrance— proceeding to announce his identity in broad daylight and with a great show of brazen self-confidence—could be counted on to bring the house down.

Another type of play known as *akubamono* (literally, "wicked old woman piece") was characterized by the appearance of a female law-breaker—but far from being an "old woman," she was as often as not an attractive girl of only seventeen or eighteen. This genre first appears in the work of Namboku, and Jokō also wrote well-known plays in the same vein, among them *Dakki no Ohyaku*, *Kijin no Omatsu*, and *Uwabami Oyoshi*. One of Jokō's best-known works, *Yowa Nasake Ukina no Yokogushi* (popularly known as *Kirare Yosa*), tells how the young master of what had been a prosperous business falls on hard times and at the instigation of evil acquaintances goes to extort money from a woman who was once his mistress; the scene between the two, of course, forms the climax of the whole play.

Despite their themes, these plays are very far from being "hard-boiled." They are noteworthy, rather, for the expression they give to the poetic sense and humanity of the ordinary people of Edo. The dialogue, partly through the influence of the story-telling and humorous narrations so popular in the latter part of the Edo period, acquired a new subtlety of inflection and content, to which the rhythmical quality derived from the accompanying music was added.

As works such as these grew more and more detailed in their portrayal of contemporary life, they inevitably irritated the authorities, and in 1866 the shogunate issued an edict complaining that in recent years *sewamono* had become too stirring to the emotions, with detrimental effects on public morals. Henceforth, it declared, plays must "avoid inflaming the emotions as far as possible." Hearing of this edict, Ichikawa Kodanji IV, the leading *sewamono* actor of the day, who was then lying sick in bed, remarked that if the edict were to be obeyed actors might just as well give up altogether. (Shortly afterwards, it is said, his illness took a sudden turn for the worse and he died.)

In the period from the Bunka and Bunsei eras on into the Tempō era, the dance-drama type of play gave birth to what was known as *hengemono* ("transformation piece"), a dance in which a single actor would appear in a number of different roles in rapid succession. Sometimes the roles would differ in age, sometimes in rank or occupation; a particular specialty that developed as time went by was the portrayal of a number of lower-class characters—for example, a nursemaid, a fireman, a peddler, and a street entertainer—which gave great scope for varied characterization.

All these developments represented a tendency for kabuki to become more diversified and diffuse than before. One further trend that marked the beginning of a decline compared with kabuki's golden age was the tendency for actors, who had hitherto specialized in a particular type of role, to undertake all kinds of different roles.

KABUKI IN THE MEIJI ERA

With the collapse of the shogunate, the restoration of the emperor in 1868, and the emergence of Japan into the modern age, the theater world, so long relegated to the lowest rank in the feudal hierarchy and restricted by an obligatory hereditary system, found itself suddenly free from restrictions and the old social stigma. The three families of theater managers in Edo found that both the restrictions and the privileges of the old system had been simultaneously removed, and a new age of free competition in the entertainment world began. Morita Kanya, twelfth hereditary head of the Morita-za, took the lead over his rivals and in 1872 established the first modern theater in the center of what was now Tokyo, the nation's capital. The following year, the Tokyo metropolitan government officially licensed ten theaters, and one by one the remaining restrictions on theatrical activities were removed.

In a sense, kabuki actors had always been outcasts, at the very lowest level of society, since they were not incorporated into any of the four classes—samurai, farmer, artisan, merchant—into which feudal society had been divided. Now, for the first time, they found themselves ordinary members of society; and their social position was still further improved when, in 1887, the emperor himself went to see a kabuki performance for the first time.

The Tokugawa shogunate's policy toward kabuki had always been one of suppression and prohibition. The Meiji government, on the other hand, correctly perceived the social potentialities of the art, and launched a campaign for its improvement. The chief instrument in implementing the government's wishes was the actor Ichikawa Danjūrō IX, as a result of whose activities kabuki, formerly an entertainment directed primarily at the common people, developed ties with the upper classes also.

The official culture of the Meiji era derived largely from that of the West, and looked to the West for all its standards. Its view of the drama, thus, quickly came to reflect Western attitudes. The type of play that mixed the historical and the contemporary was dropped, and even the words used to express such basic ideas as "actor," "theater," "play," and "libretto" were changed to unfamiliar "modern" terms, many of them direct translations from Western languages.

Danjūrō IX produced many new plays in an attempt to create a true historical drama taking advantage of the lifting of the ban on veracity about the past, and the recent past in particular. These were popularly dubbed *katsurekigeki* ("living history drama"). Many works in this genre, among them *Jishin Katō*, *Shigemori Kangen*, *Takatoki*, and *Kasuga no Tsubone*, were produced around this time, notable playwrights including the Mokuami already mentioned, and Fukuchi Ōchi, a scholar and diplomat who devoted much energy to the movement to improve kabuki.

Danjūrō had a rival in another actor, Onoe Kikugorō V, who produced plays known as *zangirimono* in which he set out to portray the new customs of the age. The word *zangiri* was a popular term for the new short hairstyle worn by men now that the old topknot had been forbidden by law, and as such was a symbol of everything new and Westernized. These *zangirimono* became a kind of *sewamono* of the Meiji era, drawing on newspaper reports and the like for their material. However, although the customs and ideas dealt with were new, the plays themselves, being written by authors trained in the old tradition, hardly differed at all from those of the Edo peiod, and far from seeming up-to-date, rapidly acquired a distinctly old-fashioned air.

In the period of new international prestige for Japan that followed the Sino-Japanese and Russo-Japanese wars, a school of modern drama known as Shimpa ("New School"; kabuki being referred to sometimes as Kyūha, "Old School") came into being. The last years of the Meiji era saw the death within a short space of years of the actors Danjūrō IX, Kikugorō V, and Ichikawa Sadanji I, and with their disappearance from the scene kabuki itself came to the end of an era.

THE NEW KABUKI

The Shimpa movement, which began in the late 1880s and 1890s, was originally inspired by political ideals, and used traditional kabuki techniques in order to portray the contemporary Meiji scene. Quite apart from Shimpa, however, the drama of the West began to be imported under the name of Shingeki ("New Drama") in the closing years of the Meiji era and had an immediate appeal for intellectuals seeking for a drama more in tune with the new age. All these developments combined to give kabuki more and more the air of a "classical" drama incapable of further development.

One method that was adopted in kabuki to counter the tendency towards ossification was to present on the kabuki stage plays written by authors other than the true kabuki playwrights who were traditionally attached to one or the other of the kabuki theaters. These plays came to be known collectively as "New Kabuki."

The first move in this direction was made in 1907, with the Tokyo-za's production of the play *Kiri Hitoha* by the celebrated scholar and novelist Tsubouchi Shōyō. The play portrays the decline of the family of Toyotomi Hideyoshi (the leader who unified the nation at the end of the sixteenth century) following Hideyoshi's death and is said to be a conscious attempt to create a Shakespearean type of drama in Japanese. The leading role was played by Shikan, later Nakamura Utaemon V. Shikan was the leading *onnagata* of the Taishō era, and it was his portrayal of Yodogimi, heroine of *Kiri Hitoha*, that secured his place as the finest actor kabuki had produced since the deaths of Danjūrō and Kikugorō.

Okamoto Kidō, who succeeded Tsubouchi Shōyō as the leading playwright working outside the theater proper, reigned unchallenged throughout the Taishō era in the field of "New Kabuki." In plays such as *Shuzenji Monogatari*, *Toribeyama Shinjū*, *Sasaki Takatsuna*, and *Banchō Sarayashiki*, he successfully clothed new ideas from the West in kabuki dress. Thanks to Kidō, the kabuki of the Taishō era achieved a genuinely fresh quality, and it is his name more than any other that the "New Kabuki" always evokes.

The actor responsible for the performance of these plays was Ichikawa Sadanji II. Successor to the first Sadanji, who with Danjūrō IX and Kikugorō V had dominated the world of kabuki in the Meiji era, he left a lasting mark on the history of Japanese theater. His greatest achievement was the foundation, with the cooperation of Osanai Kaoru, of the Jiyū Gekijō ("Freedom Theater"), which together with the Bungei Kyōkai ("Dramatic Society") started by Tsubouchi Shōyō, was one of the two leaders of the "New Drama" movement in Japan.

With Matsui Shōō, a playwright, accompanying him as his advisor, Sadanji went to Europe and studied Western dramatic techniques at the Royal Academy of Dramatic Art in London. On his return, he applied what he had learned at the Meiji-za theater, which he had inherited from his father. He presented the dramas of Ibsen, as well as new plays by Kidō and, in later years, by Mayama Seika, a playwright who was influenced by Ibsen and wrote many popular "New Kabuki" plays. He also revived old dramas such as *Narukami* and *Kenuki*, two of the "Eighteen Favorite Plays."

The new ideas abroad in the theatrical world also led to the construction of new theaters. The Yūraku-za was completed in 1908, and the Imperial Theater (Teikoku Gekijō) in 1911. The Imperial Theater was a purely Western-style theater, and its management included various prominent persons connected with the "Association for the Improvement of Drama" (Engeki Kairyōkai), among them members of the aristocracy, politicians, and businessmen. It also employed its own kabuki actors; it started presenting plays with actresses, and even put on kabuki with actresses instead of *onnagata* in the female roles.

A prominent figure in the world of entertainment in the early years of the century was Tamura Nariyoshi, manager of the Ichimura-za, who won unprecedented popularity for it by billing Onoe Kikugorō VI and Nakamura Kichiemon I on the same program. However, the Shōchiku Company (founded by two brothers, Shirai Matsujirō and Ōtani Takejirō), which had its roots in the Kyoto-Osaka area, now began to direct its gaze to Tokyo, and in 1912 Shōchiku signed an exclusive contract with Sadanji and the troupe he headed. Furthermore, in 1913 the Kabuki-za, the leading theater in Tokyo for the performance of kabuki, was taken over by Shōchiku, and from then on Shōchiku came to rule the entertainment world in Tokyo almost single-handed.

FROM EARLY SHŌWA TO THE PRESENT

The Great Kantō Earthquake of 1923 reduced Tokyo's theaters without exception to rubble. Once reconstruction was under way, the figure who came to dominate the theatrical world with his blend of histrionic skill and administrative ability was Onoe Kikugorō VI. In 1930, he founded the Japan Actors' School, through which he hoped to realize the far-seeing ideals he cherished for the Japanese drama, but the school was forced to close in 1936 for lack of funds.

In 1932 a threat to the rule of Shōchiku appeared in Tokyo in the form of the Tōhō Company founded by Kobayashi Ichizō. Besides engaging in various new dramatic activities, it also attracted a number of young kabuki actors away from Shōchiku in order to form a new Tōhō troupe, but this proved a failure. The "Tōhō Kabuki" of today is a revival of this first Tōhō troupe, achieved by enlisting the services of the actor Matsumoto Kōshirō VII and his company.

Following Japan's defeat in 1945, the occupation forces imposed various restrictions on the kabuki repertoire, but these were removed before long. Today, even the censorship system that existed from the Meiji period until the end of the war—as well, of course, as the various restrictions imposed during the war years—has disappeared, and kabuki has complete freedom as to what plays it performs.

The ten to fifteen years immediately following the end of the war saw the death of a number of the better actors who had emerged since the deaths of Danjūrō IX and Kikugorō V, but the Kikugorō and Kichiemon companies, which carried on the styles of acting of Kikugorō and Kichiemon respectively, did much good work in bringing about a revival of classical kabuki. At the same time, a large number of new works were produced, including a successful dramatization of the *Tale of Genji*.

In 1961 Tōhō signed an exclusive contract with the Matsumoto Kōshirō VIII (later Hakuō) troupe. In 1966, a newly rebuilt Imperial Theater made its debut, also under the management of Tōhō. More important still, a new National Theater was completed in 1965 and started performances in November of the same year, its aim being the preservation of the classics, and in particular a revival of the practice of performing kabuki plays in their entirety rather than in isolated scenes.

In 1972 the contract between Tōhō and Matsumoto Kōshirō VIII and his troupe was terminated, permitting the troupe to perform at the Kabuki-za Theater once again.

In 1983 the new Shimbashi Embujō Theater opened, to the delight of performers and kabuki fans alike and heralding the beginning of yet another new era of kabuki.

KABUKI ACTORS

THE TRADITIONAL name for a kabuki actor was *yakusha*, a word taken over from Nō. The word itself originally signified someone who officiated at ceremonies or religious services, and the Nō *yakusha* was a man whose service to the gods took the form of dramatic entertainment. When the word was taken over by kabuki, it lost these religious overtones. The modern word *haiyū*, often used of stage actors and always of movie actors, did not come into use until after the Meiji Restoration.

The society of kabuki actors was extremely concerned with ranks and social status. The leader of a troupe (*za*) was known as *zagashira*. He not only handled the theater personnel but sometimes allotted roles, and occasionally even produced the plays as well, since the kabuki theater maintained no "producers" as such. The post of *zagashira* was most often filled by the troupe's leading actor of male roles, but in recent times it has occasionally been filled by the *tateoyama*, the chief player of female roles, who shares the highest position in the troupe alongside the principal actor of male roles.

There were many ranks of actors beneath these two chief actors, the first and most important being the group known as *nadai*, a title taken from the list of names that appeared on the placards in front of the theaters. The next group was known as *nadaishita* or *aichū*. Below this came the *chūdōri*; the *tateshi* who choreographed the sword-fights was drawn from this class. And right at the bottom of the male actors (*tachiyaku*) came the *shitatachiyaku*, the men who played the most insignificant parts of all.

Onnagata as a class were referred to as *chū-nikai* ("mezzanine floor"). This strange name derived from the fact that the dressing rooms for the *onnagata* were on the second floor, which in the Edo period, when three-story buildings were officially prohibited, was referred to in this way. Another more respectful term applied to the *onnagata* was *tayū*, which was the title of the highest-ranking courtesan in the gay quarters; the role of *tayū* in a play was considered the best that was open to the *onnagata*.

The way of life of a comparatively high ranking actor was luxurious in the extreme, and his salary, which depended on a yearly contract, rose from one thousand *ryō* to two thousand and then three thousand as the Edo period progressed. (A male servant's average yearly wage was three *ryō*.) Where society at large was concerned, however, his position was very low. He was not allowed to live outside the theater district, and when he went out he was obliged to wear a wattle hat as a badge of his profession. Moreover, he was sometimes still referred to by such derogatory terms as "riverbed beggar" (a survival of the days when performances took place on the dry area of the riverbed in Kyoto) and "stall-man."

With the Meiji Restoration, the actor for the first time became an ordinary member of society, and made a fresh start as an artist in his own right. Even today, however, the actor's world remains rather feudal. It is still highly exclusive and it remains difficult for an actor to make a name for himself unless he comes from a well-known theatrical family. Thus, a great deal of importance is still attached to the ceremony at which an actor inherits a name. Some of the names have already passed through many generations. Thus Nakamura Kanzaburō and Ichimura Uzaemon have reached the seventeenth generation, and Kataoka Nizaemon the twelfth.

YAKUGARA

What might be called "type casting" or "specialization"—the division of all roles into a number of standard types or *yakugara* that were always played by actors specializing in that type of role—was common to the drama of both East and West in classical times. The same thing occurs, for example, in Chinese opera. The original reason behind this specialization of roles in kabuki was administrative, stemming from the edict banning the appearance of women on the stage that was issued in 1629. As a result of this edict, it became necessary to submit a declaration to the city magistrate saying that certain actors who were in fact men would be appearing as women. This marked the beginning of the profession of *onnagata*, and also of specialization in particular types of roles.

To distinguish them from the *onnagata*, actors specializing in male roles came to be referred to as *tachiyaku*. Strictly speaking, this term refers only to actors playing leading male roles. The dramatically primitive plays known as *keisei kai no kyōgen* (see p. 24) that were popular around the Kambun era (1661–1673) allowed for three parts—the "hero" who visited the gay quarters played by a *tachiyaku*; the courtesan, played by a *wakaoyama*; and the master of the house, a comic role played by a *dōkeyaku*. It was these three types of roles that formed the basis for the whole of the subsequent *yakugara* system. Somewhat later, around the Empō era, the type of role known as *akuningata* (which later came to be known as *katakiyaku*) came into being. This made it possible to base stories on an opposition between "good" and "evil"; plots became more complicated, and kabuki as drama made an important stride forward, the simple sketches of contemporary manners of the early days giving way to something closer to plays as we know them today.

In the Genroku era, the *yakugara* became still more specialized and numerous. Finally, towards the end of the Edo period, the system began to disintegrate. *Tachiyaku* would sometimes take *onnagata* roles, or *onnagata* the roles of *akuningata*. Actors appeared who were "Jacks-of-all-trades" and freely encroached on what had previously been the provinces of specialists.

The basic *yakugara*, as we have already seen, were the *tachiyaku*, the *katakiyaku* (*akunin*), and the *onnagata*, but a large number of subdivisions of these main categories developed with time. The *tachiyaku*, for example, included *wakashugata* ("youth role"), *aragotoshi* in *jidaimono*, *nimaime* ("romantic lead"), *wagotoshi* in *wagoto* pieces, *pintokona* ("soft, somewhat effeminate lead"), and *shimbōtachiyaku* ("silent sufferer lead"). In the same way, the *katakiyaku* included such catagories as *jitsuaku* ("power-seeking villain"), *kugeaku* ("wicked nobleman"), and *tedaigataki* ("clerk villain"). The *onnagata* included *musume* ("young girl"), *tayū* ("high-ranking courtesan"), *katahazushi* ("woman of a high-ranking samurai household"), and so on. The actors in these specialized fields all kept to their own type of roles, which they expressed in its typical stylized forms. The play *Kotobuki Soga no Taimen* provides an extremely good set of such standard and easily recognizable types. The villain of the piece, a *jitsuaku* role, is Kudō, traditionally played by the head of the troupe. Of the two brothers who are bent on killing him to avenge the murder of their father, Gorō is a *wakashugata* who specializes in heroic posturing, while his older brother Jūrō specializes in the more romantic *wagoto*. The chief *onnagata* plays the character Tora, while a *wakaoyama* takes the role of the courtesan Shōshō. Asaina is a *dōkeyaku*, and there is also an "elderly villain" in the character Kajiwara.

This extreme specialization also gave rise quite naturally to the theatrical families that specialized, from generation to generation, in the same roles. The characters in a play would be fitted into these different types—or in some cases, even, a play deliberately written in such a way as to provide opportunities for showing them off. The interest of a production was provided by the skillful combination and subtle interplay of the various types; there was no room for any more individual style of acting.

Especially typical of kabuki, in their use of *kata* more stylized and artificial than any of the other types of role, were the *onnagata*, the men who played the female roles. It is worth quoting here a passage from a unique work called *Ayamegusa*, an exposition of the techniques of the *onnagata* that was written by Yoshizawa Ayame, the celebrated *onnagata* of the Genroku era:

"As soon as it occurs to an *onnagata* that he might turn to male roles should female roles prove unsatisfactory, his art is finished. Whether she likes it or not, a real woman can never become a man; it is unthinkable that she should get tired of being a woman and become a man instead. In the same way, an *onnagata* who has that attitude can never truly understand and express a woman's feelings." (*Ayamegusa* in *Yakusha Rongo*)

In the attempt, not just to express femininity, but to *become* a woman, there is a kind of irrational realism that transcends ordinary common sense. The daily lives of *onnagata* of the Edo period were lived in the same way as women in almost every detail. On the third day of the third month, they celebrated the Doll Festival; they did sewing in their spare time; and their clothes were those of women in every respect. This intense effort to become a woman, by being ultimately doomed to failure, served to create for other men a kind of abstract of femininity that somehow summed up its essence better than any individual woman ever could.

PLAYS AND PLAYWRIGHTS

THE JAPANESE word *gikyoku*, meaning "play" or "drama," did not come into general use until after the Meiji Restoration of 1868, when it was adopted as a translation of these Western terms. The most common word for a play before then was *kyōgen*. There was a possibility of ambiguity here, however, since the same word was used to describe the medieval farces that used to give light relief in the Nō theater, and the word kabuki was prefixed accordingly whenever there was any possibility of misunderstanding. The Nō use of the word came in its turn from a Buddhist phrase *kyōgen kigo*, meaning something like "playful words, ornate speech" (the *kyō* here does not signify "mad," as it would in modern Japanese, but simply "playful," "not serious"). Buddhism wisely recognized that things that were in themselves neither serious nor true could be used as a convenient means of leading people into the correct paths without their realizing it. The word *kyōgen kigo* occurs, for example, in the Kamakura period classic *Heike Monogatari* ("Tales of the Heike"), which says, "How interesting it is that the most playful words and ornate speech can be a means to true worship of the Buddha!" Thus the word *kyōgen* in the Nō theater, though used nowadays to refer to the comic pieces themselves, originally meant "lighthearted (or comic) talk" intended to provide a break from the more serious Nō plays, yet basically imbued with the same Buddhistic feeling.

In kabuki, the use of the word *kyōgen* began, as we have already seen, as a way of avoiding the word *kabuki* at the time of the ban on *wakashu kabuki*, and was almost certainly taken over from Nō. The word *kyōgen* was probably chosen in preference to the word Nō itself because it would have seemed almost sacrilegious to take over the latter, with its solemn, religious overtones, for a popular entertainment such as kabuki. At the same time, it may also have been used for its suggestion that the kabuki pieces were a popularization or parody of the more aristocratic and serious Nō. The idea of amusement or frivolity was always part of the very essence of kabuki, but there has always been a slightly more moral idea also—an idea that the theater should be a means, through amusement, of instruction in ethical values and the virtues of Buddhism.

LIBRETTI

The libretto of a kabuki play is most commonly known as *daihon*, or "basic book." It is also known sometimes as *seihon*, literally "true book," a somewhat respectful term signifying the text intended to serve as a criterion for all performances of a play. In the Kyoto-Osaka area, the term *nehon* ("root book") is used with precisely the same significance.

In all these cases it is implied that a kabuki libretto is not a final, definitive text, but a kind of design or blueprint for the performance, and as such subject to amendment and addition. Significantly, no kabuki libretti were actually published until the Meiji era. It is true that in the Kyoto-Osaka area libretti were published and sold to the general public, but it seems likely that this happened only because the custom of publishing the libretti of puppet plays already existed there, and even these kabuki texts were in practice subject to considerable revision for the purpose.

The puppet plays, written from the first with the idea that they would be published, can stand in their own right as drama; that is, as works of literature. It is difficult, however, to view the kabuki texts as complete, independent works of literary value. They should be considered, rather, as being by their very nature fluid and subject to change at each performance, and this is doubtless the major reason why they were not published.

The scope left for improvisation must, in fact, be regarded as one of the positive characteristics of a kabuki text. To take two simple, concrete examples of this practice still surviving today, there are passages in both *Sukeroku* and *Benten Kozō*, both among the most popular of all kabuki plays, where it is recognized that the actors will ad-lib, with topical references or comments on the performances of the chief actors. Such passages will change with each performance of a particular play, or even sometimes from day to day. In some cases they will become an accepted part of the play, in others they will go on gathering new accretions as time passes. Most of the dialogue spoken by the chief characters is, of course, well written and of literary value, but that of secondary and minor characters is often left to those responsible for a particular production, or even to the actors themselves, who will carry on a more or less impromptu conversation. Even in the chief roles, there are some optional asides that are left to the actor himself to fill in. Such impromptu conversations are known as *sutezerifu*, and in the libretti one often comes across the direction "*Koko wa sutezerifu ari*" ("impromptu dialogue follows here"). There are even some cases, such as the *tsurane* (a passage in which the actors introduce themselves to the audience) in the well-known play *Shibaraku*, where it is laid down that the living bearer of the name Ichikawa Danjūrō shall write his own text.

Compared with the puppet theater, thus, it takes a very long time for anything approximating a definitive version of a kabuki play to evolve. Before the Genroku era, there was even a system known as *kuchidateshiki*, whereby the actors would arrange details of the plot among themselves before going on stage, then indulge in a kind of verbal free-for-all with each other once they went before the audience. Even in Genroku times, when more orderly libretti apparently came into being for the first time, the actors seem to have indulged in a great deal of dialogue not found in the text. *Yakusha Rongo*, for example, related the story of one actor who was so deeply insulted by something that another actor had ad-libbed on stage that he refused to appear in the next performance.

In short, the inventiveness of the actors themselves played a large part in the creation of the libretti at this comparatively early stage of kabuki. In the Genroku era, in fact, the overwhelming majority of playwrights were also actors; and even later, when independent authors came into existence, they were more often than not completely subject to the wishes of the actors. One of the principal characteristics of kabuki, in fact, is the persistent idea that it is not the actor who performs in order to give expression to what the author has written in his libretto, but the author who writes the libretto in order to provide a vehicle for the art of the actor. All the libretti that have survived today date from post-Genroku times, so we cannot define exactly what the typical libretto of that era was like. We do, however, have books that set down, with illustrations, the outlines of the stories (a kind of illustrated "tales from kabuki"); and it is these we must rely on to give us an idea of the nature of the plays and their libretti at the time.

Edo period volumes of kabuki libretti, which survive today in the form of handwritten copies, consist of three basic parts. First, there are the *togaki*, which lay down the basic movements of the actors. The first time such *togaki* put in their appearance in Japan was in the writings on medieval *furyū* (see p. 2), but they only became a regular feature with the texts of Nō plays. The *togaki* of the kabuki plays merely took over what the Nō theater had already started. Secondly there are the *butaigaki*, which occur at the very beginning of the libretto and lay down what scenery is to be used. In Edo, libretti always began with the words, "Within the three *ken* (approximately eighteen feet, a measurement not to be taken literally in later days) of the main stage . . ." while in the Kyoto-Osaka area the form was always "The scenery within the three *ken* . . ." Thirdly the most important part of the libretto was of course the dialogue, which was customarily given, not under the names of the characters appearing in the play but under those of the actors themselves. In the smaller stage directions occurring in the course of this dialogue itself, the kabuki did not give precise instructions in the way that modern drama does, but left most of the responsibility with the actors. Typical examples are *yoroshiku* (here meaning something like "as you see fit"), *kanashi* ("expression"), *todo* (final acting effect), and *tachimawari iroiro ari* ("various kinds of swordplay"). It was a test of an actor's skill and inventiveness to take proper advantage of the scope afforded by these deliberately vague stage directions; as we have seen, the actor's art, and not the libretto, was foremost.

TYPES OF PLAYS

Roughly speaking, kabuki plays can be classified into "pure" kabuki, that is, plays that were created expressly for performance as kabuki, and the *gidayū kyōgen* taken over from the puppet theater. The latter are also known as *maruhonmono* (*maruhon* is the libretto of a puppet play) or *dendenmono* (the *denden* representing the sound of the shamisen used in the *gidayū* music). A third category is provided by the *shosagoto* or dance-dramas. Each of these three categories in turn can be divided into historical pieces (*jidaimono*) and contemporary pieces (*sewamono*). Of the true kabuki plays, most of what are known today as the "Eighteen Favorite Kabuki Plays" are *jidaimono*; these pieces were gathered together and set in order for posterity by the actor Ichikawa Danjūrō VII (1791–1859), who chose them from among plays traditionally performed by the Ichikawa family, as representing the cream of true kabuki. Typical of the whole set is the play *Saya-ate*. In their movements and dialogue, its two chief male roles, Fuwa Banzaemon and Nagoya Sanza, typify the *aragoto* and *wagoto* styles of acting respectively. The interplay between these two elements of the *jidaimono*, and their interplay, in turn, with the accompaniment provided by the musicians, is what gives the "true" kabuki play its characteristic appeal.

In contrast to the *jidaimono* stand the *sewamono*, and the very essence of these is to be found in the plays known as *kizewamono* (see p. 31). The dialogue of these *kizewamono* is close to the ordinary speech of the time, yet it is skillfully matched to the accompaniment, acquiring in the process its own rhythms and characteristic, almost musical beauty. The plays taken over from the puppet theater can also be divided into period and social pieces, but one great difference compared with the "true" kabuki plays is that there is a narrator to one side of the stage. The actors often move in response to his words and the music of the shamisen, while at other times their dialogue and the off-stage music alternate in rapid succession. The result, especially in the historical pieces, is a sense of strong rhythmic flow and bold, dramatic emotional impulse.

The plays in the third category, the *shosagoto* or dance-dramas, can be classified, depending on the type of accompaniment they use, into *nagautamono* and *jōrurimono*. In the Kyoto-Osaka area, *shosagoto* pieces are often referred to as *keigoto*. The *kei* means "scenery," and is a reference to the *michiyuki* ("wayfaring" passages, which describe the scenery a character or characters pass through on some significant journey) that play such a prominent part in these pieces.

THE STRUCTURE OF THE PLAYS

As playwrights of the past saw it, a kabuki play was typically constructed of two elements: *shukō* and *sekai*. *Shukō* means something like the basic "plot" or "idea" of the play, while *sekai* means the "world" of the play, that is, the period and physical environment in which it takes place, or the character around which it revolves. The *sekai* provides the framework, the background, against which the ingenuities of the *shukō* are worked out. *Kezairoku*, an old work on dramaturgy, likens a play to the human body, with the plot as the bones, the setting as the flesh, and the dialogue as the skin. However, it was also a characteristic trick of kabuki plays to mix a number of different *sekai* together in the same play. Thus the story of Oshichi the grocer's daughter (based on a sensational affair that had scandalized Edo society) would appear in the same play with Ono no Komachi, a court poetess of the Heian period, and would actually be identified with her, so that the character was described as "Ono no Komachi, in reality Oshichi." Such flights of the imagination were extremely popular in Edo as a basis for kabuki plays.

In the Kyoto-Osaka area, noted for a less fanciful approach, such plays were not appreciated as they were in Edo, and less store was set by originality for its own sake. Instead, a single idea would be worked over many times in order to provide new viewpoints and new refinements of a basic theme. This process, known as *kakikae* ("rewriting") was considered to be a source of interest in itself.

The day's performances, as we have already seen, were divided into a "first piece" and a "second piece," traditionally a *jidaimono* and a *sewamono* respectively, the two being cross-related so that they shared the same plot. The inner organization of the two pieces was also more or less fixed. The *jidaimono*—the "first pieces"—would be of great length in most cases, and consist of a prologue plus five or six acts. The *sewamono*—the "second pieces"—usually consisted of a prologue, a middle scene, and a denouement, known as *ōgiri*. The term *ōgiri* in this case really refers to the last act of the whole day's performances; the word corresponding most closely to "denouement" is *ōzume*, which is used for the final scene of the first piece, and is in general use today in non-theatrical contexts as well.

The final day of a season of kabuki is traditionally known as *senshūraku*. Originally the name of a *bugaku* dance in ancient times, the word came to be used of the congratulatory chorus performed at the end of a Nō program. Although the word as such was taken over by kabuki, there is in practice no special music or dance performed to mark the end of a season. The word *senshūraku*, incidentally, was originally written with three Chinese characters signifying "one thousand," "autumn," and "delight." However, the term "autumn," with its associations of death and decay, was considered inauspicious, and a new character, incorporating half of the original together with the character meaning "turtle" (a symbol of longevity in China and Japan), was invented instead. Kabuki often uses written characters that one would seek in vain in a dictionary. A similarly elaborate ingenuity was often displayed in the titles of plays, which frequently went through terrible contortions to fit themselves into the five- or seven-character lengths that were considered to be lucky. This—as it seems to us today—rather tortuous, over-ingenious approach was one of the most striking characteristics of Edo culture as a whole.

THE AUTHORS

In the early days of kabuki, the authors who wrote the libretti of kabuki plays worked as individuals. Later, however—from the Kyōhō era (1716–1738) on—kabuki followed the practice of the puppet theater, where a number of playwrights would cooperate to produce one piece. The head of such a team of playwrights was known as *tatesakusha*; he was responsible for the basic conception of the piece as a whole, but allotted individual scenes among his pupils, matching the importance of each scene to the ability and seniority of particular pupils. There was a relationship, moreover, between the rank of a writer and the type of scene he was asked to produce. Thus the *tatesakusha* would do the *jōruri* and *shosagoto* for fourth acts and would also write *sewamono*. Men of the second rank would write third and fourth acts, or pieces without dialogue, and so on down the scale. The lowest grade of writer attended to such things as the movements of the actors, and beneath these in turn came the apprentice playwrights. Nowadays, new works for kabuki are written by playwrights working outside the theater, so that the men filling the traditional post of playwright within the theater are reduced to writing out individual parts for the actors, assisting the prompter, and making any necessary revisions in the libretto.

In the past, of course, each theater had its own resident playwrights. Nowadays, not only is the task of writing the plays left to outsiders, but the same man will write both "first" and "second" pieces. Since the Meiji era, the traditional division of the day's program into two long plays has also gone by the board, though a gesture towards the old system is still made in the inclusion in every program of a *jidaimono* and a *sewamono*.

KABUKI PERFORMANCES AND THE SEASONS

A characteristic feature of kabuki performances is their close connection with the seasons of the year, which gives them something of the ceremonial quality of annual rituals. The year is divided up for the purpose into a number of comparatively short periods. It begins with the performances known as *Kaomise* ("Face-Showing") *Kyōgen* in November, which are followed by the *Hatsuharu* ("New Year") *Kyōgen* in January; the *Yayoi* ("Third Month") *Kyōgen* in March; the *Satsuki* ("Fifth Month") *Kyōgen* in May; the *Natsu* ("Summer") *Kyōgen* in June; the *Bon* (the name for the Festival of the Dead) and *Aki* ("Autumn") *Kyōgen* in July and August; and the *Nagori* ("Farewell") *Kyōgen* in September and October.

The *Kaomise Kyōgen* is so called because in it the actors who are to appear at the theater during the following year all "show their faces" for the first time; new plays are written especially for these performances. The plays are mostly impressive *jidaimono*, and are designed to show off to the full the special abilities of the theater's new lineup of actors. In the Kyoto-Osaka area, New Year performances were referred to as the "second program," since the *kaomise* was always considered to be the first; the *Yayoi Kyōgen* became the "third program," and so on through the year. The content of the plays was also regulated according to the season. In Edo the New Year's performances always included a play about the Soga brothers, and in Osaka and Kyoto a play about the gay quarters. The Third Month performances included some play, such as *Sukeroku* or *Kagamiyama*, traditionally associated with the cherry blossom season. The fifth month is the month in which the Soga brothers are said to have taken revenge for the death of their father, so Fifth Month programs always included a piece with revenge as its theme, or else some new play on some current sensation in society. In the summer, there was a play with associations of coolness, often using real water onstage. The *Bon* performances presented a ghost play intended as an offering to pray for the peace of those who had died unhappy deaths.

The September and October performances, which marked the disbanding of the troupe of actors who had performed together at the theater throughout the year, were in the nature of a farewell to the theater's audiences. Sometimes, they would represent a farewell to Edo audiences for an actor who had come temporarily from Osaka. On such occasions, it was customary to present a play—for example, *Kuzu no Ha no Kowakare* or *Shigenoi Kowakare*—on a theme associated with parting.

All of these performances naturally came to partake of the nature of annual rituals, and this was emphasized still further by the fact that many of the performances began on traditional festival days; thus the Third Month performances began on the third of the third month, the Fifth Month performances on the fifth of the fifth month, and the Autumn performances on the ninth of the ninth month.

There seem to have been subtle differences between Edo and the Kyoto-Osaka area both in the plays produced and in the things that audiences looked for in the plays. The authors were well acquainted with the distinctions between Kyoto, Osaka, and Edo, and were apparently obliged to take account of them in their work. According to the *Kezairoku*, the tastes of the Edo public were coarser, and the plays written for it had to be spectacular *jidaimono* with plenty of fighting, gambling, and the like. They typified the outlook of the average samurai, and for Osaka audiences the same plays were too stiff and inhuman. The people of Osaka—the same work states—were fond of abstract theory, so that their plays tended to revolve around questions of social obligation and the like, and the plots had to be more rationally worked out.

As we have seen, the first writers of kabuki plays were also actors, and it was only gradually that the playwright achieved independence. The first man to work from the outset as a writer of plays without first becoming an actor was Chikamatsu Monzaemon. In later years the authors of puppet dramas and kabuki plays merged with each other, the precise point at which this happened being marked by Namiki Shōzō and his pupil Namiki Gohei (see p. 30). Important playwrights in later years, who have already been dealt with in the section on the history of kabuki, include Tsuruya Namboku, famous for his ghost play *Yotsuya Kaidan* and for developing the type of social drama known as *kizewamono*; other writers in the same vein were Segawa Jokō and Kawatake Mokuami. In the Meiji era, the scholar Fukuchi Ōchi began to write new dramas for kabuki, and was followed by other writers such as Tsubouchi Shōyō and Okamoto Kidō, all of them without the traditional ties with the theater that had bound earlier playwrights.

PRODUCTION AND PERFORMANCE

WHENEVER ONE watches a kabuki performance, one must bear in mind that the action on the stage is governed by a special set of conventions and a special type of formalization. To take one of the simplest examples, there is the concept of *kamite* and *shimote*, terms meaning literally "upstage" and "downstage" respectively, but in the kabuki theater signifying right and left facing the stage. According to the conventions of kabuki, the *kamite* is superior in position to the *shimote*, and entrances and exits are accordingly always made from the left. The actor who appears from the *hanamichi* and makes his way to seat himself on the right side of the stage is always either a guest, a messenger from someone of high rank, or himself of high rank, and due account of this must be taken in the production.

In the celebrated play *Terakoya*, for instance, there is a scene in which Takebe Genzō, the head of the "private school" that gives the play its title, encounters Matsuō, who has come to identify the head of the slain son of his master's rival. Matsuō has come as a messenger under orders from his master, so he passes from the left to the right. Gemba, the assistant messenger, does the same. The schoolmaster, on the other hand, moves from right to left to pay his respects, but on the way collides with Matsuō, and the two of them try to sound out each other's intentions. This is a typical instance of the way traditional Japanese manners are reflected in kabuki production as a means of heightening the emotional impact of the action.

A similar difference of social station is shown by the different levels created by a raised platform on the stage. In *Kumagai Jinya*, for example, the hero Kumagai delivers his celebrated narration standing on the raised platform, while his wife, Sagami comes down from the platform in order to deliver a piece of *kudoki* ("lamentation"), one of the techniques particular to the *onnagata*. The difference of level between the two figures is not only unusually effective in creating a stylized stage picture, but also symbolizes the different positions held by men and women in feudal society.

There are other similar conventions. An *onnagata*, for instance, must not step out in front of an actor in a male role, but must seat himself half a pace behind. There is a strict distinction, again, between right and left in other connections besides the *kamite* and *shimote* of the stage, and the left is always considered more "noble" than the right (the *kamite*, of course, is on the left from the point of view of the actor). Thus in all his actions, whether dressing, walking, or climbing stairs, a man always moves his left foot first, whereas a woman moves her right. A well-known example of this in a kabuki play occurs in the fourth act of *Kanadehon Chūshingura*, in which Enya Hangan commits suicide by disembowelment.

Enya Hangan is waiting for his faithful retainer Ōboshi Yuranosuke to rush to his side, but the hour appointed for the suicide arrives and Yuranosuke still does not appear. Since there is nothing that can be done about it, Hangan prepares to position himself on the overturned tatami mat that is the prescribed seat for a man about to commit *seppuku*. In doing so, he inadvertently raises his right foot first, then realizes with a start what he has done and places his left foot first on the mat instead. This small action, which is likely to pass unnoticed by anyone who does not know the convention, is intended to suggest his distracted state of mind at the time (in fact, it must be accounted a piece of artistic license, since the more preoccupied a man is the more he is likely, physically, to obey a habit instilled in him since childhood).

STYLIZATION

The insistence on the conventions of everyday life is only one of the various factors that contribute to what is often referred to as the stylized quality of kabuki. Another, possibly still more important factor is the strong influence of the puppet theater on kabuki; yet another is the large part played in kabuki, ever since its origins, by the dance. Whichever is the most important, the stylization itself is undeniable. One of the chief considerations in the acting is that the picture formed by the actors should be beautiful, and a great deal of thought is devoted not only to the colors but to the postures of individual actors and the composition of the whole. Every scene, for example, invariably ends with a general pose that creates a visually pleasing picture. This tendency is particularly strong in *jidaimono*. The action may culminate in a group of figures divided into two opposing parties that balance each other in a kind of tug-of-war, open up to form the two arms of an inverted ''V,'' or create some similar kind of pattern that is held as the curtain is drawn. In *sewamono*, on the other hand, the pose is struck momentarily, then broken again, and the curtain closes on a more realistic note.

It is generally held that kabuki acting can be divided into the stylized techniques of the *jidaimono* and the realistic techniques of the *sewamono*. In practice, however, the two are frequently interwoven, their alternation forming the basic rhythm, as it were, of the action.

JIDAI AND *SEWA*

Not only do these two elements occur together within the same play; they also occur within the same piece of acting. They are used freely from moment to moment to strengthen the action and give a kind of accent to the whole. The *sewa* style of acting cannot, strictly speaking, be called realistic. It is convenient to use the term in order to distinguish *sewa* acting from the *jidai* style, but it might be more accurate to describe the style as based in its broad outline on real life. Ultimately, the style is a manifestation of the interest in the contemporary shown by kabuki from the days of Okuni onward. That interest gave rise to the type of play centering around the gay quarters; it gave birth to the characteristic *wagoto* techniques; and it can similarly be traced right through to the characteristic acting style of the social dramas. It is in this sense that the *sewa* style of acting can be called realistic.

In contrast to this style stand the *aragoto*, which developed in Edo, and the particularly stylized forms of acting that arose when the actors in plays adapted from the puppet theater attempted to imitate the movements of the puppets themselves, as in the Prologue of *Kanadehon Chūshingura*. It was the blending of these two contrasting styles that gave rise to what we now think of as kabuki acting.

As these conventions of kabuki acting became an integral part of kabuki and were passed on by generations of actors in turn, there gradually emerged what are known as *kata*—distinct styles, or patterns of acting. One of the most celebrated of these is what is known as *kimari* or *mie*, in which a conventionalized series of movements culminates in a picturesque pose that is held for a few seconds. Characteristically, this pose requires intensely energetic motion; just before a *mie*, there will be a crescendo of violent emotion at the very peak of which the actor or actors freeze into stillness.

The *mie* is effective in conveying extremely strong emotion to the audience. A related technique is what is known as *roppō*. In the early days of kabuki, *roppō* was used when an actor first made his appearance, but later it came to be used instead as a way of making an effective exit. A famous example is the exit of Benkei along the *hanamichi* at the end of *Kanjinchō*; a combination of alternating postures and violent movements, it provides a strongly rhythmical, highly exciting climax to the play that only ends when Benkei finally disappears through the curtain at the back of the theater. A technique similar to *roppō* that is used nowadays for entrances is *tanzen*, which is a gentler, more elegant kind of *roppō*. The combination of such techniques with the *mie* constitutes the very essence of kabuki's special appeal. The plays known as *dammari* ("silent," because they contain no dialogue) are made up of these techniques, consisting of a string of *kata* in pantomime with musical accompaniment.

In the *dammari*, the pattern of techniques used by the actors is laid down according to the type of role and the actor's rank. The role played by the head of the troupe, for example, has the awesome hairstyle known as *ōbyakunichi* or *daibyaku*, and he performs a *mie* known as *hashiramaki* around a column, which is only allowed to an actor in this position; then, after the curtain has been drawn, he performs a *roppō* on the *hanamichi* as he makes his exit. However violent the emotions expressed, it is characteristic of kabuki acting that its primary aim is always to entertain.

In the *sewamono*, the type of acting required is more realistic, but it is never allowed to imitate real life to the extent that the restraints controlling the picture presented to the audience are relaxed. Even here, the actors must never lose control of the line of their movements or let themselves be carried away into naturalistic gesturing. A small indication of what is required of them is seen in what is known as *aibiki*, a tall black stool placed on the stage on which an actor seats himself. Although he is in fact seated, he is supposed to be standing, which means that he cannot settle back and relax, and must keep delicate control over his muscles.

It is also laid down that in speaking some particularly important piece of dialogue an actor must always face the audience. In modern drama, for example, two actors engaged in an argument will quite naturally face each other, but in kabuki, the more important the matter, the more essential it is that the speech should be addressed to the audience. In *Kumagai Jinya*, for instance, there is a celebrated passage in which the hero Kumagai is to speak to Atsumori's mother. The conventions of kabuki require that at this point, as the musicians sing "Now he takes his seat to embark on his story," he deliberately turn his back on the actor playing Atsumori's mother and deliver his speech to the audience. Such is the importance attached to this convention in kabuki acting that one of the criticisms frequently leveled at an immature actor is that "he hasn't learned to face the audience."

PATTERNS OF ACTING

As the preceding suggests, one of the main aims of kabuki production is to highlight important climaxes in the performance; the part is emphasized rather than the whole, and interest is focused on the handling of each individual situation. The plot of the play is a thread, as it were, on which these situations are strung like a row of beads. The beads themselves consist of exercises in any of a number of fixed patterns—*aragoto*, *wagoto*, and so on—which determine the general content and style of each. Not only is the general pattern for the acting in each situation laid down, but different families of actors have different traditions as to how the details should be handled. It is these patterns of acting that are known as *kata*. However, if kabuki were no more than the faithful handing-on from generation to generation of the acting traditions embodied in these *kata*, it would degenerate into mere technique. The true test of an individual actor is his ability to use the predetermined *kata* as a means of gripping the audience and swaying it emotionally.

All kinds of conventions, thus, govern the performance of kabuki, yet the outstanding characteristic, perhaps, is the extremely important part played in response to the requirements of successive *kata* by color, form, and sound, which blend together to compose a series of visually beautiful and stirring scenes.

COLOR AND FORM

Some of the colors used are simple and strong—the black curtain that signifies darkness, for example, or the red cloth covering the floor or the dais on which the musicians sit. They have a kind of bold refinement that is characteristic of kabuki, and at the same time provide a background against which the shapes and colors of the actors' costumes form a subtle variation. These costumes can be loosely classified into two types: those that reproduce realistically the everyday clothing worn during the period in question, and stylized, exaggerated costumes such as were never seen in real life. Generally speaking, the former appear in the *sewa-mono*, the latter in the *jidaimono*. An example of the stylized type of clothing is the costume symbolizing a feudal lord in a period play. Its chief feature is an outer kimono of brocade with a large, biblike appendage at the back of the collar. In the same way, a princess conventionally wears a red embroidered costume and a wig done in a special hairstyle known as *fukiwa*. Fixed types of characters, in short, wear fixed types of costumes and hairstyles.

Sometimes, the costume and hairstyle undergo a quick change on the stage. There are two methods of effecting a quick costume change, known as *hikinuki* and *bukkaeri* respectively. With *bukkaeri*, a thread holding the garment together at the shoulders is pulled out so that it falls off the shoulders at both front and back. *Hikinuki* involves an arrangement whereby the clothing on the upper half of the body pulls out of the *obi*. *Bukkaeri* is used to indicate a change in the nature of the character, while *hikinuki* is used solely for the visual appeal of the costume change. A good example is the dance in *Musume Dōjōji*, where there are many changes. The *hikinuki* changes are introduced solely for their visual appeal, but at the point where the dancer Kiyohime is transformed into a serpent, it is *bukkaeri* that is used. Another good illustration of *bukkaeri* is seen in the play *Narukami*. This includes a scene in which a holy recluse, finding himself morally corrupted by the charms of a woman, is seized with a fit of anger and transformed into a devil, the change being marked by the application of blue *kumadori* makeup and a *bukkaeri* change. These changes take place, in kabuki, onstage in full view of the audience. Another similar change is the baring of one or both shoulders by a character who has been wounded or is about to perform a dance or engage in swordplay.

The actors are aided in making these changes by assistants known as *kurogo* ("black fellows"), who are muffled in black from head to foot. Black is the color of nonexistence, and although they appear on the stage they are not in fact there according to kabuki tradition. The one exception occurs in *shosagoto* pieces, where realism is less important than stylization and the assistants wear *kamishimo*—the formal kimono with wide, triangular shoulder pieces and *hakama* divided skirt.

With plays such as *Sukeroku*, one of the "Eighteen Favorite Plays," half the value of the piece would be lost without the elements of color and spectacle. The colors—representing the taste of the common people of Edo—are often rather garish, yet the result is a richness and brilliance hard to match elsewhere. The attitude to color of the popular *ukiyo-e* artists of the same period has much in common with that of kabuki, but kabuki is bolder in its colors, richer, and more dynamic.

WIGS AND MAKEUP

Changes of costume necessarily involve changes of hairstyle also. The expression *katsura* (''wig'' in modern Japanese), used to refer to the whole hairstyle with any added accessories, is peculiar to kabuki; in Nō, for instance, there is no such general term. The word *katsura* originally meant ''vines'' or ''creepers.'' The *Kojiki*, Japan's first national history, in the section dealing with the age of the gods, relates that the goddess who danced in front of the cave in which Amaterasu was hiding bound her hair with a creeper for the purpose. This is, essentially, the same as the *katsura* used in kabuki, which originally meant an ornament for the hair; the *kazura-obi* used in Nō corresponds to this *katsura* (*obi* here means ''band''). In the early days of kabuki, a piece of purple cloth was frequently worn over the front of the head in order to hide the portion which all adult males were required to shave. This was known as *katsura*, and the name was retained even when the cloth came to be replaced by a wig of real hair. Even nowadays, *onnagata* appear in some old dramas with a purple cloth over their front hair—a relic of the days when it was a necessary disguise for them.

Perhaps to make up for any monotony of color in a country where everyone's hair is black, kabuki employs a great variety of hairstyles. Generally speaking, the wigs can be divided, like the costumes, into those that approximate the actual hairstyles of the day, and those that are stylized and would never have been worn in real life. These hairstyles change on the stage along with the costumes. For example, a style known as *shike*, which is a little of the hair sticking out at the ears, undergoes subtle changes depending on the type of character. There are many different varieties, and when it is pulled the hair falls out long. The result is known as *obakege* (''ghost-hair''), and indicates that the character has become a supernatural being.

There is another device known as *gattari*, which involves pulling a fastener out of a carefully done hairstyle so that the piled-up superstructure tilts to one side. If the fastener is pulled out still farther, the hair falls about the head in disorder—a process known as *sabaki*, used in battle and death scenes. *Sabaki* sometimes leaves the front hair in place, sometimes not. When the whole head of hair falls loose, it is known as *sōsabaki*. In this way, changes in costume and hairstyle—as well as in makeup—help greatly in giving kabuki visual variety.

Mention should be made here of the various hair ornaments, known as *kakemono* (''stuck on''), *sashimono* (''poked through''), and so on. These include *kanzashi* (large ornamental hairpins) and spotted bands, and differ according to the age and nature of the characters portrayed by the actor and the costume he is wearing. In the case of a female character, a glance at the hairstyle is enough to tell whether it is a princess, a married woman, an unmarried woman, a courtesan, or what have you. With male characters similarly, the social status, type of occupation, and so on can be told at once by the hairstyle.

The men who dress the actors' hair are known as *tokoyama*, and are divided into two groups, the ''second-floor *tokoyama*'' and the ''third-floor *tokoyama*,'' who specialize in female and male characters respectively.

Changes in costume and hairstyle also necessitate changes in makeup. The most characteristic form of makeup in kabuki is known as *kumadori* (literally, ''making shadows''). The two basic colors are crimson and dark blue, but black, terracotta, bronze, and gold are also used. Generally speaking, red signifies justice or strength, and blue, evil or the supernatural. A character with a completely red face is either a superman of some kind or an evil man. The style of makeup employed in the Peking opera and known as *lien p'u* resembles the Japanese *kumadori* somewhat, but whereas *lien p'u* creates the effect almost of a mask, *kumadori* remains something painted on the face.

In early times, when *tsura-akari* (''face light,'' see p. 58) was employed to light up the face of an actor on the *hanamichi*, the *kumadori* makeup, in the flickering light of the candle, must have leapt into vivid life. With modern electric lighting, the effect is mostly flat and lifeless.

MUSIC

In many cases, the more stylized passages of kabuki are accompanied by music. Music in the kabuki theater can be divided roughly into three categories. First, there is what might be called ceremonial music, which is used to mark, for example, the beginning and end of a performance, and in which the stick drum plays a large part. Another characteristic kabuki sound that may be classified with ceremonial music is the wooden clappers known as *hyōshigi* (or simple as *ki*). These not only mark the beginning of a play, but at times—as when they are beaten while the curtain is being drawn—become almost an integral part of the production. They are also used in the course of a performance to add excitement to a swordfight; for various onomatopoeic purposes; and—perhaps most important of all—to point up the moment when an actor strikes a *mie*. At the beginning and end of an act, two blocks of wood are beaten together, but when clappers are used to suggest other sounds, a pair of wooden blocks is beaten against a flat board laid on the floor—a process known as *tsukeuchi*. *Tsukeuchi* is a specialized skill, and nowadays there are men employed who do nothing else but formerly it was the job of the scene-shifters alone.

The second type of music is known as *geza* music. It is used chiefly for special effects, and the musicians are hidden in the *geza*, a black box with a slatted window situated on the left of the stage facing from the audience. The principal instruments used are shamisen, stick drum, hand drum, and various types of flutes, but these are supplemented by a whole variety of other instruments. The *geza* musicians are known as *o-hayashi*. Since they are invisible to the audience, they are sometimes called *kagebayashi* ("hidden musicians").

The third type of music is performed onstage in full view of the audience, and is called *debayashi* ("onstage music") to distiguish it from the *kagebayashi*. *Debayashi* can be divided into two main types, *nagauta* and *jōruri*. The former consists of accompanied song or chant, the latter of a highly dramatic recitation with shamisen accompaniment. Both make use of shamisen and voices, but *nagauta* is performed on a tiered platform (*hinadan*) at the back of the stage, whereas *jōruri* is performed on a *yamadai* (see p. 57) at the left of the stage. There are two styles of *jōruri*, known as *tokiwazu* and *kiyomoto* respectively. In the *gidayū kyōgen*, that is, the plays taken over from the puppet theater, a reciter accompanied by shamisen is situated to the right of the stage; sometimes, they are hidden from sight in a box behind a blind.

Kabuki makes considerable use of sound effects that are suggestive or symbolic rather than literal; for example, there is the "sound of snow," or the clappers used to herald the emergence of the moon. A large proportion of these sound effects use the stick drum—the sounds representing rain, snow, water, waves, and wind, for instance. There is also a typical combination of flute and drum, popularly known as *hyūdorodoro* (an onomatopoeic word) that is used to mark the appearance of ghosts. It is popularly believed in Japan that the flute has the power to summon up departed spirits. Mention should also be made here of the music that is played while scenery is being raised through the floor of the stage. This derives from the music played by groups of musicians on the floats that are pulled through the streets at Japanese festivals. Another characteristic feature is the "theme music" that often accompanies the appearance of a particular character; such music differs according to the character's disposition, status, circumstances at the time, and so on.

THEATERS AND STAGE MACHINERY

THE TRADITIONAL Japanese word for the theater as a form of entertainment is *shibai*. One use of the word indicates the drama itself. In this sense, it is still used today—in phrases such as "*shibai o mi ni iku* ("to go to the theater") or "*shibai ga suki de aru*" ("*to be fond of the theater*")—alongside such post-Meiji Restoration innovations as *gekijō* ("theater building") and *gikyoku* (an individual "play" or "drama"). Originally, however (and this is the literal meaning), the word referred to the stretch of turf on which the audience sat to watch a theatrical performance. In this sense, it first came into use sometime in the middle ages, and was used not only for the drama, but also for the place where audiences sat to watch sumo matches.

It was not until well into the Edo period that the word *shibai* came to be used of the theater as a form of entertainment and of the theater building itself. (There was a word *shibaigoya*, "theater stall," which meant, specifically, the theater building.) Until not long before the Genroku era, it continued to signify the place where the audience sat, the large open space in front of the stage that in later Edo times came to be known as *doma* (literally an unfloored space in a building, but in Japanese architecture used of any area that is not boarded and raised above the level of the ground).

In opposition to the *shibai* in this sense there were special seats for the privileged, which were known as *sajiki*, or sometimes *shajiki* or *sanjiki*. The word originally signified a raised platform, and the first *sajiki* was in fact a kind of dais made of boards and raised above the surrounding earth. The word itself is extremely ancient, appearing in the *Kojiki*. *Sajiki* seem to have been constructed originally as temporary structures for the gods to dwell in on their visits to earth, but the meaning gradually changed to that of special seats constructed for the benefit of privileged persons, and of the nobility in particular. At shrine and temple performances of *dengaku* and *sarugaku*, early dramatic forms that were very popular in medieval times, *sajiki* were always set up for the privileged. The same custom was taken over by kabuki at an early stage in its history.

THE STAGE AND THE *YAGURA*

The use of the word *butai*, still used of the stage itself, dates from the introduction of *bugaku*, the ancient court dances. Although in its early stages the *bugaku* stage was quite large, it later became standardized as a platform twenty-four feet square with a dais eighteen feet square standing on top of it. This type of stage derived directly from that imported from China along with *bugaku* itself.

In medieval times, the Nō stage came into being. The most distinctive difference between it and the old *bugaku* stage was the addition of a roof, which made it resemble

52

the dancing stage of a Shinto shrine or the type of stage used for performing the sacred dance known as *kagura*. The Nō stage, in fact—although since the Meiji Restoration it has often been incorporated into buildings more resembling the theaters of the West—is still in essence a place for performing solemn dances in homage to the gods. This was the stage that was to give birth to the kabuki stage; the stage on which Okuni danced her *kabuki odori*, on the dried-up part of the Kamo riverbed or in the grounds of shrines and temples, was the same as that used for the performances given by Nō actors to benefit the shrines and temples. As yet, there was no special kabuki stage, but it was the same stage that was gradually to develop into the characteristic kabuki stage we know today.

Whenever theatrical performances were given in temple or shrine grounds, a square wooden boxlike structure would be set up at the entrance. It was known as *yagura* ("tower" or "turret"), and became just as essential to theatrical performances and sumo matches as real turrets were to castles. It was on top of this *yagura* that the big drum was beaten to announce the commencement and close of a performance. Originally, however, the purpose was to provide a place for the gods to come down to earth so that the performance could be held in their presence. It was adorned with strips of white paper in the manner of a Shinto shrine, and a curtain was hung around it to signify that it was the temporary abode of a god.

In the early days of kabuki also, a *yagura* with the same paper decorations was set up as a kind of symbol of the theater. Sometimes lances and the like were arranged on top of it, partly as a charm to ward off evil spirits and also—in all likelihood—as a practical means of self-defense in what was still a barbarous age. In the early days, there was no roof over most of the audience—only the *sajiki* and the stage had shelter. Thus performances were impossible when it rained, but on fine days it was the beating of the big drum that confirmed that things would go ahead as scheduled. It was not until after Genroku times, in the Kyōhō era, that theaters came to have roofs; until the Genroku era, it seems that there was no more than a kind of temporary roof over one section of the audience.

In the Edo period, the *yagura* became a kind of symbol of a theater's special privilege to give performances. Even today, a square boxlike structure, the last vestige of the *yagura*, stands over the entrance of the Kabuki-za in Tokyo, and the Naka-za in Osaka also makes a similar gesture. In the past, however, the *yagura* had a vital significance for a theater, since it was a sign that the theater had been officially licensed by the magistrate representing the shogunate. What was known as *yagura ken* ("*yagura* right") was in fact the right to give public performances. As we have already seen, during the Edo period this right was granted to only three theaters—the Nakamura-za, the Ichimura-za, and the Morita-za, which were all managed by successive generations of the same families.

In the play *Soga no Taimen*, there is a scene in which one of the chief characters, Kudō Suketsune, mounts a dais and seats himself upon it. Before he does so, he traditionally faces toward the audience and gives a deep bow. This bow is not really directed at the audience, but is an act of obeisance directed at the god residing in the *yagura* at the entrance to the theater. The role of Kudō is always played by the head of the troupe, and the gesture can also be considered as a ceremony marking his assumption of the leader's position. Either way, this small piece of business is a sign of the reverence that was once paid to the *yagura*.

THE *ZA*

The theater of whose life the *yagura* was such an eloquent symbol was known in Japanese as *za*. The word is still used today in the names of some Tokyo theaters—Kabuki-za, Yūraku-za, Haiyū-za—but it is also used in the sense of a company, or troupe of actors, one well-known example being the Bungaku-za in Tokyo. In this latter sense, which is closer to that in which it was used in kabuki in pre-

Meiji days, the name *za* was not confined to actors only, but signified a union or guild of artisans or merchants in any one of a large number of trades. These *za* first came into being in the middle ages. In the field of entertainment, for example, there were two *za* of *dengaku* performers known as the *honza* ("original guild") and *shinza* ("new guild") respectively. These were zealous in stressing their own authority in rivalry to each other, and equally zealous in protecting their own rights against intruders. With the development of Nō, similar *za* were formed by Nō actors, and the "four guilds of Ōmi province" and "four guilds of Yamato province" were particularly famous. When kabuki came into being, there naturally arose *za* of kabuki actors also, and the head of a particular *za* of actors also became the manager of the theater at which they performed. Thus the term *za* did not originally signify the theater building at all.

The theater of Okuni's day was a space surrounded by a simple bamboo palisade, the latter being covered with straw matting to keep outsiders from peering in and getting a free show. The entrance, situated beneath the *yagura*, was known as *nezumi kido* or "rat gate," presumably since it was so small and had such a high threshold that people had to bend up double to get in. The verb *haneru*, meaning originally to "flip" or "flick," which people used to use in the sense of "to be over" in speaking of a theatrical performance, is traditionally said to have derived from the custom of covering the entrance with a straw mat that was "flipped up" as soon as the performance came to an end.

Since in the early days of kabuki the greater part of the audience sat on the ground, it was customary to spread out carpets or straw mats as protection against the damp. At first, people probably brought their own, but later the practice arose of hiring out mats half the size of a tatami for people to sit on. A member of the audience who took a strong dislike to a particular actor's performance would sometimes pick up his half-mat and hurl it onto the stage. The expression *hanjō o ireru* ("to throw in half-mats") is used even today in the sense of "to heckle" or "to jeer." There are any number of similar idioms that have come into everyday conversation from the world of kabuki—so closely was the kabuki theater at one time bound up with the lives of the common people.

THE *HANAMICHI*

The first step in the development towards the characteristic kabuki stage familiar today occurred after the transition to *yarō kabuki* (see p. 22), and took the form of a *tsukebutai* or "added stage." This was a forward extension of the *hashigakari* of the Nō stage—a kind of covered passage running from the left side of the stage to the greenroom—to the point where it came level with the stage proper. The next step was the development of the *hanamichi* ("flower way"), the raised gangway that runs through the auditorium from the stage to the back of the theater.

Something known as *hanamichi* had existed from around the Kambun and Empō eras, the time when *yarō kabuki* began, but at this stage it was used, not to permit the entrance and exit of actors through the audience during a performance, but to give the audience itself access to the stage. The "flower" of "flower way" originally signified a gratuity, and referred to gifts of money presented to an entertainer, which in early times were fastened to the branch of a flowering tree. The "flower way" was the route members of the audience took in presenting such gifts (which continued to be referred to euphemistically as "flowers" even when the original charming method of presentation had died out). Such being its purpose, the original *hanamichi* ran from the front of the audience to the center of the stage at the front.

It seems likely that this *hanamichi* was an extension of the three steps, known as *sandan* or *shirasubashigo*, that stood at the front of *bugaku* and Nō stages, and not, as has been suggested, an extension of the *hashigakari* that ran from the side of the stage. The *shirasubashigo* of the Nō stage was used when the shogun made a formal present of costumes to a Nō actor, the actor descending from the stage in order to receive the gift. The original *hanamichi* was similar to this, with the exception that it was the donor—or his envoy—who mounted the stage to make the presentation. It was after Genroku, at the beginning of the Kyōhō era, that the *hanamichi* began to be used in actual performances and actors first made their exits and entrances along it.

As the functions of the *hanamichi* changed, its position gradually shifted from the center towards the left-hand side of the stage, and to balance it another, narrower *hanamichi* put in its appearance on the right-hand side. This extra *hanamichi* was known as *kari-* (temporary) *hanamichi* or *higashi no ayami* ("east walk"), while the original *hanamichi* was referred to as *honhanamichi* ("main *hanamichi*"). The "east" derived from the fact that the stage was, in theory at least, supposed to face south, which meant that the right side was facing east and the left west. It was this, incidentally, that led to the use of of the words "*Tōzai! Tōzai!* ("East-west! East-west!)" to summon attention and secure quiet for some address to the audience. The use of the twin *hanamichi* had the effect of making the acting and production much more complex and varied than before; with the increasing development of the stage and stage machinery, kabuki itself gradually became more spectacular, and the plays themselves began to change in their turn.

Typical cases of the use of the *hanamichi* are found in *Shiranami Gonin Otoko*, where five actors put in their first appearance together on the main *hanamichi* and introduce themselves to the audience one at a time; and in *Gosho no Gorozō*, where two groups of men, one group wicked and the other virtuous, appear on the two *hanamichi* and engage in a verbal exchange across the heads of the audience. In another play, *Imoseyama*, the chief male and female characters advance towards the stage proper along the two *hanamichi*, exchanging conversation as they go, the *hanamichi* in this case being intended to represent the two banks of the Yoshino River, with the audience in between as the river. In *Nozaki Mura*, the story of the famous lovers Osome and Hisamatsu, the final scene has Osome on a boat on the main *hanamichi* moving towards the exit behind the audience and disappearing behind the curtain, while Hisamatsu, in a palanquin, proceeds down the *kari-hanamichi*. In this case, the main *hanamichi* is the river and the smaller *hanamichi* the bank; the audience, paying attention alternately to the two *hanamichi* as well as to the stage proper, has a kind of composite picture formed in its mind. The *hanamichi*, in short, created the possibility of all kinds of varied effects in the production of plays. The possiblities were increased still further by two more characteristic features of the kabuki stage—the revolving stage and the curtain.

THE REVOLVING STAGE AND CURTAIN

The revolving stage, a unique product of kabuki, rivals the *hanamichi* as one of the twin glories of the kabuki theater. The idea that inspired its inventor, Namiki Shōzō, was that of showing at one and the same time two events that occur simultaneously in different places. Its invention had a great effect on the construction of plays.

In 1829, a variation on the revolving stage known as *janome mawashi* ("bull's-eye revolving stage"), in which a second circle was cut within the first and revolved separately from it, came into use. The invention of the revolving stage also encouraged the development of various other kinds of stage machinery such as the *seridashi*, *suppon*, *gandō gaeshi*, and *hiki dōgu*, complex mechanisms that added to the variety of the plays. Of these, the *seridashi*, which is still in common use today, consists of a rectangle cut in the center of the revolving stage to make it possible to raise scenery from beneath the stage. For example, in the play *Sammon Gosan no Kiri* the great gateway of the Nanzenji temple is raised from below, while in the "Palace Scene" in the play *Sendai Hagi* the palace itself is raised so that a scene can be enacted in a cellar beneath the floor. The use of the *seridashi* is always accompanied by special music known as *seri no aikata*; and the moment when a large set piece begins to move carries with it precisely the same atmosphere of excitement as when one of the great floats used in a religious festival shudders and slowly begins to advance. One might almost say that at such times the scenery of kabuki ceases to be a simple background, or just so much apparatus to be pushed and pulled into place, and becomes one of the leading actors in a piece.

The same kind of thing is true of the curtain. The Nō theater, of course, has no curtain, and it was kabuki that first discovered and exploited its uses. Its whole nature, moreover, is different from that of the curtain in the theater of the West. The curtain of theaters in the West is a drop curtain that is either raised in one piece or else divided in two down the center and raised in two pieces towards the upper corners of the proscenium arch. The kabuki curtain is drawn aside horizontally, from the left of the stage to the right. The three theaters of Edo used a curtain known as *jōshiki maku* ("standard curtain"), made up of narrow vertical strips of black, green, and light brown cloth (the colors, of course, varied slightly from theater to theater). The reason for the name was probably that such a curtain was considered a rather dignified, formal affair. Only the officially licensed theaters could use this type of horizontal curtain; the small, unofficial theaters known as *hyakunichi shibai* were obliged to use drop curtains—for which reason the term *donchō shibai* ("drop curtain theaters") was used disparagingly of these small unlicensed establishments. Various other kinds of curtains are used in kabuki to achieve various different stage effects, but none of them separates the stage from the audience.

The kabuki curtain, like Western curtains, serves the purpose of marking off divisions in time and space, yet it possesses the added characteristic that it is, in itself, an integral part of the performance—one of the props, as it were. It is not simply a piece of machinery that opens and closes mechanically in response to a bell, but is utilized positively in the production. Thus the opening of the curtain is always accompanied by the beating of the clappers at the side of the stage, which steadily mark its progress, the whole process being timed so that the curtain finally disappears into the wings on precisely the last beat. The beating of the clappers in this way is in itself a technique that requires many years of practice to perfect, and is still more difficult when the production also calls for music, which forms a kind of counterpoint with the clappers. The Prologue to *Kanadehon Chūshingura* and the opening of *Kotobuki Soga no Taimen* are two instances where such a complex technique is required.

There is a difference between the way the clappers are sounded and the way the curtain is drawn at the end of an act depending on whether the piece is a *sewamono* or a *jidaimono*. In certain cases, the curtain is drawn without accompanying clappers, a process known as "curtain without the clappers." That such distinctions should be made is itself an indication of the conscious use made of the curtain to heighten the effect of the play.

A special curtain used for effecting sudden changes of scene and other dramatic effects is the type that can be opened by releasing along its whole length at the top, so that it falls to the stage, suddenly revealing whatever has been concealed behind it until now. The curtain is usually light blue, of red and white stripes, or black—symbolizing darkness—and is suspended by rings hooked onto knobs arranged in a row along the long bamboo pole from which the curtain hangs. At a signal from the clappers, this bamboo pole is suddenly twisted by pulling on a rope, so that the knobs along its length dip, disengaging simultaneously all the rings along the top of the curtain, which thereby drops in one piece. This method of opening a curtain, which is probably not to be found anywhere outside kabuki, also affords what is, except in films, the quickest method of all of "cutting" to a new scene.

The cloth known as *keshimaku* ("concealing curtain") in not a true curtain in the preceding sense at all, but is a black cloth held up in front of a character who is supposed to have died onstage, so that he can effect his exit without spoiling the illusion.

Whereas in the West the drawing—or the dropping—of the curtain invariably signifies the end of the play, it is a characteristic of kabuki that the emotional climax of a piece occasionally comes *after* the curtain has been drawn. Perhaps the most famous example of this occurs in *Kanjinchō*. At the end of the play, the closing of the curtain leaves the hero Benkei alone on the *hanamichi*, along which he executes a highly exciting *roppō* (see p. 48) before finally making his exit through the curtain at the opposite end of the theater from the stage. Such an idea is, of course, unfamiliar to Western audiences, and it is reported that when a kabuki troupe presented *Kanjinchō* in America a few years ago, the audience prepared to leave immediately after the curtain had gone across, thereby disrupting what should be the emotional climax of the whole piece.

There are various special terms associated with the curtain. The theater people who work on the audience's side of the curtain are known as *omotekata* ("front-men") while those who work behind the curtain—and this includes the actors, the scene-shifters, and the musicians in the *geza* box alike—are known as *urakata* ("behind-men"). The word *makumi* (literally "curtain-seeing") means to go to see one act of a play only, and the term *maku* is used as a translation of the Western word "act" in modern drama. *Maku no uchi* ("between the curtains") is familiar in everyday life as the name of a particular type of box lunch, so called because it was originally eaten in the theater during the interval between acts. The term *nobetsu makunashi* ("straight on without curtain") signifies the method whereby changes of scene are indicated by shifting scenery and props, or by use of the revolving stage, without resorting to use of the curtain, and consequently has come into ordinary speech as an adverb meaning "uninterruptedly," "non-stop."

SCENERY AND PROPS

There is an extremely intimate relationship in kabuki between techniques of acting and production on the one hand, and the special nature of the stage machinery and scenery on the other. One interesting characteristic of kabuki scenery is the concept of *jōshiki dōgu* ("standard scenery"), which refers to various typical arrangements of the stage that may occur in many different plays. Thus *hirabutai* ("plain stage") refers to the stage used without any special scenery or props at all. The stage with a simple platform stood on it is known was *nijū* ("double"). This platform comes in various heights, low, medium, and high, known in Japanese as *tsune-ashi* ("normal step"), *chū-ashi* ("medium step") or *chū-daka* ("medium height"), and *taka-ashi* ("high step") respectively. The measurements are 1 *shaku* 4 *sun* (approximately one foot five inches), 2 *shaku* 1 *sun* (approximately two feet one inch), and 2 *shaku* 8 *sun* (approximately two feet nine-and-one-half inches) respectively. The *tsune-ashi* platform is used in *sewamono* plays, the others in *jidaimono* plays. The *shosagoto*, the dance pieces, make use of two special platforms known as *hinadan* and *yamadai*. The *hinadan* ("doll stand," so called because of the terraced stand on which dolls in ancient court dress stood for display at the time of the Doll Festival on March 3) is for the use of *nagauta* musicians, and occupies the rear center of the stage; the *yamadai* ("mountain dais," so called because it has a low mountain painted on its side), is occupied by the musicians who perform *tokiwazu* and *kiyomoto* shamisen music, and other types of *jōruri* music, and usually stands somewhat to the left of the stage. In Japan, the principal musicians are not placed out of sight in a box, but are situated on top of an inverted box in full view of the audience.

Long years of experience with scenery and props, and increasing division of labor among those responsible for them, has resulted in a very strict distinction between the two categories. To take only one example, a piece of scenery representing a cherry tree will be the responsibility of the scene-shifters, but a spray of blossom that is to be broken off the tree and will thus come into contact with an actor's hand is a prop, and as such is the responsibility of those in charge of props in general.

A word should be said here about lighting. The only means of illumination used in theaters during the Edo period was candles, but since regulations required that all performances should take place in the daytime, use was made of natural daylight—allowed in, when theaters acquired roofs, through skylights. In the late afternoon, or when the day was especially dark, this was supplemented with candles. Lighting effects, in short, were not particularly developed, and were restricted chiefly to the opening and shutting of skylights to suggest night scenes, rainy days, and the like. One special effect that is worthy of mention, however, was known as *tsura-akari* (''face light'') or *sashidashi* (''thrusting out''). This was a kind of spotlighting effect used when the head of the troupe performed, achieved by means of a candle on a long holder, which an attendant thrust out so as to illuminate the actor's face. It is still used even nowadays when it is particularly desired to create a ''period'' effect.

AUDIENCES AND PERFORMANCES

DRAMA IS unthinkable without audiences. Good audiences are essential if drama is to come into being as an art, and equally essential if it is to achieve maturity. In Japan, the characteristic entertainments of each age naturally reflected the tastes and culture of the audiences to which they catered. Among the classical stage arts, *bugaku* had its survival guaranteed by its position within the culture of the court, and the nobility furnished the audiences that made it thrive. In the same way, the growth of Nō was fostered by the samurai class.

The kabuki and puppet theater, which developed in Tokugawa times, differed from these earlier forms in that they were encouraged chiefly by the merchant class. Even so, the term "merchant class" covered a section of society that differed considerably from period to period in its education, economic status, and general culture, and the nature of kabuki fluctuated correspondingly. Even within a single period, several levels can be distinguished in the merchant class; it varied from district to district within the city, and there was a great difference between the merchants of Edo and those of the Kyoto-Osaka area. There were other obvious differences in taste dictated by age and sex. In fact, the single term "merchant class" covers a whole range of nuances of taste and outlook, all of which were incorporated into kabuki.

Our only knowledge of audiences of the days when Okuni originated the *kabuki odori* is derived from illustrated books and screen paintings of the day. These suggest that kabuki audiences at the time were rather aristocratic: among them one can even distinguish women of the nobility, priests, and high-ranking samurai. It is interesting also to find, mingling with the other spectators, foreigners in the dress of Portuguese traders and seamen of the day.

Early kabuki, thus, would seem to have drawn its patrons from a comparatively high level of society. Contemporary accounts suggest, moreover, that during the period of *onna kabuki* the popular stars frequently found patrons among the daimyo of the various provinces. In the period of *wakashu kabuki* and on into that of *yarō kabuki*, no less a personage than Iemitsu, the third Tokugawa Shogun, frequently invited a troupe led by Nakamura Kanzaburō to perform kabuki dances for him in Edo Castle. In the period preceding the Genroku era—during the Manji (1658–61) and Kambun eras, for example, some extremely ardent devotees of kabuki appeared among the ranks of the daimyo. Lord Naonori of Yamato, for instance, left many accounts of kabuki and puppet theater performances in his personal diary.

This diary affords much invaluable material for the modern scholar, since he regularly summoned kabuki and puppet troupes to his mansion to perform for him and painstakingly set down what he saw. It was of course unthinkable that a daimyo should go personally to a theater stall in order to see kabuki on its home ground. Yet such was his infatuation with the theater that whenever he heard rumor of some new play or other item of interest, he would send a retainer especially to see it, and afterwards set down the report in writing.

Even in later times, there were cases of a daimyo living in retirement patronizing a particular actor, but generally speaking the daimyo's interest in kabuki ceased with the Genroku era. From Genroku on, an estrangement occurred, on the surface at least, between the samurai class and kabuki. Even after this members of the samurai class still continued to go to the theater surreptitiously, but, in theory at least, the theater was lumped together with the gay quarters as a place of ill repute from which the samurai and his family should stay clear. And from the Kyōhō era on, the perfection of the feudal system and the reinforcing of the caste system led to an increasingly repressive attitude towards kabuki on the part of the authorities.

As we have already seen, however, things were not always so, and it is believed that *rōnin*—masterless samurai—played a role of considerable importance in the early, formative stages of kabuki. Even as late as the Genroku era, the great playwright Chikamatsu Monzaemon is said to have come from a samurai family, and Sawamura Sōjūrō I, founder of a celebrated theatrical family, is said to have been of samurai stock himself. Moreover, until quite a late date good-for-nothing second and third sons of shogunate retainers commonly became musicians in the kabuki theater orchestra. (It is apparently for this reason that—alone among those who participated in kabuki performances—the musicians [*hayashi*] were given the honorific prefix *o-* as well as the suffix *-san*, and were known as *o-hayashi-san*; it is said that for the same reason the musicians' room in the theater was equipped with a sword rack.) Thus the influence of the samurai class on kabuki cannot be entirely ignored, but it is safe to say that, as time went by, it increasingly came to reflect the culture of the merchant class to the exclusion of all others.

The samurai class did not necessarily dislike kabuki, and it was even considered rather stylish to imitate this aspect of merchant culture. The women of the shogun and feudal lords had dancing masters called *kyōgenshi* who came to their houses and performed kabuki dances for them. There were also dilettantes among the samurai who showed a positive interest in one or the other aspect of kabuki—there was a shogunate official, for example, who became known as a master of the shamisen. On the surface, however, the samurai were officially forbidden to have contact with the theater as such, and there is a story that the daughter of a daimyo was imprisoned, and the retainers accompanying her forced to commit suicide, because she stopped her palanquin in front of a theater and looked inside.

For open encouragement, therefore, kabuki had to look to the merchant class. As we have seen, the merchant class embraced a wide range of varying tastes, all of which were reflected in kabuki. Before examining such distinctions, however, one can make one further, more basic classification—between the true connoisseur of the theater and the easy-to-please rabble. Although differences of social status, rank, and age play a certain part here, the distinction is primarily one that transcends such external considerations. The drama critics of the day (the men who wrote the *yakusha hyōbanki*) divided the members of an audience into two sections, the *sajiki* and the *doma*. In the early days, the *doma* (nowadays an unfloored section of a building, level with the ground outside) was the stretch of turf immediately in front of the stage, and was known as *shibai* (see p. 52), or sometimes *oikomiba* (literally, "place to pack them in"). The *sajiki*, on the other hand, was a raised wooden section on either side of the *doma*, divided up into sections like the boxes of a Western theater. There was a great difference in the entrance fee, of course, but the contemporary use of the terms *doma* and *sajiki* also shows that, much as in the Elizabethan theater, there were differences in education and dramatic sophistication between the two.

Only merchants of a certain standing could afford to go into the *sajiki* in the first place, of course. Entrance to the *sajiki* was effected via the *shibaijaya* ("theater teahouses"). These resembled the other teahouses common at the time, but served the special purpose of providing meals for the better-class patron and also providing him with a place to change his clothes, relax during the intermissions, and even entertain. When the play was over, he could hold parties there to which he would invite the actors or geisha. There were *ōjaya* ("large teahouses") and *kojaya* ("small teahouses"), both of which owned shares in the theater. Their influence on theatrical circles was considerable, and they apparently sometimes took a hand in planning programs.

No doubt, despite the official ban, the *sajiki* patrons included many high-ranking samurai who came incognito to see the play. Toward the end of the Edo period, they even included some of the *oyashikikata*, the majordomos who supervised the Edo mansions of the feudal lords while they were away in their own fiefs. More often than not, the latter came at the expense of wealthy merchants who did business with their establishments. The play *Kirare Yosa* includes one character, a merchant, who obtains enormous privileges by entertaining such a man at the theater. Color prints of the interiors of Edo period theaters dating from around the Meiwa and An'ei eras sometimes show a row of women with cotton head-coverings seated in the audience. These are obviously ladies-in-waiting from the shogun's private quarters, taking advantage of a short leave of absence to see kabuki. Their vacation usually came around the third month, and they provided quite a distinguished clientele.

For the benefit of patrons such as these, brilliantly spectacular plays such as *Sukeroku* or *Kagamiyama* would be put on. At the time, there were commonly corridors leading from the *sajiki* to the greenroom or the manager's quarters and to the teahouses, an arrangement that favored the growth of intrigues between patrons and the actors who appeared in such plays. One of the more spectacular scandals that arose as a result was the "Ejima-Ikushima affair" (p. 27) involving a maid in the shogun's private apartments and the actor Ikushima Shingorō, whom she invited to a party with disastrous results for kabuki as a whole.

A clue to the nature of theatergoing at the time is given in *Kyakusha Hyōbanki* by the popular novelist Shikitei Samba, who wrote in the Bunka and Bunsei eras, toward the end of the Edo period. The work gives patrons of the theater (as the punning title suggests; *kyakusha* means "patron") the same attention normally accorded to actors by the *yakusha hyōbanki*, and is valuable for the picture it gives of audiences of the day. For instance, Samba classifies the ladies-in-waiting just mentioned as "extra-upper-upper," which almost certainly carried a flavor of "putting on airs," and not merely "high-class."

It is certain, indeed, that the patrons of the *sajiki* considered themselves to be a cut above the common people in the *doma*, and that to the latter they seemed to inhabit a kind of remote world above the clouds. There is a satirical verse of the time that runs: "Viewed from the *sajiki*, ordinary mortals seem somehow mean"; and another that says, "Invited to sit in the *sajiki*, one leaves the common herd." Both verses effectively point up the distinction between the two classes of patron. It should be noted that there was also a steadier, less spectacular inhabitant of the *sajiki*, different from these flashier types. This was the man of substance who had a genuine interest in the theater, the type of man referred to in late Edo times as *kabesu*. This was a portmanteau word made up of the first syllables of *kashi* ("cake"), *bentō* (box lunch), and *sushi*, and referred to the type of patron who, hating to miss the play, had food sent from the teahouse and munched his way through it at his seat, without having to take his eyes off the performance on the stage.

A system peculiar to kabuki was that of *hiiki*, or patronage. The patronage in question was directed by members of the audience towards particular actors, and was doubtless beneficial to the development of the theater. As the *Kyakusha Hyō-banki* said, "The prosperity of the theater depends on the patrons; if an actor gets on in the world, it is thanks to his supporters, without whom he would not last a single day, a single moment even." Such patrons were often organized into associations called *renjū*. These *renjū*, especially in Osaka, seem to date back to a very early stage in the history of kabuki. By the Genroku era, there was one known as Ō *renjū*. Somewhat later, by the Shōtoku era (1711–16), there was another known as Sasase, and by the Kyōhō era an Ōte *renjū*. In Edo, the *renjū* were formed somewhat later. These associations, it should be noted, were very different in nature from the drama societies and playgoing parties of today, and were more like supporters' associations having close links with particular actors.

Whenever a special piece was put on, for example, a new play or one of the "Eighteen Favorite Plays" such as *Sukeroku*, it was the custom for these associations of patrons to give presents. Thus whenever *Sukeroku* was performed, the Yoshiwara association would be responsible for supplying the umbrella the hero carried and the purple band he wore around his head. The members would also attend the actual performance and engage in direct verbal exchange with the actor concerned.

This kind of exchange, a very important feature of kabuki, ensured that there was always a close rapport between an actor and his audience. It was very different from the state of affairs in modern theater, in which the audience is remote from the events on the stage—an outsider, as it were, peering into a box from which one side has been removed. An actor would even address his audience directly as he left the stage by the *hanamichi*, and members of the audience would try to grasp him by the hand. There was also a ritual known as *teuchishiki* and somewhat resembling a toast, in which, halfway through a performance, actor and audience would clap hands together. Quite often, an actor who was going to some other part of the country would read an address to his audience, whereupon a member of the supporters' association would go onto the stage and deliver a eulogy.

The humblest members of a kabuki audience were the frequenters of the *doma* seats. The "pit," now considered the best place of all, was in the Edo period the cheapest and the most vulgar. The audience that watched the play from the *doma* was largely made up of shop assistants, apprentices, and serving men and women, who would come to watch the play during *yabuiri*, the annual holiday for apprentices and servants. "The Danjūrōs of the pit go out on their ears" said one humorous verse of the day, evoking what must have been a familiar scene—a group of apprentices at the theater swaggering about drunkenly in fond imitation of their idol, the actor Danjūrō, until they finally fell to blows and were ejected from the theater in disgrace.

There were, in fact, other seats still cheaper than the *doma*—the *mukōsajiki* ("farther *sajiki*"), also known as *ōmukō* (the "great beyond"), which faced the stage at the very back of the theater. The rearmost seats of all in the "great beyond" (the "back of beyond"?) were known as the "deaf gallery," since it was almost impossible to hear the dialogue at all. Samba has some amusing descriptions of the way patrons of the "back of beyond" tried to make the best of a bad situation. "This is the best place in the house," one of them says. "Not hearing makes it twice as enjoyable, as you have the fun of working out for yourself what's happening on the stage."

There were other seats too, equally cheap, but because they were too near the stage rather than too far from it. These were located on top of a raised platform popularly known as the "saints' pedestal," while the actual space on top of the platform was called "Yoshino." These seats had the disadvantage of being situated on the left-hand side of the stage itself and of providing nothing but rear views of the actors most of the time. Their occupants would disappear from general view whenever the curtain was drawn; when it was up, they bore a remarkable resemblance to the conventional sculptural representations of the Sixteen Saints that one finds in Buddhist temples, arranged in rows on one single pedestal. Yoshino is the name of a hill near Nara celebrated for its cherry blossoms, and the seats were given this name because the best view they afforded was not of the play but of the sprigs of artificial cherry blossom that hung down from above the stage.

Admission fees in the Edo period were based strictly on supply and demand, and one of the most distressing features of the Edo theater must have been the way the price of seats rose as a play's popularity increased. On the other hand, they fell sharply whenever there was a poor box office. Thus although admission fees were fixed in theory, they fluctuated sharply in practice, which meant that to invest money in the theater was a kind of speculation, an uncertain affair at best. The man who put up the money for a production, referred to at the time as *kinkata*, was accordingly regarded as little better than a gambler.

Whenever there was a rush at the box office, the policy was naturally to cram in just as many spectators as possible. There was no question of fixed capacities in the theaters of the day, and in a pinch spectators would even be allowed on the stage, which came to resemble the dancing stage at some small Shinto shrine during its annual festival, when the local children were allowed onto the stage to watch. "What a hit!" said one humorous verse, "Only a few square feet left to dance in." Another verse of the day conjures up an even more amusing picture: "Such a hit! The corpses are cleared away with difficulty." The press of spectators, in other words, was so great that only with difficulty could they remove the "corpses" strewn about the stage after one of the great swordfights so popular in kabuki.

The spectacle presented by the kabuki theater on such occasions (with "actors and audience rubbing shoulders," as another verse put it) must have been unlike anything imaginable in the theater today. Nor were the audiences themselves well-mannered in the modern sense. Cries of approval and bellows of "Ham!" ("radish" would be nearer to the Japanese expression) were the order of the day, and the audience ate and drank freely as it watched. Shouts of encouragement to the actors were an important element in creating the special aura of excitement surrounding the kabuki. These calls varied from age to age: the late Sadanji II, for example, was customarily hailed with the novel cry of "*Daitōryō!*" ("President!"); but in the early days of kabuki cries such as "*Yo! Tento-sama!* (literally "Sun!" but "Light of my life!" might convey the feeling better) were common. A special cry used for the *wakashu kabuki* was "*Annami no o-saku!*" ("creation of Annami"), a reference to the work of the famous sculptor Annami, whose statues of the bodhisattva Jizō were considered to represent an ideal of masculine beauty. Still more commonly, however, the audience simply called out the *yagō* ("shop name") of the actor—Nakamura-ya, Harima-ya, etc. This *yagō* was probably a survival from the days when many actors ran hair-oil shops and other similar establishments while they were not appearing at the theater.

The very lowest grade of spectator was, of course, the man who got in free; such people were referred to as *aburamushi* ("cockroaches," for obvious reasons) or *dempō*, a name stemming from the old custom of allowing free admission to anyone wearing the habit of the Dempō-in, a subsidiary temple of the great temple of Kannon at Asakusa.

The audiences obviously varied greatly in the degree of education and sophistication they brought to bear on the proceedings. One of the *hyōbanki*, for example, remarked scathingly of an actor playing to the gallery: "He must have been aiming at the *doma* audience; certainly the servants and apprentices on their annual outing went home greatly contented." Another *hyōbanki* upbraided an actor directly in the following terms: "That kind of acting may please the pit, but don't expect the connoisseurs in the boxes to come to see it. Put an end to it, now!''

During the first half of the Edo period the Kyoto-Osaka area was the headquarters of the kabuki world, and audiences in that area prided themselves on possessing a more highly developed critical faculty than their counterparts in Edo. It is recorded that when Danjūrō II, an Edo actor, went to Osaka, his audiences were outraged at what they considered his ''crude ranting.'' The type of theatergoer who prided himself on being well informed and noticing details that escaped the average man was known as *migōsha*. An earlier word with the same sense was *mezuishō* (''eye-crystal''). Crystal was originally the material used for making spectacles, and the implication was that such a man could discern well what was going on on the stage.

There were several ways in which audiences actually gained admission to the theater. The patrons of the *sajiki* entered via the teahouses, where they would rest and refresh themselves on the way. Those going to the *doma* bought tickets at the gateway by the *yagura*, and passed through directly into the ''auditorium.'' Towards the end of the Edo period, the theaters were all situated in Saruwaka-chō (in the Asakusa area) where they formed a kind of theater district. This meant that, transportation being poor, patrons from the residential districts that lay on higher ground far removed from the more plebeian lowlands bordering the Sumida River were obliged to leave home before dawn if they wanted to see the beginning of the program.

In the Edo period, there were no evening performances. The day's program ran from early morning until dusk; actual times varied from period to period, but generally speaking things started at six o'clock in the morning and went on until five o'clock in the evening. A resident of the more distant areas of the city who wanted to miss nothing had to make his preparations the day before and set forth, with the aid of paper lanterns, while it was still pitch dark. For women, it was a particularly arduous undertaking; there were kimono to be put on, difficult obi to tie, and hair to be done up in elaborate coiffures, so that all in all a trip to the theater was likely to consume the better part of two days.

With *kaomise* performances, the first drum warning of an approaching performance was struck at two in the morning. A contemporary record referring to ''the first drum tearing one from one's dreams in the middle of the night'' must have summed up the feelings of many a theatergoer of the day. By the time a patron from the highlying residential districts had reached the Kyōbashi district, near the center of modern Tokyo, dawn would be breaking. A little further on at Nihombashi, he would be joined by other theatergoers, from different parts of the city, all converging into one steady stream flowing towards the theater district in Saruwaka-chō. Around the time when it became fully light, he would drop into a shop for a quick bowl of rice, tea, and pickles, then go on to Saruwaka-chō, where brightly colored banners bearing the names of popular actors of the day would be fluttering in the morning breeze, setting the hearts of the ladies beating faster. Finally, in front of the theater, he would find the *kido* (''wicket'') *geisha*, the men who were the equivalent of Western circus barkers. These *kido geisha* wore gay clothes and their patter was enlivened by imitations of well-known actors. There were also men paid to haul in patrons—known as *kappa* (river imps), presumably because the *kappa* believed to lurk in rivers were similarly fond of grabbing the unsuspecting wayfarer and dragging him in.

A second signal from the big drum, and a dance called *Sambasō* would begin. This dance, always performed before the program itself began, is a ceremonial piece and is known in theatrical circles as *bandachi*. It was performed each day by lower-ranking actors from the *ōbeya* (communal greenroom). In order to see everything, including this preliminary *Sambasō*, one needed to be at the theater at a very early hour indeed. A popular verse of the day pokes fun at the *kido geisha* as they announce that *Sambasō* is about to start: "Brushing their teeth as they announce it—*Sambasō*." "*Sambasō*—people from afar come to see it," says another contemporary verse, the idea being that it was only the people who had to make a special effort to go to the theater at all who insisted on getting their full money's worth and seeing the program right from the beginning. On the other hand, the people of Sakai-chō (where the Nakamura-za stood before the shift to Saruwaka-chō) are laughed at because they prided themselves on being connoisseurs and deliberately did not turn up until the afternoon.

Because a visit to the theater required a whole day—or two days in some cases—the audience was liable to get tired well before the proceedings were over. The better-class patrons in the *sajiki*, therefore, would often retire to the *chaya*, where they would rest, eat, or even put on a fresh change of clothes before returning to their seats. The wives and daughters of wealthy merchants, for example, would sometimes wear different kimono for the morning, afternoon, and evening respectively. "They change so often," one humorous verse said, "one wonders if *they* are putting on a show for the actors." Another verse, in a reference to the Seven Komachi (the seven episodes associated with the Heian poetess Ono no Komachi that occur so frequently as a theme in art) speaks of "the Komachi of the *sajiki*, who changes her clothes seven times."

Programs were illustrated booklets known as *ehonbanzuke* and *yakuwaribanzuke* with likenesses of idols for devotees to pore over in rapture. On their way home they could buy prints of those same idols, while the teahouses, in the hope of encouraging larger tips, would present them with hair decorations, hand towels, fans, and the like, all with their favorite actors' names on them. For the people who had stayed at home, they could buy rice crackers, cakes, or cosmetics, also with the actors' names inscribed on them. Actors and the theater were so popular at the time that a large number of fashions and fads were started at the theater, in which respect it was rivaled only by the gay quarters. We have already seen, in the discussion of the *hanamichi* (p. 54), how close the relationship between audiences and actors was in the theater. There was even a custom—which in some cases has survived to the present day—whereby an actor would throw something to the audience from the stage or *hanamichi*. In *Musume Dōjōji*, the lead actor would toss to the audience the cotton towel he had been using.

A word should also be said about admission fees. There was a great discrepancy between the *doma* and the *sajiki*. The charge in the *sajiki* during the 1810s and 1820s was said to be the equivalent of three bales of rice, which in monetary terms must have corresponded to at least 1.2 *ryō*. On the other hand, a place in the *doma* could be obtained for as little as 12–15 *momme* (60 *momme* = 1 *ryō*), plus incidentals such as the charge for renting a mat to sit on.

In practice, this meant that the majority of kabuki fans among the common people had to content themselves with what was known as *koshibai* ("little theater") or *hyakunichishibai* ("hundred days' theater"), which was performed in the grounds of shrines and temples or at popular gathering places in the city. In a way, these performances had a function similar to the cheap cinemas found in the vicinity of large railway stations in modern Japanese towns. They were far less dignified than the real theaters; they used a simple drop curtain instead of a proper curtain that was pulled across in front of the stage, and for this reason were often referred to slightingly as *donchōshibai*, "drop curtain theaters" (see p. 56). Nevertheless, they played an important role in popularizing kabuki among the lower, less educated classes of the large cities.

By the latter part of the Edo period, kabuki had spread throughout the whole country. Performances were given in all the castle towns, and even in the smaller country towns and villages the farmers would take matters into their own hands and present their own performances, which were known as *ji shibai* ("local theater").

The enthusiasm of the provinces for kabuki reached its peak in the period from the Bunka and Bunsei eras until the Meiji Restoration (1811–1868). So widespread, in fact, was popular interest in the theater that any history of kabuki that deals only with the great theaters in the three great urban centers and does not take account of these local performances must be considered biased and incomplete.

THE PLATES

FAMOUS STAGE SCENES

Pl. 10. *Ame no Gorō*
This kabuki dance-drama is a rendering in dance form of Soga no ▷
Gorō visiting the Ōiso gay quarters in the rain and displays softness
within the rough, dashing *aragoto* style. In kabuki, Soga no Gorō always
wears a costume with a swallowtail butterfly design. His youthfulness
is suggested by the red leggings (*kyahan*), while the shawl covering his
head indicates that he is trying to remain incognito. The costume
overall is an exaggerated, old-fashioned style. (*Gorō*, Ichikawa Danjūrō)

Pl. 11. *Narukami*

This is one of the *aragoto* pieces in the "Eighteen Favorite Kabuki Plays." Hatred of the Court has led the holy man Narukami to use his divine powers to confine all of the dragon gods in the land, thus causing a terrible drought. The Court sends a beautiful woman to the hills where Narukami and his followers live. She seduces Narukami. The spell is broken and rain falls. This scene depicts the corruption of Narukami, whose white robes symbolize his saintliness, by Taema, a court lady dressed as a *hime* ("a young woman of noble birth"). Narukami's robes change into a flame pattern after his corruption. The purple band (*bōshi*) on the front of Taema's wig is an old costume style, and Taema's eyebrows, called *bōshi mayu*, are drawn in this manner when the purple band is worn. (*Taema*, Bandō Tamasaburō; *Narukami*, Ichikawa Danjūrō)

Pl. 12. *Kuruwa Bunshō: The Yoshida-ya Scene*
Izaemon has come to the brothel Yoshida-ya, only to find that his favorite courtesan, Yūgiri, is with another patron. In this scene he is shown complaining to her. Plays centering around Yūgiri and Izaemon date back to 1679, but it was not until 1808 that the story was incorporated into the play *Kuruwa Bunshō*. This scene provides an example of *wagoto* acting at its most typical. (*Yūgiri*, Onoe Kikugorō; *Izaemon*, Nakamura Senjaku)

Pl. 13. *Kumo ni Magō Ueno no Hatsuhana: The Ōguchi-ya Retreat Scene in Iriya*
This scene depicts a secret meeting between the Yoshiwara courtesan Michitose and her lover Naojirō (Naozamurai). In kabuki the placement of actors back to back indicates a love scene. Since this is a *sewamono* play, the acting and costumes are more realistic than those in *jidaimono*. (*Michitose*, Bandō Tamasaburō; *Naojirō*, Ichikawa Danjūrō)

Pl. 14. *Kanjinchō*
This is one of the "Eighteen Favorite Kabuki Plays." Benkei, dressed as a *yamabushi*, looks back at Togashi, the guard at the Ataka barrier, as he thanks him for letting Yoshitsune and his band (who are all in disguise) pass through the barrier safely. Benkei then follows after the band. (*Benkei*, Ichikawa Danjūrō)

Pls. 15–16. *Ichinotani Futaba Gunki*,
ACT III: *Kumagai Jinya*
Kumagai realizes the significance of the
warning against cutting flowers that appears on a signboard put up by the
Minamoto general Yoshitsune. At the
battle of Ichinotani, he accordingly kills
his own son Kojirō instead of Taira no
Atsumori, the young noble who is his
enemy, thus fulfilling the directive to
cut off one's own finger rather than cut
a flower. He hands the head of his son
to Yoshitsune when he comes to inspect
what is supposedly the head of Atsumori. The lamentations of Kumagai's
wife Sagami are silenced when she
realizes what he has done. In the end,
Kumagai becomes a Buddhist monk
and sets forth to wander the country
alone. (*Kumagai*, Onoe Shōroku)

Pl. 17. *Kagotsurube Sato no Eizame*, ACT IV: *Shin Yoshiwara Nakano-chō*
Sano Jirōzaemon, a country bumpkin, makes his appearance in Edo's
Yoshiwara gay quarters. By chance, he encounters a procession of
courtesans in Nakano-chō, the main thoroughfare, and is at once infatuated, with disastrous effects on his whole life. (*The courtesan Yatsuhashi*, Nakamura Utaemon; *Jirōzaemon*, Nakamura Kanzaburō)

Pl. 18. *Koibikyaku Yamato Ōrai*, ACT II: *The Seal-breaking Scene*
This play is a celebrated *sewamono* by Chikamatsu telling how Chū-bei, adopted son of a man in the express messenger (*hikyaku*) business, becomes involved with the courtesan Umegawa and, needing money, makes improper use of public funds. His friend Hachiemon comes to the gay quarters and discusses Chūbei's lack of money in front of many people. Chūbei himself hears this and flies into a rage in which he (half-inadvertently) breaks the seal of the money he has in his charge and uses all of it. (*Umegawa*, Nakamura Senjaku; *Chūbei*, Kataoka Takao)

Pls. 19–20. *Heike Nyogo no Shima*, ACT II: *Kikai ga Shima*

Pl. 19. In this play popularly known as *Shunkan*, a messenger comes from the capital to the island of Kikai ga Shima to inform Shunkan and his followers—who have been banished for allegedly plotting treason—that they have been pardoned. Shunkan gives up his place on the boat to a young woman of the island who has fallen in love with one of his followers, and is left alone on the island, gazing sadly at the boat as it recedes into the distance. (*Shunkan*, Matsumoto Hakuō)

Pl. 20. *Shunkan*, Nakamura Kan'emon; *Tanzaemon*, Kataoka Takao; *Naritsune*, Arashi Keishi; *Chidori*, Arashi Yoshisaburō)

Pl. 21. *Kasane*

Yoemon kills his wife Kasane, badly disfigured through retribution, with a sickle when she falls into a jealous rage. Her unravelling *obi* heightens the effect of the *tachimawari*, while the crescent moon in the night sky increases the eeriness of the scene, and the wild pinks (*nadeshiko*) by the waterside add a sorrowful touch. (*Kasane*, Nakamura Utaemon; *Yoemon*, Ichikawa Danjūrō)

Pl. 22. *Seki no To*
Shown here is a typical kabuki dance piece. Sekibei, officer of the barrier at Osaka, but in reality the archvillain Ōtomo no Kuronushi, is about to chop off a branch of a cherry tree when Sumizome, the spirit of the cherry, appears and exerts her charms on him. The pose adopted by Sumizome, in the guise of a courtesan, as she bends back to avoid the axe wielded by Kuronushi, is known as *ebizori* (''prawn bend'') *mie*. (*Sumizome*, Nakamura Jakuemon; *Kuronushi*, Onoe Shōroku)

Pl. 23. *Sagi Musume*
The last scene at the end of this kabuki dance-drama is of a white heron, which has taken the form of a young girl, turning into a dying heron. The hairdo has come undone, indicating that the actor is playing a supernatural role. In making the play conclude with the white heron on the verge of death, Kikugorō VI drew on the ballet about a dying swan. (Nakamura Utaemon)

Pl. 24. *Fuji Musume*
This piece is a translation into dance terms of the popular *Ōtsu-e*, a crude type of picture sold as souvenirs to travelers passing through Ōtsu, near Kyoto, on their way up or down the Tōkaidō highway. A favorite image was a young woman (*musume*) with wisteria flowers (*fuji*) on her shoulder. Here, a young woman dances before a background of wisteria in full bloom (*Fuji Musume*, Onoe Kikugorō)

Pls. 25–26. *Musume Dōjōji*

Pl. 25. This piece is the celebrated Nō play *Dōjōji* turned into a kabuki dance-drama. On the day on which a dedication service for the temple bell is to be held at the Dōjōji Temple, a dancing girl arrives at the ceremony. Strictly speaking, women are not allowed within the precincts, but she is admitted so that she can perform a dance. As she is dancing, however, her true identity is revealed as Kiyohime, the snake demon who destroyed the original bell. Here she is shown as the dancing girl Hanako, just beginning her performance with her eyes fixed in hatred on the bell. (*Hanako*, Nakamura Shikan)

Pl. 26. After jumping into the bell and knocking it down, Kiyohime the snake demon perches on it defiantly.

1–2. *Kotobuki Soga no Taimen*
In this scene the two Soga brothers, Jūrō and Gorō, come face to face with their dead father's foe, Kudō Suketsune, at the latter's mansion, and resolve that they will kill him in revenge for their father's death. All three theaters in Edo invariably presented this piece at the New Year, so both the costumes and production are extremely stylized. In the scene illustrated here, the two brothers, summoned by Asaina, advance on Kudō, who sits on the high dais. Gorō tries to dash forward impetuously, but Jūrō restrains him gently. (*Gorō*, Onoe Shōroku; *Jūrō*, Nakamura Kanzaburō; *Asaina*, Ichimura Uzaemon; *the courtesan Shōshō*, Nakamura Shikan; *the courtesan Tora*, Nakamura Utaemon; *Suketsune*, Ichikawa Danjūrō XI)

3. *Kanjinchō*

Yoshitsune, who is on bad terms with his elder brother, the Shogun Yoritomo, is on his way to the country in disguise with a band of his retainers. At the Ataka barrier on the way, he arouses the suspicions of the captain of the guard, Togashi, but is allowed to go on his way thanks to the cunning of his retainer Benkei. The play, an adaptation from the Nō, was first performed in 1840. It is one of the "Eighteen Favorite Kabuki Plays." In the scene shown here, the musicians who perform the accompanying *nagauta* are lined up in front of the backdrop painted with a pine tree that characterizes plays taken over from the Nō. Togashi has just seen through Yoshitsune's disguise as a porter, and Yoshitsune's followers are about to attack him, but Benkei holds them back with his priest's staff. (*Benkei*, Onoe Shōroku; *Togashi*, Ichikawa Danjūrō XI)

4-5. *Ya no Ne*

On a fine spring day when the plum blossoms are just coming into bud, Soga no Gorō is sharpening the head of a giant arrow he plans to use to kill his enemy, Kudō, when he falls asleep and has a dream that warns him that his elder brother is in danger. Upon awakening, he leaps onto the horse of a passing vegetable vendor and hastens off to the aid of his brother, urging his horse on with a large radish. The play is one of the *aragoto* pieces of the "Eighteen Favorite Kabuki Plays." (4. *Gorō*, Ichimura Uzaemon; *groom*, Nakamura Matagorō. 5. *Gorō*, Onoe Shōroku)

6. *Kenuki*

The daughter of the Ono family falls ill with a mysterious disease that makes her hair continually stand on end. As he sits waiting, Kumedera Danjō, who has come as a messenger, takes out a pair of tweezers (*kenuki*) to pluck his beard, but the tweezers begin to move of their own accord. He guesses that there is a magnet concealed in the ceiling, and realizes that the fact that the daughter's hair stands on end is caused by the metal ornaments she wears in her hair. He roots out the wicked chief retainer who is responsible, and goes home leaving the family in peace of mind once more. The play was first performed in 1742 as part of *Narukami Fudō Kitayama-zakura*, and is one of the "Eighteen Favorite Kabuki Plays." (*Danjō*, Ichikawa Danjūrō XI)

7. Narukami

The Court has sent a beautiful woman to seduce the holy man Narukami and break the spell he has cast over the country. Arousing himself from his infatuation, Narukami flies into a rage. His hair stands on end, his clothes change to a flame-colored robe, and he sets off in pursuit of the woman. The play was first performed in 1742 as part of *Narukami Fudō Kitayama-zakura*. (Narukami, Onoe Shōroku)

8. Kagekiyo

This is one of the "Eighteen Favorite Kabuki Plays." The Heike general Kagekiyo goes down to the camp gate of the Genji forces and is thrown into prison, but breaks out in order to take revenge on Yoritomo. In this scene, Kagekiyo has just broken out of prison and holds one of the prison's square pillars as he exits down the *hanamichi* doing a *roppō* after the curtain is closed. (Ichikawa Danjūrō)

9–10. *Dammari (Mime Interlude)*
Various characters search, perhaps for treasure, in the dark deep in the hills. The entire action is performed in a highly stylized manner without dialogue. At the end of a *kaomise dammari*, the actor who is head of the troupe conventionally appears from inside a wayside shrine and advances onto the *hanamichi*, where he strikes a pose.

9. The head of the troupe, dressed as a bandit, has just advanced onto the *hanamichi*. The other actors on the stage all strike various *mie*.

10. The *ishinage* (''stone-throwing'') *mie* calls for an actor holding a rolled banner to have a fight with constables and pose as if he were throwing a stone at them. (Ichikawa Danjū-rō XI)

11. *Kataki Uchi Tengajaya Mura*, ACT III: *Tenjin Forest*

Iori, whose father, Hayase Gemba, has been murdered, is wandering about the countryside with his followers in search of the assassin. Iori's retainer Motoemon joins the enemy side, and through his machinations Iori—who by now has become a cripple living in a wretched hovel—is cut to pieces by the enemy. This kind of death by the sword in a dramatic, highly stylized fashion is one of the specialties of a kabuki actor. (*Motoemon*, Nakamura Kanzaburō; *Iori*, Morita Kanya XIV)

12. *Dannoura Kabuto Gunki*, ACT III: *Akoya no Kotozeme*

Shigetada summons the courtesan Akoya to an inquest and asks the whereabouts of her lover, Taira no Kagekiyo, who is in hiding. She insists that she does not know, whereupon Shigetada makes her play three instruments—the koto, the shamisen, and the *kokyū* (a three-stringed bowed instrument)—and from the sounds she produces tries to detect what is in her mind. Here, Shigetada is shown listening intently to Akoya's playing of the koto. The way he "plays" these instruments is one of the tests of an *onnagata*'s skill and affords one of the highlights of this play. (*Akoya*, Nakamura Utaemon; *Shigetada*, Kataoka Nizaemon)

13. *Imoseyama Onna Teikin*, ACT IV: *Palace Scene*
The young woman Omiwa is following her lover Motome by means of a string attached to him. Reaching Iruka's palace, she is tormented by malicious ladies-in-waiting, and loses consciousness. When she awakens and sits up, she finds the string attached to an ornament, and a piece of paper fastened to her hair. She blazes with fierce jealousy. (*Omiwa*, Nakamura Utaemon)

14. *Meiboku Sendai Hagi*, ACT II: *Palace Scene*

The nurse Masaoka, protecting her lord's infant son—who is involved in a family succession struggle—has retired with the boy to an inner room on the pretext of the boy's "illness." The enemies Sakae Gozen and Yashio bring cakes as a gift for the supposed invalid. Masaoka's own son Semmatsu promptly kicks the box and takes one of the cakes and eats it to test it for poison. To avoid discovery of the fact that the cakes are indeed poisoned, Yashio stabs Semmatsu to death. (*Yashio*, Nakamura Ganjirō II; *Masaoka*, Nakamura Utaemon)

15. *Meiboku Sendai Hagi*, ACT II: *Yukashita Scene*

The "Yukashita ("under the floor")" scene begins as the palace rises from beneath the stage floor. At the same time, Arajishi Otokonosuke rises from a trapdoor in the stage with his foot on a rat, which in actuality is Nikki Danjiō. Otokonosuke smacks the rat's forehead and it runs away into an opening in the *hanamichi*. The magic spell broken, Nikki Danjō, with a scar on his forehead, emerges from the opening in the *hanamichi*. (*Danjō*, Matsumoto Hakuō; *Otokonosuke*, Bandō Mitsugorō VIII)

◁ 16. *Ōshū Adachigahara*, ACT III: *Sodehagi Saimon*
Sodehagi, who has been disowned by her father because of a love affair, and is now blind and a social outcast, comes one snowy day to visit her father, who is reported to be in difficulties. Her mother Hamayū laments the lot of a samurai's wife who is not permitted to take in her arms the grandchild she has never seen before. Sodehagi is led in by her daughter Okimi, and recites a ballad. Her mother listens, full of emotion yet unable to show it. (*Sodehagi*, Nakamura Kanzaburō; *Hamayū*, Onoe Kikujirō)

17–18. *Mekura Nagaya Ume ga Kagatobi*, ACT II: *Hongō Tōrimachi Gate*
The play is a *kizewamono* based on actual incidents that occurred in Edo at the end of the Edo period: a quarrel between fire-fighters/scaffolders employed by the Lord of Kaga and the official Edo fire brigade; and the machinations of a supposedly blind masseur. In these two scenes, the Kaga men line up on the *hanamichi* before moving to the stage. Led by Matsuzō, they are about to set off to start a quarrel, when they are restrained by Umekichi, chief of the Kaga fire brigade. (*Matsuzō*, Matsumoto Hakuō; *Umekichi*, Onoe Shōroku)

◁ 19. *Sonezaki Shinjū: Temmaya Scene*
Tokubei, a clerk in a soy sauce shop, has been ruined by his friend Kuheiji and can no longer meet with his beloved Ohatsu, a courtesan. In this scene he is hiding under the floor, unable to enter Ohatsu's sitting room. Kuheiji is with Ohatsu and utters a string of insults about Tokubei. Hearing this, Tokubei takes Ohatsu's foot and puts it to his throat, communicating to her his determination to die. (*Tokubei*, Nakamura Ganjirō II; *Ohatsu*, Nakamura Senjaku)

20. *Edo Sodachi Omatsuri Sashichi: The Killing on the Yanagiwara Embankment*
The fireman/scaffolder Sashichi kills his mistress Koito, a geisha, on the Yanagiwara embankment, thinking that she has betrayed him, but then realizes from a note she has left behind that he had been mistaken. The highlight of the scene is the murder by the dashing Sashichi, a typical Edokko (literally, "child of Edo," that is, a person born in Edo). This is a typical *kizewamono*. (*Koito*, Nakamura Utaemon; *Sashichi*, Ichikawa Danjūrō XI)

21. *Kagotsurube Sato no Eizame: Yatsuhashi's Room*
Sano Jirōzaemon, a tradesman from the country whose face is pitted from smallpox, falls madly in love with Yatsuhashi, a Yoshiwara courtesan, and frequents the Yoshiwara district. He tries to ransom her and take her back to the country with him, but Yatsuhashi, who has another lover, reviles him in public, driving him to despair. This develops into the *koroshiba* ("killing scene") later on. (*Jirōzaemon*, Nakamura Kanzaburō; *Yatsuhashi*, Nakamura Utaemon)

22. *Masakado*
Takiyasha, daughter of Masakado, who has been defeated by imperial forces, becomes a courtesan called Kisaragi, and in this guise seeks to use her charms to make Mitsukuni, who has come to arrest Masakado's family, change his allegiance. However, Mitsukuni sees through her wiles, and she is obliged to use magic to escape. (*Takiyasha*, Nakamura Utaemon)

23. *Seki no To*
This is a classical dance-drama typical of the Tokiwazu style of accompaniment. Yoshimune Munesada is protecting the Ōsaka Barrier with a servant, Sekibei. Sekibei in reality is the archvillain Ōtome no Kuronushi, who is scheming to take over power. Munesada's mistress Ono no Komachi comes to visit, and a *teodori* ("hand dance") is performed before Sekibei reveals his true identity. (*Sekibei*, Matsumoto Hakuō; *Komachi*, Nakamura Utaemon; *Munesada*, Nakamura Kanzaburō)

24. *Momijigari*
It is autumn, and the maples are at their most beautiful. Taira no Koremochi, who has come to Mt. Togakushi to hunt deer, is offered saké by a noblewoman who is having a saké party under the trees. Koremochi drowses, and has a dream in which the mountain god warns him that the woman is really a demon in human form. He wakens and kills the demon just in time to prevent it from setting on him. The play is a kabuki dance-drama version of the Nō *Momijigari*, and was first performed in 1887. It is one of the "New Eighteen Favorite Kabuki Plays." (*Koremochi*, Matsumoto Hakuō; *Demon*, Nakamura Utaemon)

25–26. *Kagamijishi*
On the day of the "rice cake cutting" at the New Year, a serving woman in the inner quarters of the shogun's castle in Edo is dancing. She puts a "lion mask" on her hand to dance with, but as she is dancing the spirit of the lion takes over and she loses control of it. (25. *The serving woman Yayoi*, Nakamura Shikan. 26. *The spirit of the lion*, Ichimura Takenojō)

27. *Futa-Omote* (*Twin Faces*)
This type of dance is performed by two actors in identical costumes. In the course of the dance, it proves that one of them is the ghost of, for example, a former lover that has taken possession of the other's shape and has come to torment him or her. In the version shown here, the ghost of Hōkaibō, a wicked priest who fell in love with Okumi, appears in the same costume as Okumi and torments her. (*Hōkaibō's ghost*, Nakamura Kanzaburō)

28. *Ōmi no Okane* (*Danjūrō Musume*)
This play is based on a legend about Okane, a young girl in Ōmi province possessing great strength, who subdued an untamed horse with her *geta*. Girlishness is expressed beneath the strength. At the end, when she is performing with a long sash, a throng of men appear around Okane and make fun of her. Okane performs with the sash while taking the men to task. The men's *tenugui* ("hand towels") are worn on their heads in the fighting style (*kenka-kaburi*); their cotton kimono bear the *mimasu* ("three rice measures") pattern used in the Danjūrō crest. Because Danjūrō VII first performed the play, it is also known as *Danjūrō Musume*. (*Okane*, Nakamura Jakuemon)

SUGAWARA DENJU TENARAI KAGAMI

Pl. 27. ACT IV: *The Terakoya Scene*
This is the climactic head inspection scene, fraught with tension. Genzō
and his wife Tonami, having handed over a different head whose identity they are unaware of, press in upon Matsuō, who proceeds to inspect it. The head, in fact, is that of Matsuō's own son, who has served
as a substitute. (*Tonami*, Nakamura Jakuemon; *Genzō*, Ichimura
Uzaemon; *Matsuō*, Nakamura Kanzaburō)

29. ACT I: *The Court Scene*
An envoy from the kingdom of Pohai wishes to make a portrait of the emperor to take back to China with him. When the Minister of the Left Fujiwara no Shihei tries to have his own likeness painted in place of the emperor who is ill, the Minister of the Right Sugawara no Michizane stops him, and suggests a portrait of Prince Tokiyo. On the right is Fujiwara no Shihei, on the left Sugawara no Michizane.

PLOT OUTLINE

One of three great masterpieces written for the puppet theater (along with *Kanadehon Chūshingura* and *Yoshitsune Sembonzakura*), this play was first performed at the Takemoto-za in Osaka in the eighth month of 1746. The playwrights were Takeda Izumo, Namiki Senryū, and Miyoshi Shōraku. A kabuki version was soon produced in the tenth month of the same year. Chikamatsu's *Tenjin-ki* ("A Chronicle of Tenjin") already existed, and there are other pieces in which Sugawara no Michizane is cast as the hero, but folk-tale elements were added and innovations made in the plot for the kabuki production. The parts of the triplets Matsuō, Umeō, and Sakuramaru were included along with Takebe Genzō and his wife, and Michizane's aunt Kakuju. In particular, the three playwrights were said to have vied with each other in depicting the separation between parent and child in the "Dōmyōji scene" at the end of Act II, the "Ga no Iwai scene" (also known as the "Sata Village scene") at the end of Act III, and the "Terakoya scene" at the end of Act IV. Of them, Terakoya is the most famous and most frequently performed. (Michizane is referred to as Kan Shōjō, the Sinicized reading of the characters for his name, in kabuki.)

The audience at court of the envoy from T'ang China depicted in the prologue is hardly ever performed today, and the scene that follows, "On the Banks of the Kamo River," is rarely presented. Ordinarily, the beautiful love scene involving the four young people provides the starting point for the events that follow. Through the intercession of the groom Sakuramaru and his wife, the emperor's younger brother Prince Tokiyo meets Michizane's adopted daughter Kariya-hime. Meanwhile, Michizane has summoned Takebe Genzō, in order to transmit to him the family secrets of calligraphy. The courtier Mareyo, who plays the role of villain, fights with Genzō over the scroll containing the secrets, providing a comical touch. Michizane is falsely accused by Fujiwara no Shihei and his court cap falls off, an ill omen. Genzō and his wife flee, bearing Michizane's son Kan Shūsai with them. This last scene too is hardly ever performed. (ACT I: *At Court; On the Banks of the Kamo River; At Michizane's Mansion, The Transmission of the Secrets of Calligraphy*)

Kakuju beats her daughter Kariya-hime, whom Michizane had adopted, in punishment for her misconduct, which has caused all the trouble. Kakuju's son-in-law Sukune Tarō and Tarō's father Haji no Hyōei try to make a cock crow at night in order to hand Michizane over to an imposter posing as the official escort. Michizane parts with Kariya-hime before going off to Tsukushi safely, aided by the wooden statue which the official escort mistakenly takes away, thinking that it is Michizane. (ACT II: MICHIYUKI, *Yasui Village; Dōmyōji—The Chastisement, The Crowing of the Cock*)

The famous "Kuruma-biki" scene at the beginning of Act III involves the fight between the three brothers, Umeō, Sakuramaru, and Matsuō. After his carriage is pulled apart, Shihei stands in a formidable *mie* pose on top of the carriage.

The three brothers gather at Sata Village to celebrate Shiratayū's seventieth birthday (*ga no iwai*). Matsuō and Umeō fight with straw rice bales in the garden, breaking the branch of a cherry tree. As the broken branch suggests, Sakuramaru takes responsibility for the incident involving Kariya-hime and Prince Tokiyo and eventually commits suicide. (ACT III: *Kuruma-biki; Sata Village—Rice Bales Tawaradate, Sakuramaru's Suicide*)

The *aragoto* style of acting is used for Michizane's part in the "Mount Tempai" scene of Act IV. The last scene in the act is "The Private School" (*terakoya*). After the curtain opens, a well-behaved child brought by his mother is placed in the private school where Genzō lives in obscurity hiding Michizane's son Kan Shūsai. This is called *tera-iri* ("entering the school"), but the scene ordinarily begins with the appearance of the anguished Genzō on the *hanamichi*. He has been ordered to cut off the head of Shūsai and discusses with his wife the possibility of substituting the boy Kotarō, who has newly entered the school that day.

Shundō Gemba, Shihei's retainer, and Matsuō, arrive at the school. The inspection of the school children begins at the gate. This passage, enlivened by the comical part of Yodarekuri, makes an effective pause before the ensuing tragedy. During the head inspection, Matsuō puts his hands on the lid of the box holding the head and stares down. This tense passage is the climax of the play. After everyone leaves, the substitution a success, Kotarō's mother Chiyo comes to get her son and Genzō slashes at her with his sword. Chiyo parries it with Kotarō's writing box, whereupon a white shroud with Buddhist prayers on it falls out, heightening the pathos. Matsuō soon comes out wearing a black robe, and reveals his real intention; half laughing through his tears he rejoices that his son has served as a substitute. At the end of the act, Matsuō and his wife put on white robes. There is then a touching speech on the burial of Kotarō, called *iroha-okuri*, into which the *iroha* alphabet has been woven. (ACT IV: *Mount Tempai; Terakoya—Tera-iri, The Head Inspection, Iroha-okuri*)

Michizane is transformed into lightning that falls on the court destroying the villains, and the play comes to an end. (ACT V: *At Court*)

30. ACT I: *On the Banks of the Kamo River*
Going to the Kamo Shrine to pray on behalf of the emperor who is ill, Prince Tokiyo secretly meets Michizane's adopted daughter Kariya-hime with the help of Sakuramaru, the carriage attendant, and his wife Yae. They are discovered by the opposition, and the prince and Kariya-hime disappear to avoid trouble. The photograph shows the love scene between Sakuramaru and Yae after the prince and Kariya-hime have gone into the carriage. (*Sakuramaru*, Onoe Baikō; *Yae*, Nakamura Jakuemon)

31. ACT I: *At Michizane's Mansion, The Transmission of the Secrets of Calligraphy*
Commanded by the emperor to transmit the secrets of calligraphy, Michizane—more commonly known as Kan Shōjō in kabuki—summons to his mansion Takebe Genzō, a former pupil who had been banished because of an illicit affair, and transmits the secrets to him. The courtier Mareyo becomes resentful and makes a nuisance of himself. (*Kan Shōjō*, Ichikawa Danjūrō XI; *Genzō*, Bandō Mitsugorō VIII; *Mareyo*, Ichikawa Yaozō)

32. Hiding under the robe of Sonoo no Mae (Michizane's wife), Tonami (Genzō's wife) secretly bids farewell to Michizane as he is about to set out for the Court. Michizane's court cap falls off, an ill omen. (*Shōjō [Michizane]*, Kataoka Nizaemon; *Sonoo no Mae*, Sawamura Sōjūrō; *Tonami*, Onoe Baikō)

Pl. 28. ACT II: *Dōmyōji, Michizane's Farewell*
Kariya-hime cannot openly bid farewell to Michizane, and so she does so from behind Kakuju, her real mother. (*Shōjō*, Kataoka Nizaemon; *Kakuju*, Jitsukawa Enjaku; *Kariya-hime*, Bandō Tamasaburō)

Pl. 29. ACT III: *The Sata Village Scene, The Rice Bales Tawaradate*
Umeō and Matsuō fight with rice bales. There are a number of fixed *kata* in the *tachimawari*; the character of the brothers is revealed through their costumes, wigs, and makeup. This is a beautiful, stylized scene. (*Umeō*, Onoe Tatsunosuke; *Matsuō*, Ichikawa Ennosuke)

33. Genzō and his wife Tonami punish Mareyo for being a nuisance by making him carry a small desk on his back. (*Tonami*, Onoe Baikō; *Mareyo*, Ichikawa Nedanji; *Genzō*, Kataoka Nizaemon)

34. ACT I. *Outside the Gate of Michizane's Mansion*
As a result of Shihei's slander, Michizane is put under house arrest. Attempting to save Michizane's son Shūsai on behalf of the Sugawara family, Umeō leads him over the wall and entrusts him to Genzō and his wife Tonami. (*Tonami*, Nakamura Jakuemon; *Umeō*, Bandō Minosuke)

35. ACT II: *Michiyuki, Yasui Village*
Disguised as a peddler of sweets, Sakuramaru hides Prince Tokiyo and Kariya-hime in his boxes and heads for the village where Kariya-hime's real mother Kakuju lives. (*Kariya-hime*, Kataoka Hidetarō; *Sakuramaru*, Onoe Baikō; *Tokiyo*, Kataoka Takao)

36. ACT II: *Dōmyōji, The Chastisement*
On his way to exile at Dazaifu in Kyushu, Michizane stays at the mansion of his aunt Kakuju. Learning that the love between Prince Tokiyo and her daughter Kariya-hime was the cause of Michizane's exile, Kakuju becomes angry and beats Kariya-hime, but her older daughter Tatsuta no Mae stops her. (*Kariya-hime*, Bandō Tamasaburō; *Tatsuta*, Kataoka Hidetarō; *Kakuju*, Jitsukawa Enjaku)

38. ACT II: *Dōmyōji*
Tatsuta no Mae, who overhears the evil scheme between her husband Sukune Tarō and her father-in-law, is killed by Sukune. (*Tatsuta*, Kataoka Hidetarō; *Sukune Tarō*, Nakamura Tomijūrō)

37. ACT II: *Dōmyōji: The Crowing of the Cock*
Tatsuta no Mae's husband Sukune Tarō and father-in-law Haji no Hyōe try to make a cock crow during the night in order to hand Michizane over to men posing as his real escort. (*Sukune Tarō*, Bandō Mitsugorō; *Hyōe*, Ichikawa Shōhaku)

39. ACT II: *Dōmyōji*
Michizane's spirit lodges inside a wooden statue that he had carved as a keepsake. The statue comes to life, and the impostor posing as Michizane's official escort takes the statue, thinking that it is Michizane. (*Shōjō* [*Michizane*], Kataoka Nizaemon)

40. ACT III: *Kuruma-biki*
Umeō and Sakuramaru lie in wait for Shihei in order to avenge their master Michizane. (*Sakuramaru*, Nakamura Fukusuke; *Umeō*, Nakamura Kankurō)

41. ACT III: *Kuruma-biki*
Umeō and Sakuramaru stop Shihei's carriage which is being guided by their brother Matsuō. An altercation ensues between the brothers and they push and pull at the carriage until it falls apart. Shihei then appears above the carriage. Intimidated by his strength, Umeō and Sakuramaru abandon their plans. (*Shihei*, Bandō Hikosaburō; *Sakuramaru*, Nakamura Fukusuke; *Umeō*, Nakamura Kankurō; *Matsuō*, Nakamura Kichiemon)

42. ACT III: *The Sata Village Scene*
The wives of Umeō, Sakuramaru, and Matsuō gather at the home of Shiratayū, the father of the three brothers, to celebrate his seventieth birthday. (*Yae*, Nakamura Kotarō; *Chiyo*, Ichikawa Monnosuke; *Haru*, Ichimura Manjirō)

43. ACT III: *The Sata Village Scene, Rice Bales Tawaradate*
Matsuō and Umeō, who have become enemies, fight with straw rice bales. A cherry branch breaks, foreshadowing Sakuramaru's death. (*Umeō*, Onoe Shōroku; *Matsuō*, Matsumoto Hakuō)

44. During the fight, Shiratayū comes back, and Umeō and Matsuō hurriedly straighten their clothing with the help of their wives. (*Umeō*, Onoe Tatsunosuke; *Matsuō*, Ichikawa Danjūrō)

45. Following Matsuō's wishes, Shiratayū disowns him and chases him away with a broom. (*Matsuō*, Ichikawa Danjūrō; *Shiratayū*, Ichimura Uzaemon)

46. *Sakuramaru's Suicide*
Taking responsibility for the disappearance of Prince Tokiyo and Kariya-hime which led to Michizane's exile, Sakuramaru commits suicide. (*Sakuramaru*, Onoe Kikugorō; *his wife Yae*, Ichimura Manjirō; *his father Shiratayū*, Ichimura Uzaemon)

47. ACT IV: *Mount Tempai*
Shiratayū serves Michizane in exile at Mount Tempai. Michizane dies here; transformed into thunder, he flies to the capital to avenge himself against Shihei. (*Shiratayū*, Bandō Mitsugorō VIII; *Shōjō* [*Michizane*], Ichikawa Chūsha VIII)

48–54. ACT IV: *Terakoya*

48. This is a typical kabuki substitution story (*migawarimono*). After receiving the secrets of calligraphy, Genzō and his wife Tonami open a school in the countryside. Matsuō's wife Chiyo brings her son Kotarō to enroll him in the school. Inside the schoolroom, Kan Shūsai (Kan Shōjō's [Michizane's] son), in disguise, is practicing calligraphy. The child on the desk at the right has been forced to stand there as a punishment. (*Chiyo*, Nakamura Senjaku; *Tonami*, Nakamura Shikan)

49. Matsuō and Shundō Gemba, who have come to apprehend Kan Shūsai, examine the faces of the children one by one. (*Matsuō*, Matsumoto Hakuō; *Gemba*, Bandō Minosuke)

50. Matsuō and Genzō (along with Tonami) confront each other as they try to find out what the other side is really thinking. (*Matsuō*, Onoe Shōroku; *Genzō*, Nakamura Kanzaburō; *Tonami*, Nakamura Shikan)

51. *The Head Inspection (Kubi Jikken)* In place of Kan Shūsai, Genzō and his wife cut off the head of the child who had entered the school that morning (Matsuō's son), and have Matsuō inspect it. (*Matsuō*, Matsumoto Hakuō)

52. After Matsuō and his men take the head and depart, Kotarō's mother Chiyo comes to get her son. When Genzō strikes at Chiyo with his sword trying to kill her, she parries his thrust with Kotarō's writing box and a shroud falls out. (*Chiyo*, Nakamura Utaemon; *Genzō*, Kataoka Nizaemon)

53. Changing into a black robe, Matsuō reappears and reveals that his son has served as a substitute for Kan Shūsai. (*Matsuō*, Matsumoto Hakuō)

54. This is known as the "Iroha-Okuri" scene. Dressed in white mourning robes at the end, Matsuō and Chiyo lament the death of their son. Inside, Michizane's wife Sonoo no Mae and Shūsai also mourn Kotarō's death.

Pl. 30. ACT IV: *The Yoshino-yama
Michiyuki*
Tadanobu and Shizuka hurry to
Yoshitsune's hiding place. Performing tradition stipulates that since
they are not lovers, their acting must
convey the mistress-servant relationship. (*Tadanobu*, Onoe Kikugorō;
Shizuka, Nakamura Shibajaku)

55. ACT I: PROLOGUE, *The Horikawa Mansion*
The scene is Yoshitsune's mansion at Horikawa in Kyoto. Yoshitsune has been pursuing the defeated remnants of the Taira forces, but now a messenger comes from his brother, the Shogun Yoritomo in Kamakura, accusing him of plotting treason. Yoshitsune's wife, Kyō no Kimi, is a member of the Taira side, and Yoshitsune is suspected of having entered into a secret agreement with the Taira on account of this relationship. Hearing of this, Kyō no Kimi commits suicide, with her own father as her assistant in the act. Yoshitsune's mistress, Shizuka, also appears in this scene. (*Shizuka*, Sawamura Sōjūrō; *Yoshitsune*, Ichimura Uzaemon; *Kyō no Kimi*, Nakamura Shibajaku; *her father Kawagoe Tarō*, Ichikawa Danshirō)

PLOT OUTLINE

This *jōruri* drama in five acts is a *jidaimono* jointly written by Takeda Izumo, Miyoshi Shōraku, and Namiki Senryū. It was first performed as a puppet play at the Takemoto-za in the eleventh month of 1747, and then as kabuki at the Nakamura-za in Edo in the fifth month of 1748. In recent times the fifth act has seldom been performed. The main theme of the story is provided by the attempts of the Taira generals Tomomori, Koremori, and Noritsune to restore the fortunes of their clan following its defeat by the Minamoto clan. Secondary themes are provided by the flight of Yoshitsune of the Minamoto from his jealous relatives and by the visit paid him at his hiding place in Yoshino by the fox/Tadanobu and Yoshitsune's mistress, Shizuka Gozen.

Kawagoe Tarō, Yoshitsune's father-in-law, comes to question him concerning his loyalty to his elder brother, the shogun Yoritomo in Kamakura. Yoshitsune's wife Kyō no Kimi commits suicide as a testimony to his loyalty, but just then Tosabō, sent by Yoritomo to capture Yoshitsune, arrives with a troop of men. Benkei, Yoshitsune's retainer, routs them, then cuts off the heads of the slain soldiers and, placing them in a great rain cistern, makes a show of stirring them in the water. The ritual is, of course, purely a piece of kabuki bravado. (ACT I: *The Horikawa Mansion*)

Shizuka Gozen has followed Yoshitsune, now fleeing from his elder brother's wrath, as far as the Fushimi Inari Shrine on the outskirts of Kyoto, but now he bids her farewell, giving her the famous "Hatsune" drum as a parting present. Just then Hayami no Tōta, one of Tosabō's retainers, arrives and tries to take Shizuka prisoner, but she is saved by Satō Tadanobu—in reality a fox who has taken human form and come so as to be near the drum, which was made from the skin of its parents. (ACT II: *Before the Gate of the Fushimi Inari Shrine*)

Yoshitsune proceeds to Daimotsu Bay, where he intends to board a boat in his flight. Here Tomomori of the Taira, believed to have been killed by Yoshitsune, is living in disguise as a boatman named Tokaiya Gimpei until he can take his revenge on Yoshitsune. Dressed as his own departed spirit, he attacks Yoshitsune, but is defeated and throws himself into the sea. (ACT II: *The Tokaiya Scene; The Daimotsu Bay Scene*)

Kokingo, a retainer of Koremori, is accompanying Wakaba no Naishi, Koremori's wife, as she flees from Yoritomo. They stop to rest at a tea shop, and are gathering pasania nuts to amuse Rokudai, Koremori's young son. A ruffian named Igami no Gonta appears and seems friendly, but takes their money. (ACT III: *The Pasania Tree Tea Shop*)

Constables are pursuing them, and Kokingo becomes separated from Wakaba and Rokudai and is killed. Yazaemon, proprietor of a *sushi* shop, finds the body and cuts off the head to use as a substitute for the head of Koremori when the constables come looking for him. (ACT III: *In the Bamboo Grove*)

Koremori is living in hiding in the *sushi* shop under the name of Yasuke. Igami no Gonta, who is the son of the proprietor, has given information of Koremori's whereabouts, but Yazaemon's daughter Osato, who is in love with Koremori, helps him escape. Yazaemon, enraged at his son's betrayal, stabs him to death. But Gonta repents in death, and by passing off his own wife and son as Wakaba no Naishi and Rokudai, enables Koremori and his family to escape. (ACT III: *The Sushi Shop*)

Shizuka Gozen, in the company of the fox/Tadanobu, passes through the hills of Yoshino in the cherry blossom season on her way to find her lover, Yoshitsune. (ACT IV: MICHIYUKI)

Yoshitsune and Shizuka, reunited, discover the true identity of the fox/Tadanobu; Yoshitsune gives him the Hatsune drum. The grateful fox responds by using his supernatural powers against Yokokawa no Kakuhan (in reality Noritsune of the Taira) and a band of soldier-monks who make a surprise attack on Yoshitsune. (ACT IV: *The Mansion of Kawazura Hōgen*)

Yoshitsune intervenes and stops the fight between Tadanobu and Noritsune. Yoshitsune tells Noritsune that he has rescued the emperor Antoku. Noritsune expresses his gratitude to Yoshitsune and decides to become a monk so that he can pray for the souls of those who died in the battle between the Taira and the Genji. (ACT V: *The Hanayagura Scene*)

56–57. ACT I: PROLOGUE, *By the Moat of the Imperial Palace*
This is an *aragoto* episode. Tosabō has come under orders from Yoritomo in Kamakura to hunt down Yoshitsune. Benkei has killed and cut off the heads of Tosabō and various low-ranking samurai, and now goes through the ritual of placing the heads in a great tub of rainwater and stirring them. (Known as *imo-arai*, ''potato washing,'' the ritual is, of course, purely a piece of kabuki bravado.) (*Benkei*, Bandō Hikosaburō)

58. ACT II: *Before the Gate of the Fushimi Inari Shrine*
Yoshitsune and his followers, in flight from the capital, have reached the entrance to the Fushimi Inari Shrine just outside Kyoto. Here, Yoshitsune bids farewell to his mistress Shizuka, giving her as a parting present a famous drum called ''Hatsune'' that he had been given at the Court. Hayami no Tōta, a retainer of Tosabō, seeks to take Shizuka prisoner, but a fox appears in the guise of Tadanobu and rescues her. The fox has come in order to be close to the drum, which is made from the skin of its own parents. In the company of Tadanobu, Shizuka sets out for Yoshino. (*Tadanobu*, Ichikawa Ennosuke; *Shizuka*, Sawamura Sōjūrō; *Yoshitsune*, Ichimura Uzaemon)

Pl. 31. ACT II: *Fushimi Inari Shrine*
Tadanobu fighting with Tōta's men.
(*Tadanobu*, Ichikawa Ennosuke)

Pl. 32. ACT II: *The Daimotsu Bay Scene*
In the final scene, Tomomori ties the rope of
the anchor around his body and flings the anchor into the sea so that the weight pulls him—
he does a spectacular somersault—under the
waves. (*Tomomori*, Ichikawa Ennosuke)

59-60. ACT II: *The Tokaiya Scene*
The action switches to follow the fortunes of the Taira side. Taira no Tomomori, generally believed to have been killed by Yoshitsune, is in fact alive and living as a boatman, under the name of Tokaiya Gimpei, until such time as he can take his revenge on Yoshitsune. Yoshitsune and his followers arrive at night asking for lodging and passage over the bay. Tomomori sees his opportunity, and, bidding farewell to the infant Emperor Antoku and his nurse, Suke no Tsubone—who have been living disguised as his own child and wife—he lures Yoshitsune out onto the sea.

59. Gimpei's retainers surreptitiously come to observe Yoshitsune. They are "caught" by Gimpei who wants to allay any suspicions that Yoshitsune may have about him. (*Sagami Gorō, a retainer*, Ichikawa Danshirō)

60. Gimpei appears as the ghost of Tomomori and performs a dance of farewell to Emperor Antoku and Suke no Tsubone. This episode is based on the celebrated Nō play *Funa Benkei*. (*Tomomori*, Ichikawa Ennosuke)

61-63. ACT II: *(the stage revolves) The Daimotsu Bay Scene*

61. Suke no Tsubone, with the Emperor Antoku in her care, is watching the struggle between Yoshitsune and Tomomori out at sea. A messenger, Irie Tanzō, arrives to say that Tomomori and his men have been taken unawares from the rear and defeated. (*Suke no Tsubone*, Nakamura Jakuemon; *Irie Tanzō*, Ichikawa Danshirō)

62. Before long, Tomomori appears, wounded by an arrow, with Yoshitsune hot on his heels. (*Tomomori*, Ichikawa Ennosuke)

63. Tomomori ties himself to a great anchor. Then, committing the infant emperor to the care of Yoshitsune, throws himself into the sea. (*Tomomori*, Onoe Shōroku)

64–65. ACT III: *The Pasania Tree Tea Shop Scene*

64. This act interpolates the story of the Taira general Koremori, who is living in hiding in the hills of Yoshino (near Nara). Koremori's wife, Wakaba no Naishi, and his child Rokudai, accompanied only by a young retainer, Kokingo, approach a tea shop beneath a great pasania tree in Shimoichi village on their way to visit Koremori. Suddenly a ruffian called Igami no Gonta appears and, under pretense of helping them gather pasania nuts, substitutes his own bundle for theirs and extorts money from them. (*Gonta*, Ichikawa Ennosuke; *Wakaba*, Nakamura Tōzō; *Kokingo*, Nakamura Karoku)

114

65. Gonta mocks Kokingo, who, angered at having lost his money, attempts to draw his sword.

66. ACT III: *(the stage revolves) In the Bamboo Grove* Pursued by the constables sent to catch them, Kokingo becomes separated from Wakaba no Naishi and Rokudai, and is killed. The swordfight in this scene is particularly famous. (*Kokingo*, Nakamura Karoku)

67. The proprietor, Yazaemon, comes across Kokingo's body on his way home, and decides to cut off the head with the idea of using it as a fake "proof" of Koremori's death. He hides the head in a *sushi* tub. (*Yazaemon*, Ichikawa Yaozō)

68–75. ACT III: *The Tsurube Sushi Shop Scene*

68. Taira no Koremori is being given shelter in a *sushi* shop, disguised as an assistant called Yasuke. The proprietor's son Gonta, who has been disowned by his father and is the ruffian who mocked Kokingo earlier, comes to try to find out who "Yasuke" really is, in the hope of making some money out of it. Here Gonta holds the portrait with which he is checking Koremori's identity. (*Gonta*, Ichikawa Ennosuke; *Yasuke*, Sawamura Sōjūrō)

69. The proprietor's daughter Osato, unaware that Yasuke is a nobleman, has fallen in love with him. The scene affords wide scope for both *yatsushi* and *nureba*. She is shown here confessing her love for Yasuke. (*Osato*, Sawamura Tanosuke)

70. Osato reveals her love for Yasuke, and they are about to retire for the night when Wakabe no Naishi and Rokudai arrive. (*Wakabe*, Nakamura Tōzō; *Yasuke*, Sawamura Sōjūrō)

71. Kajiwara Kagetoki arrives to take Koremori prisoner. Gonta picks up a *sushi* tub and goes out after Koremori, saying that he will catch him and earn a reward. (*Gonta*, Ichikawa Ennosuke)

72. Yazaemon sets out after Gonta, but bumps into Kagetoki and is brought back home. (*Kajiwara Kagetoki*, Ichikawa Danshirō; *Yazaemon*, Ichikawa Yaozō)

73–74. Yazaemon gets out the *sushi* tub in which he put the head that he says is Koremori's, but it is empty. Then Gonta appears with the missing head and a woman and her child bound in ropes who, he says, are Koremori's wife and child. (*The woman*, Ichikawa Monnosuke; *Kagetoki*, Ichikawa Danshirō)

75. Enraged at his son's apparent wickedness, Yazaemon attacks him with a sword. But as he dies, Gonta confesses that the supposed Wakaba and Rokudai are in fact his own wife and child, and the head is that of Kokingo. He dies a reformed character. Koremori and his wife and child appear and pray for Gonta's peace in the next world.

76–78. ACT IV: MICHIYUKI
A *michiyuki* describing the journey of Shizuka and Tadanobu to the hills of Yoshino, where Yoshitsune has taken refuge. The scene is a dance piece set in the Yoshino hills at the time of the cherry blossoms, and Shizuka and Tadanobu recall various episodes of the past as they go. Tadanobu, in reality a fox in human shape, relates in mime the story of the battle at which his elder brother Tsuginobu was killed. (*The fox/Tadanobu*, Ichikawa Ennosuke; *Shizuka*, Sawamura Sōjūrō)

79–84. ACT IV: *The Mansion of Kawazura Hōgen*

79. The real Satō Tadanobu comes to see Yoshitsune at the mansion of Kawazura Hōgen in the Yoshino hills where he is living in hiding. Yoshitsune treats him as a traitor since he does not have Shizuka with him even though she is supposed to be in his charge. (*Shizuka*, Ichikawa Monnosuke; *the real Tadanobu*, Ichikawa Ennosuke; *Yoshitsune*, Nakamura Ganjirō II)

80. Suddenly, the fox/Tadanobu arrives. At Yoshitsune's command, Shizuka beats the Hatsune drum, whereupon the fox/Tadanobu assumes his true form and tells how he has come after the drum because it is made from the skin of his parents. During his narration, he performs various acrobatics.

81. Yoshitsune, to the fox's great delight, gives him the drum. (*Yoshitsune*, Nakamura Ganjirō II)

82. The fox is overjoyed and holds the drum in its paws.

83. Just then, a band of soldier-monks commanded by Yokokawa no Kakuhan (Taira no Noritsune in disguise) rushes in to attack Yoshitsune, but they are defeated by the fox's supernatural powers. Kakuhan (Noritsune) retreats, but tells Tadanobu that he will return.

84. After defeating the monks, the fox flies off over the *hanamichi*.

85–86. ACT V: *The Hanayagura Scene*

85. As he promised, Tadanobu returns to fight Noritsune. Several foxes then appear to attack Noritsune and his men. (*Noritsune*, Ichikawa Danshirō)

86. Yoshitsune intervenes and stops the fight between Tadanobu and Noritsune. Yoshitsune tells Noritsune that he has rescued the emperor Antoku. Noritsune expresses his gratitude to Yoshitsune and decides to become a monk so that he can pray for the souls of those who died in the battle between the Taira and the Genji.

Pl. 33. *The Puppet Announcement*
Unlike any other kabuki play, the prologue to *Chūshingura* is preceded by an "announcement" made by a puppet, which, after much preliminary throat-clearing, introduces the cast for the whole play. It is manipulated from the rear by a puppeteer in black, who moves its head, mouth, and arms to great humorous effect.

Pl. 34. ACT I: *Prologue*
The prologue is played with an extraordinary degree of solemnity and stylization. It is the only play of all those derived from the puppet theater in which the traditional prologue is preserved. When the curtain opens, the characters who appear in the play are presented sitting motionless, as if they were indeed puppets. Then, as the music begins and their names are called one by one, they lift their heads in turn and become "human beings."

87. ACT I: *At the Hachiman Shrine*
This scene is referred to as the "Helmet Inspection Scene" because Kaoyo Gozen, the wife of Enya Hangan, is called on, in the presence of the shogun's brother at the Hachiman Shrine in Kamakura, to identify the helmet that had belonged to the deceased warrior Nitta Yoshisada.

PLOT OUTLINE

This is a *jōruri* play in eleven acts in the *jidaimono* style. It was written jointly by Takeda Izumo, Miyoshi Shōraku, and Namiki Sōsuke. First performed as a puppet drama in the eighth month of 1748 at the Takemoto-za, it was first performed as a kabuki play at the Arashi-za in Osaka in the eleventh month of the same year. The story is loosely based on the Genroku era heroes, forty-seven *rōnin* (masterless samurai), who broke into the mansion of their late master's enemy and killed him.

The play opens with Kaoyo, the wife of Enya Hangan, identifying the helmet of the warrior Nitta Yoshisada at the Tsurugaoka Hachiman Shrine in Kamakura. One of the officials, the villain Kōno Moronō, tries to give her a love letter. His advances are checked by a young daimyo, Momonoi Wakasanosuke, for whom he accordingly conceives a violent hatred. (ACT I: *Before the Tsurugaoka Hachiman Shrine in Kamakura*)

Following his return to his mansion, Wakasanosuke, still indignant at Moronō's behavior, resolves that he will slay him. His chief retainer Kakogawa Honzō, who realizes what is afoot, hastens off to Moronō's mansion to try to bribe him into an apology to Wakasanosuke. (ACT II: *Momonoi's Mansion*)

Placated with gifts given him by Honzō, Moronō apologizes to Wakasanosuke. However, he vents his spleen at having been rejected by Kaoyo on Enya Hangan, and finally drives him to the point of drawing his sword in the shogun's palace. In the meantime, by the rear gate, Hangan's retainer Hayano Kampei is dallying with Okaru. Too late, he realizes what has happened to his master. (ACT III: *The Gift-giving; The Pine Tree Chamber in the Palace; The Rear Gate*)

Hangan is ordered to commit suicide as punishment for the crime of having drawn his sword in the shogun's palace. He does so, and his wife offers incense for him. His retainers leave the mansion of their dead master; they are now *rōnin*. (ACT IV: *Hangan's Suicide; Offering Incense; Vacating the Mansion*)

Kampei, ashamed of failing his master, decides to go off with Okaru to her home in the country. The two of them set out in secret. ("The Fugitives," a dance-drama with *kiyomoto* accompaniment. The full title is MICHIYUKI: *The Bridegroom's Journey*. First performed at the Kawarazaki-za in the third month of 1833, it is an independent, choreographed elaboration of the "Rear Gate Scene" of Act III, which is sometimes omitted and the *michiyuki* performed in its stead later in the play.)

Yoichibei, Okaru's father, sells his daughter into prostitution for money to help Kampei participate in the plan to avenge the death of his lord. Half the money is stolen from him by Sadakurō, and Yoichibei is murdered. Kampei, out hunting, accidentally shoots Sadakurō, and the money falls into his hands. (ACT V: *The Yamazaki Highway; The Two Shots*)

Kampei, meeting the brothel-keeper and hearing about the transaction, is convinced that it is he who has killed Yoichibei. To atone for it, he kills himself. (ACT VI: *Kampei's Seppuku*)

The leader of the *rōnin* who are secretly bent on revenge is Ōboshi Yuranosuke. He is spending his days in apparent dissipation to deceive the enemy. Okaru, now a courtesan, has a chance encounter with her elder brother Heiemon. Yuranosuke becomes convinced of their sincerity, and Heiemon is permitted to join the band. (ACT VII: *At the Ichiriki Teahouse in Gion*)

Honzō's daughter Konami, accompanied by her mother, is traveling along the Tōkaidō highway towards Kyoto on her way to be betrothed to Rikiya, Yuranosuke's son. (ACT VIII: MICHIYUKI: *The Bride's Journey*)

Yuranosuke's wife spurns them because Honzō has disgraced himself by giving bribes to Moronō. Honzō overhears the conversation, and goads Rikiya into mortally wounding him. He bequeaths him his own head and a plan of Moronō's mansion. (ACT IX: *Yuranosuke's Country Retreat in Yamashina*)

Amakawaya Gihei, a merchant who has been judged worthy by Yuranosuke to share the secret of their enterprise, is assembling a stock of weapons. (ACT X: *The Amakawaya Scene*)

The forty-seven *rōnin* break into Moronō's mansion, and after much fighting finally discover Moronō and take his life. (ACT XI: *The Storming of Moronō's Mansion*)

88. Having identified the helmet, Kaoyo is about to retire when Moronō embraces her from behind and hands her a love letter. She quietly lets the letter fall to the ground. (*Kaoyo*, Nakamura Utaemon; *Moronō*, Matsumoto Hakuō)

89. Moronō abuses Wakasanosuke so intemperately that the latter loses his self-control and grasps the handle of his sword. Seeing what is about to happen, Enya Hangen intervenes. The curtain falls on a scene of intense emotion, with Moronō glaring down at Wakasanosuke from the raised section of the stage, Wakasanosuke shaking with barely contained rage, and Hangan making a dramatic gesture of restraint. (*Wakasanosuke*, Ichimura Uzaemon; *Hangan*, Onoe Baikō; *Moronō*, Bandō Mitsugorō VIII)

90. ACT II: *The Momonoi Mansion*
This scene is popularly known as the "Pine-cutting Scene." The retainer Kakogawa Honzō, realizing that he cannot dissuade his master Momonoi Wakasanosuke from killing Moronō, cuts off a pine branch and gives it to Wakasanosuke as a token of his agreement with his intention. He then hurries off ahead of Wakasanosuke in order to intercept Moronō and offer him a bribe to make him more amenable. (*Kakogawa Honzō*, Bandō Mitsugorō VIII)

91. ACT III: *The Gift-giving Scene before the Gate of the Ashikaga Palace*
Moronō is on his way to the palace in a palanquin when Wakasanosuke's retainer Honzō rushes up and presents him with gifts intended to placate him. Moronō himself, who is hidden inside the palanquin, does not appear, and the transaction is carried out via his retainer Sagisaka Bannai, a comic figure. Bannai puts on lofty airs, so Honzō slips a gold coin inside his sleeve as a bribe, whereupon Bannai's whole attitude instantly changes. This amusing passage, and the passage in which Bannai instructs his henchmen how to kill Honzō, are the highlights of the scene. (*Honzō*, Ichikawa Enzaburō; *Bannai*, Arashi Rikaku)

Pl. 35. ACT III: *The Pine Tree Chamber in the Palace*
Hangan is enraged by Moronō's insults. He lunges at Moronō, and
the daimyo rush to restrain him. (*Hangan*, Onoe Kikugorō)

92. ACT III: *The Rear Gate Scene*
Hangan's retainer Hayano Kampei has been dallying with Okaru, a waiting woman in Hangan's service. (*Hayano Kampei*, Jitsukawa Enjaku; *Okaru*, Nakamura Senjaku)

93–95. ACT III: *The Pine Tree Chamber in the Palace, popularly known as the "Quarrel Scene" or the "Pine Tree Room Scene"*

93. (The stage revolves) Wakasanosuke, fired with the desire to kill Moronō because of the insults he has received, encounters Moronō in the Pine Tree Chamber. Moronō's attitude, mystifyingly, has changed completely; he flings down his sword and grovels abjectly before Wakasanosuke. Wakasanosuke leaves, deprived of the excuse to kill Moronō. (*Wakasanosuke*, Ichikawa Ennosuke; *Moronō*, Nakamura Tomijūrō)

94–95. Hard on Wakasanosuke's heels appears Enya Hangan. Moronō, ill-tempered on account of the scene that has just passed, vents his spleen on Hangan by accusing him of being late. A box is then delivered containing a poem in which Kaoyo tells Moronō that she cannot respond to his illicit advances. Still more incensed by this, Moronō begins to jeer at and revile Hangan, telling him that he is a blockhead samurai. After a great deal of this, Hangan is driven to the point where he draws his sword and wounds Moronō, but Honzō, Wakasanosuke's retainer, restrains Hangan from killing Moronō, and Moronō flees with nothing worse than a wound on his forehead. (*Enya Hangan*, Onoe Baikō)

96. (The stage revolves) Hearing a great commotion, Hangan's retainer Hayano Kampei rushes to the palace, only to find that his master has finally been goaded into drawing his sword and has wounded Moronō. Ashamed that he failed his master in his time of need, he decides to go off with Okaru to her home in the country. (*Hayano Kampei*, Jitsukawa Enjaku; *Okaru*, Nakamura Senjaku)

97–100. ACT IV: *Hangan's Suicide*

97. The law declares that whoever dares to draw his sword within the shogun's palace shall be sentenced to suicide by disembowelment and his estate confiscated. Hangan has broken that law, and two messengers arrive from the shogun to hand him the order demanding that he commit *seppuku*. (*The messenger Ishidō Umanojō*, Ichikawa Sadanji III)

98. Dressed in robes of pure white, Hangan steps onto the dais on which custom demanded that *seppuku* should be performed—an overturned tatami mat swathed in white cloth, with sprigs of anise in vases at each corner. He eagerly awaits the arrival of his favorite retainer, Ōboshi Yuranosuke, hoping to pass on his dying wishes, but the time for the suicide arrives and Yuranosuke has still not come. He plunges in the sword, and at that moment Yuranosuke arrives, just in time for a last word with his master. (*Yuranosuke*, Onoe Shōroku; *Enya Hangan*, Onoe Baikō)

99. *The Offering of the Incense*
The body of Hangan is placed in a palanquin. His wife Kaoyo, who has cut her hair (as a sign that she is taking holy vows), takes the lead in burning incense to pray for her husband's soul. Tradition dictates that in this scene the actors playing female roles should use no rouge whatsoever on their cheeks. (*Yuranosuke's son Rikiya,* Onoe Kikugorō; *Kaoyo,* Nakamura Shikan)

100. *Vacating the Mansion*
As the retainers of the late Enya Hangan leave their former master's residence for the last time, Yuranosuke takes out the short sword with which Hangan committed suicide and swears that he will take revenge. (*Yuranosuke,* Onoe Shōroku)

101–105. MICHIYUKI: *The Bridegroom's Journey*
This scene is a dance piece with *kiyomoto* accompaniment and is popularly known as "The Fugitives." Kampei and Okaru are shown making their way, avoiding as far as possible being seen, to Okaru's home in the country. Most of the action centers around the baffling of an attempt to halt the fleeing couple made by Sagisaka Bannai, the comic villian, and comic constables, who are routed ignominiously by Kampei.

101. The amorous couple sets out. (*Okaru,* Onoe Baikō; *Kampei,* Nakamura Kanzaburō)

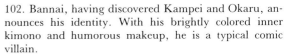

102. Bannai, having discovered Kampei and Okaru, announces his identity. With his brightly colored inner kimono and humorous makeup, he is a typical comic villain.

103. Bannai, who is infatuated with Okaru, attempts to take her away with him.

104. Kampei throws his outer kimono off his shoulders, revealing his red undergarment, and one by one routs the constables whom Bannai has brought to capture him. The constables, who are referred to as *hanayoten*, wear gaudy costumes, and attack Kampei with flowering cherry branches. This type of variation on the usual swordfight is known as *shosadate*.

105. Realizing that he is no match for Kampei, Bannai retrieves his sword, which has been flung to one side, and using it as a stick, beats an undignified retreat.

106–107. ACT V: *The Yamazaki Highway, The Two-Shots Scene*

106. In this scene, Kampei is taking shelter from the rain while hunting.

107. Okaru's father, Yoichibei, has sold his daughter into prostitution for the sum of one hundred *ryō*, in order to help his new son-in-law Kampei. Yoichibei takes fifty of the hundred *ryō* with him and is on the way home when he is killed and robbed by Sadakurō, son of a former samurai in Enya Hangan's household, who has become a bandit. Next, Sadakurō himself is shot mistakenly by Kampei, who is hunting wild boar. The fifty *ryō* Sadakurō stole from Yoichibei now falls into Kampei's hands. The scene is referred to as "Yamazaki Highway," since the action takes place on a dark night along this road. (*Kampei*, Ichikawa Sadanji III; *Sadakurō*, Morita Kanya XIV)

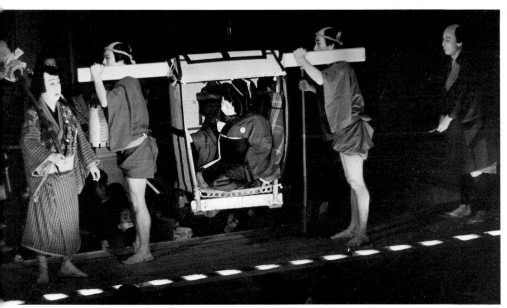

108–112. ACT VI: *Kampei's Seppuku*

108. Okaru has allowed herself to be sold into prostitution in order to provide the money that Kampei needs to prove his own good faith and be admitted into the band of those who are out to avenge Hangan's death. She is being taken away in a palanquin by the brothel-keeper when, on the *hanamichi*, she encounters Kampei, who has been out hunting boar. (*Okaru*, Nakamura Utaemon; *Kampei*, Nakamura Kanzaburō)

109. Kampei and Okaru part sorrowfully. (*Kampei*, Nakamura Kichiemon; *Okaru*, Bandō Tamasaburō)

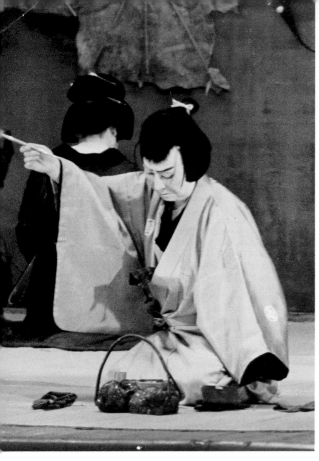

110. Hearing the brothel-keeper say that she gave his father-in-law half the money for Okaru in a cloth bag, Kampei compares the bag he took from the dead Sadakurō with the bag containing the other half, and realizes to his horror that he has—he thinks—killed his own father-in-law. The passage is considered one of the most difficult and rewarding for the actor playing the part. (*Kampei*, Nakamura Kanzaburō)

111. The body of Yoichibei is brought in, and Okaru's mother, Okaya—who is, like Kampei himself, misled by the purse—bitterly reproaches him. Kampei makes no attempt to defend himself, convinced that he has committed a great wrong. (*Okaya*, Onoe Taganojō)

112. As the only possible gesture of atonement for his "crime," Kampei commits suicide. But two of his fellow samurai examine Yoichibei's body, and discover that he was killed by a sword and not a bullet; thus Kampei's final gesture is seen to have been all for nothing. The part of Kampei is always played by a well-known actor. For many years, the name Kampei was a synonym for an attractive but ineffectual, weak-willed young man. (*The samurai Senzaki Yagorō*, Nakamura Tomijūrō; *the samurai Fuwa Kazuemon*, Bandō Mitsugorō VIII)

113. This gay, colorful scene is in the celebrated Gion gay quarters of Kyoto. The act begins by showing Yuranosuke playing blind man's bluff with the maids of one of the better-known houses; he is pretending to give himself up to a life of dissipation in order to allay the suspicions of his enemies. Ono Kudayū, in the service of Moronō, knows that it is the anniversary of the death of Yuranosuke's former master, Enya Hangan, and to test his true feelings, offers him a piece of octopus (seafood was prohibited on the anniversary of someone's death), which Yuranosuke eats without hesitation. (*Kudayū*, Nakamura Kasen; *Yuranosuke*, Onoe Shōroku)

114. Yuranosuke reads a letter from Kaoyo. Watching him from an upper window is Okaru, who is now a courtesan. Yuranosuke summons Okaru and announces that he will ransom her. (*Yuranosuke*, Onoe Shōroku; *Okaru*, Nakamura Utaemon)

115. Okaru's elder brother Heiemon arrives. His is convinced that Yuranosuke has no intention of taking revenge for his master's death, but Okaru, who has seen the letter, whispers the truth in his ear. (*Okaru*, Nakamura Jakuemon; *Heiemon*, Jitsukawa Enjaku)

116. Hearing that his sister Okaru has seen the secret letter and is to be ransomed by Yuranosuke, Heiemon concludes that she is to be murdered, and tries to kill her with his own sword, saying that it is better that she should be killed by him so that he can at least demonstrate his faithfulness to his master Yuranosuke and be allowed to join them. (*Okaru*, Nakamura Utaemon)

117. Yuranosuke realizes the loyalty of Okaru and her brother. He kills Ono Kudayū, who has been hiding beneath the veranda hoping to sell information to the enemy, and orders Heiemon to throw him into the river.

118. Act VIII, Michiyuki: *The Bride's Journey*
This dance scene shows Honzō's daughter Konami, accompanied by her mother Tonase, on her way to be married to Yuranosuke's son Rikiya. The dance relies for much of its effect on the contrast between the grace and dignity of a middle-aged woman of samurai birth and the unspoiled charms of a well-bred young girl. (*Tonase*, Nakamura Utaemon; *Konami*, Nakamura Matsue)

119–120. Act IX: *Yuranosuke's Country Retreat in Yamashina*

119. Honzō's wife Tonase, arriving with her daughter Konami for the promised nuptials, is spurned by Yuranosuke's wife Oishi. Ashamed and despairing, she is about to kill her daughter and die herself when the silence is broken by the sound of a flute, and a voice cries "Stop!" from the room at the right. The scene, which takes place on a day of heavy snow at Yuranosuke's unpretentious country dwelling, is remarkable for its dignified drama and pathos. (*Konami*, Nakamura Tokizō IV)

120. The flute was played by Honzō, who is in the guise of a wandering monk. He deliberately goads Rikiya into fatally wounding him with a halberd; then, before he dies, he reveals his true motives and gives them a plan of Moronō's mansion as a wedding gift. (*Yuranosuke*, Ichikawa Jukai III; *Yuranosuke's wife Oishi*, Sawamura Sōjūrō; *Honzō*, Nakamura Ganjirō II)

121. ACT X: *The Amakawaya Scene*
Amakawaya Gihei, a merchant who at Yuranosuke's request has been assembling the weapons required by the forty-seven *rōnin* for their revenge, is the stereotype of the upright, loyal merchant. He has divorced his wife to prevent her from knowing what he is doing, and his loyalty to Yuranosuke's cause does not swerve even when some of Yuranosuke's men, sent to test him in the guise of constables, threaten to kill his infant son. This scene is the most infrequently performed of the whole play. (*Amakawaya Gihei*, Bandō Mitsugorō VIII)

122–124. ACT XI: *The Storming of Moronō's Mansion*

122. Ōboshi Yuranosuke carries the war drum before the main gate of Moronō's mansion. (*Yuranosuke*, Onoe Shōroku)

123. The band of *rōnin* rush into Moronō's mansion to avenge their former lord's death. They are shown here fighting with Shimizu Ikkaku, Moronō's bodyguard, and his men. (*Ikkaku*, Nakamura Tomijūrō)

124. Moronō, discovered hiding in the charcoal shed, has been beheaded, and the band of *rōnin* are triumphant, their mission accomplished.

SPECIAL TECHNIQUES

125. *The Genroku Mie*
So called because it is one of the classic *mie* that originated in the Genroku era, the Genroku *mie* illustrates very clearly how the actor's pose combines with costume and makeup in a *mie* to create a single, integrated effect. (*Kamakura Gongorō* in *Shibaraku*, Onoe Shōroku)

126. *The Fudō Mie*
A type of *mie* peculiar to *aragoto* is based on poses taken from Buddhist iconography. This *mie* is known as the "Fudō" *mie* since the actor strikes a pose suggestive of the conventional representations of the Buddhist deity of that name. (*Fudō Myō-ō* in *Narukami Fudō Kitayama-zakura*, Onoe Shōroku)

127. *The Sutra Scroll Mie (Kyōmon no Mie)*
The holy recluse Narukami, corrupted by Taema-hime, makes a quick costume change into a flame-colored robe. The monks around him try to prevent him from running wild with rage, but he flings a sutra scroll at them and strikes the grand pose shown here. (*Narukami*, Ichikawa Danjūrō)

128. *The Tide-Watching Mie (Shiomi no Mie)*
This is Kezori's pose just before curtain, as he stands in the prow of the boat watching the movement of the tide. In one variation, he carries a hatchet on his shoulder and gazes downwards. (*Kezori* in *Hakata Kojorō Nami Makura*, Ichikawa Danjūrō XI)

129. *The Pillar-Winding Mie (Hashiramaki Mie)*
In the *hashiramaki mie*, which may be performed only by the head of the troupe, the actor twines his arms and legs around a pillar and glares in typical *mie* fashion. At the same time, an assistant standing behind him holds out his costume so that it opens up like a peacock's tail. The character Narukami, shown here, is a holy recluse who is enraged by the realization that a beautiful woman has corrupted him. He performs a quick *bukkaeri* change into a costume suggesting the flames of wrath, then grasps the pillar of his hermitage and strikes the *mie*. (*Narukami* in *Narukami*, Ichikawa Danjūrō)

130. *The Curtain-Close Mie (Makugire no Mie)*
The character Watanabe no Tsuna, who has just failed to capture the demon Ibaragi, strikes a *mie* as he sets off in pursuit. (*Watanabe no Tsuna* in *Ibaragi*, Onoe Shōroku)

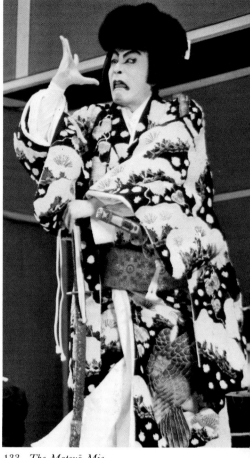

131. *The Umbrella Mie (Kasa no Mie)*
This dashing pose is struck by Soga no Gorō (one of the two brothers in the famous tale of the Sogas' revenge), who appears in wooden clogs and carrying an umbrella. (*Soga no Gorō* in *Ame no Gorō*, Onoe Shōroku)

132. *The Signboard-Holding Mie (Kōsatsu no Mie)*
There are two forms of this *mie*, the "Shikan" type, in which the signboard is carried on the shoulder, and the "Danjūrō" type; in which it is held pointing downwards. "Shikan" and "Danjūrō" are, of course, the names of the actors who favored the two versions respectively. (*Kumagai Naozane* in *Ichinotani Futaba Gunki*, Matsumoto Hakuō)

133. *The Matsuō Mie*
A *mie* is struck by the ailing Matsuōmaru (also known simply as Matsuō) in a moment of intense excitement. He sticks his sword on the ground to support his weakened body. The costume, with its pattern of snowladen pine trees, is traditional to this scene. (*Matsuōmaru* in *Sugawara Denju Tenarai Kagami*, Kataoka Takao)

134. *The Tenchi Mie*
This pose is struck by Maizuru and Soga no Gorō as the former holds the latter back from attacking somebody. (*Soga no Gorō* in *Kusazuri-biki*, Nakamura Tōzō; *Maizuru*, Nakamura Utaemon)

138. *The Murderer's Mie (Koroshi no Mie)*
In *Natsu Matsuri Naniwa Kagami*, the chivalrous Danshichi, who is covered all over with tattoes, kills his father-in-law Giheiji in a rice paddy. There are thirteen fixed *mie* poses during the murder. (Matsumoto Kōshirō)

◁ 135. *The Curled-Up Prawn (Ebizori) Mie*
This is the pose from *Seki no To* in which, after his true identity
is revealed, Sekibei (in reality Ōtomo no Kuronushi) swings an
axe around his head and Sumizome, the spirit of the cherry,
bends over backwards. (*Kuronushi*, Nakamura Kichiemon; *the
spirit of the cherry*, Bandō Tamasaburō)

136. *The Jōge Mie*
Fuwa Banzaemon, an *aragoto* role, and Nagoya Sanza, a *wagoto*
role, have a quarrel in which they cross (sheathed) swords, and
finally strike a highly stylized pose in which they tug at each
other's sedge hats. (*Fuwa Banzaemon* in *Ukiyozuka Hiyoku no Inazuma*, Ichikawa Danjūrō XI: *Nagoya Sanza*, Ichikawa Sadanji
III)

137. *A Sewamono Kimari*
In *sewamono* plays, the word *mie* is replaced by *kimari*. The
character Yosaburō in *Yowa Nasake Ukina no Yokogushi*, who has
degenerated into a good-for-nothing, meets his former mistress
after a long separation. As he reveals his true identity, he strikes
the pose shown here. (*Yosaburō*, Ichikawa Danjūrō XI)

139. *Use of Two Hanamichi as River Banks*
In the "Mountain Scene" of Imoseyama Onna Teikin, the widow Sadaka and Daihanji make their way through the audience along two separate *hanamichi*. Sadaka is on the main *hanamichi*, Daihanji on the secondary *hanamichi*, the two *hanamichi* representing the two banks of the Yoshino River.

140. *Lineup on the Hanamichi*
In the play *Aoto Zōshi Hana no Nishiki-e*, five men appear on the *hanamichi* at one time, walking in time to music illustrating various personalities, and proceed to identify themselves. An umbrella that one could twirl and strike manly poses with was considered a kind of necessary accessory to the dashing young male in the kabuki. The designs on the costumes of the five characters are intended to suggest their respective names. The different roles each have their own *kata*, even extending to the way the cotton towel is flung over the shoulder.

141. *Use of the Hanamichi as a Road*
In the ''Numazu (no Sato) Scene'' of the play *Iga-goe Dōchū Sugoroku*, Jūbei and an old palanquin bearer leave the stage via the secondary *hanamichi*, make their way behind the audience to the main *hanamichi*, and then return to the stage, engaging in conversation all the while. While they are doing so, the scenery representing a pine grove in the background of the stage shifts to indicate the distance they have covered.

142. *Use of Two Hanamichi as a River and as a Riverbank*
Shown here is the end of the ''Nozaki Mura Scene'' in *Shimpan Utazaimon*, in which the lovers Osome and Hisamatsu, for fear of what people will think, start home for Osaka by separate routes. Osome goes by boat along the main *hanamichi*, while Hisamatsu goes by palanquin along the secondary *hanamichi*, which here represents the bank of the river.

143. *Flying Through the Air–1*
Iwafuji, who has died once, comes to life again endowed with occult powers, and in the brilliant costume she wore in her heyday flies through the air chasing a butterfly with a fan. She holds a parasol as she flies above the massed cherry blossoms of spring. (*Iwafuji*, Nakamura Kanzaburō)

144. *Flying Through the Air–2*
This is Ishikawa Goemon in the play *Zōho Futatsu Domoe* which is based on the real life exploits of a famous robber. (*Ishikawa Goemon*, Jitsukawa Enjaku)

145. *Use of a Substitute Actor*
In the "Suma Bay Scene" of *Ichinotani Futaba Gunki*, there is a passage in which the hero Kumagai calls to Atsumori, who has ridden into the sea on his horse. At this point, a small boy actor is used for Atsumori, to make him appear to be in the far distance. When Kumagai rides out after him, one more boy actor is used in the same way. When the two fight and fall from the saddle, a curtain is lowered and adult actors replace the boys again.

146. *An Onnagata Acting in Puppet Style*
A puppet-style of acting (*ningyō-buri*) is used when a beautiful woman expresses very strong emotions, as in the case of Yuki-hime in the "Kinkakuji Scene" of *Gion Sairei Shinkōki*. Yuki-hime, whose hands are tied behind her, draws the shape of a rat by gathering cherry blossom petals with her toes, whereupon the rat comes to life and gnaws through the rope. Pretending that Yuki-hime is a puppet, a black-robed actor plays the role of a puppeteer while she imitates puppet movements. (*Yukihime*, Nakamura Jakuemon)

147. *A Male Role in Puppet Style*
Among actors playing male roles, the puppet style is seen most frequently in *dōke* ("comic") and *kataki* ("enemy") roles. The villain who torments the courtesan Akoya in *Dannoura Kabuto Gunki* acts in puppet style. He even has false eyebrows that move mechanically and is "supported" by two "puppeteers." (*Iwanaga Saemon*, Ichikawa Danshirō)

148. *Roppō Exit*
The head of the troupe is shown executing a *roppō* along the *hanamichi* in a *dammari* play. His hair is done in a style known as *kikubyaku*, and his costume is a colorful brocade kimono. He proceeds along the *hanamichi* at a rapid pace, gesturing vigorously with his arms as he goes. (Ichikawa Ennosuke)

149. *Leaping Roppō*
In the "Kuruma-biki Scene" of *Sugawara Denju Tenarai Kagami*, three men, triplets by birth, meet and have a quarrel, after which one of them, Umeōmaru, who has a violent disposition, leaves along the *hanamichi*. As he does so, he performs a vigorous version of the *roppō* known as *tobi roppō* that calls for him to leap up and down as he goes, traditionally with rounded back. (*Umeōmaru*, Kataoka Gatō)

150. *Spider-Hands-and-Octopus-Legs Roppō*
Expressive of an old and thoroughly wicked character, the *kumode tako-ashi roppō* is used in *Shinrei Yaguchi no Watashi* when Tombei pursues his daughter Ofune's lover, Nitta Yoshimine, in an attempt to kill him. The actor's feet imitate the movements of an octopus, his hands the movements of a spider. The sword hilt is designed to make a ringing sound when the actor runs. (*Tombei*, Ichikawa Danshirō)

151. *Fox Roppō*
At the end of the scene before the shrine in *Yoshitsune Sembonzakura*, Tadanobu—in reality a fox in the guise of a human being—shoulders his armor and executes a *kitsune roppō* along the *hanamichi* with his hands in the "fox's paws" position. The scene has an atmosphere at once brilliant and eerie. (*The fox/Tadanobu*, Onoe Shōroku)

152. *Single-Handed Roppō*
In the final scene in *Kanjinchō*, Benkei goes out after Yoshitsune, executing a *katate roppō* with one hand spread out and the other holding an itinerant monk's staff. Note that he moves from right to left on the stage. (*Benkei*, Matsumoto Hakuō)

155. *Exit along the Hanamichi in a Kizewamono Play* ▷
Naozamurai, the charming scoundrel in the play *Kumo ni Magō Ueno no Hatsuhana*, has met one of his cohorts, Ushimatsu, in the paddy fields close to the gay quarters. After some small talk he bids him farewell, and walks off alone along a snowy path (the *hanamichi*), watched from the stage by Ushimatsu. (*Naozamurai*, Ichikawa Danjūrō XI)

153. *Exit Along the Hanamichi by a Monk*
Kumagai, the hero of *Ichinotani Futaba Gunki*, has become a Buddhist monk. Here he sets off along the *hanamichi* after the curtain has been drawn. In the background can be seen a shamisen musician, who comes out to accompany him with a special piece of music. Kumagai makes his way along the *hanamichi* in time with it, covering his ears as he goes to shut out the hateful sound of the battle music (*donjan*) being played in the *geza*. (*Kumagai*, Matsumoto Hakuō)

154. *Exit Along the Hanamichi by a Sorcerer*
In the fourth act of *Meiboku Sendai Hagi*, Nikki Danjō, who dabbles in the occult, and has just made an appearance as a monstrous grey rat, quietly—almost stealthily—makes his way out along the *hanamichi* following the drawing of the curtain. Assistants hold out towards him the candles that in the Edo period performed the functions of a spotlight. (*Nikki Danjō*, Ichikawa Ennosuke)

156. *Exit along the Hanamichi by a Popular Hero*
Gorozō, in a towering rage, makes an excited exit along the *hanamichi* in the play *Soga Moyō Tateshi no Gosho-zome*. He wears wooden clogs, and his kimono is tucked up above his knees. As he proceeds along the *hanamichi*, his excitement mounts, and he quickens his pace until he finally rushes out of sight. (*Gorozō*, Onoe Shōroku)

157. *Exit along the Hanamichi in a Love-Suicide Piece*
One of the special features of this type of play is the special manner of walking—distracted, almost as though the characters were already no longer of this world—that is adopted by the hero and heroine as, watchful all the time for their pursuers, they go hand in hand to their death. (*Umegawa* in *Koibikyaku Yamato Orai*, Nakamura Shikan; *Chūbei*, Jitsukawa Enjaku)

158. *Exit of an Onnagata—1*
The lady-in-waiting Yayoi in *Kagami-jishi* has been dancing with a lion mask in her hand, but the mask has taken on a life of its own, and she cannot release it. It starts to chase two butterflies and she is dragged willy-nilly after it. The two "butterflies" are attached to long wires held by an assistant. (*Yayoi*, Nakamura Shikan)

159. *Exit of an Onnagata—2*
Hachimonji is a special manner of walking used by actors representing courtesans in scenes in which they are shown outside in the street. The styles differ according to whether the gay quarters are those of Kyoto or Edo, and are known as *uchi-hachimonji* in the former case and *soto-hachimonji* in the latter. The photograph shows the courtesan Yatsuhashi in the play *Kagotsurube Sato no Eizame* walking a *soto-hachimonji* on the *hanamichi* in high wooden clogs with three crosspieces. (*Yatsuhashi*, Nakamura Utaemon)

Pls. 36–37. *Bukkaeri*
When the officer of the barrier guard in the play *Seki no To* reveals his true identity as the archvillain Ōtomo no Kuronushi, his costume undergoes a *bukkaeri* change (aided by an assistant), switching from a commonplace padded kimono to a nobleman's dress. At the same time, his hood is removed to allow his hair to fall into the style known as "prince wig," and he uses a mirror and makeup concealed in an axe to make up his face. (*Kuronushi,* Nakamura Kichiemon)

Pls. 38–39. *Hikinuki*
Hikinuki permits a rapid change of costume in the course of a dance. With the aid of an assistant, the outer garment is pulled out from the *obi* around the waist, and falls down to form a different costume, the mood of the dance itself altering at the same time. (Bandō Tamasaburō in *Musume Dōjōji*)

STYLIZED SCENES AND KATA

160–166. *Head Inspection*

The head inspection *kata* is an essential ingredient of the type of scene, common in *jidaimono*, in which somebody is killed or commits suicide as a substitute for another. The head of the deceased, however, must be inspected to make sure that it is indeed the right person, and the crux of the situation is the manner employed to pass off the substitute head as the real thing, or to allay the other side's suspicions. The "Moritsuna Head Inspection" shown here is one of the most famous of all such scenes. (*Sasaki Moritsuna* in *Ōmi Genji Senjin Yakata*, Ichikawa Danjūrō IX)

160. With soft paper, Moritsuna wipes the blood from the head to be inspected.

161. He prepares himself to inspect the head of his younger brother. He shuts his eyes, steels himself, and presses down hard on the handle of his sword.

162. Slowly, he opens his eyes—but stare as he may, the head, beyond all doubt, is not that of his younger brother Takatsuna.

163. His expression shows that he realizes there must be some cunning plot behind what has happened. As he watches, various expressions of contemplation and consideration pass over his face.

164. With a start, he realizes that this must be a plot hatched by Takatsuna himself.

165. He raises the lid containing the head in both hands, and at the words "Reverently, he proffers the head with both hands," he holds the container out.

166. Takatsuna's son Koshirō kills himself to help his father succeed in his plot. As the accompaniment excitedly declares, "Praise him! Praise him!" Moritsuna makes a gesture in praise of the young boy's suicide.

Pl. 40. *Yasuna's Mad Scene*
This is one of the most famous ''mad scenes.'' Clasping in her arms
a kimono (not visible here) that once belonged to her dead lover,
Yasuna wanders distractedly through the spring countryside. The
piece, called *Yasuna*, is a dance-drama with *jōruri* accompaniment.
(*Yasuna*, Onoe Baikō)

Pl. 41. *Jidai Dammari*
Shown here is one kind of *jidai dammari*, a *jidaimono* piece that is entirely mimed, in which the shrine at Miyajima, with its *torii* gateway standing in the sea and its impressive shrine buildings, forms a background against which various characters, each a famous figure, appear and seek each other out "in the dark." The actor who climbs up the three steps covered with red cloth in the center of the stage is the head of the troupe.

Pl. 42. *Sewa Dammari*
The end of the "Onbōbori Scene" in *Tōkaidō Yotsuya Kaidan*. The actors grope around in the dark, leaving something behind that serves as evidence in the following act when the story is resolved. In *sewa dammari* (stylized passages without dialogue in a *sewa-mono* play), costumes are based on everyday dress, and the action generally takes place at the water's edge. (*Iemon*, Ichikawa Danjūrō; *Naosuke*, Nakamura Kichiemon; *Omon*, Nakamura Utaemon)

167–169. *Kata in Monogatari Passages*

For a male actor in a *jidaimono* piece, one of the most important types of passage in the play, around which much of the action revolves, is the *monogatari* or "narrative," in which he relates some particularly stirring or moving episode. Many of these are tales of battles, accompanied by *gidayū* music, with mime by the actor himself. The "Kumagai Jinya Scene" of *Ichinotani Futaba Gunki* is celebrated for "Kumagai's Narration." (*Kumagai Naozane*, Onoe Shōroku)

167. Kumagai, back at his camp, is relating how he killed Atsumori. He sweeps his battle fan in a great circle and points it out over the heads of the audience.

168. As the reciter declares "He hails Atsumori with his fan," the actor playing Kumagai opens his battle fan, with its gold sun on a red background, and strikes a *mie*.

169. At the words "From the mountain to the rear" in the accompaniment, he holds the open fan upside down to suggest the shape of a mountain, then strikes a grand *mie*. The accompaniment at this point is describing how Kumagai, having Atsumori at his mercy, notices that he is as young as his own son, and is tempted to spare him.

170. *Kudoki*

The *onnagata* equivalent of the "narrative" or "head inspection" of male roles is the *kudoki* or "lamentation." It occurs in both *sewamono* and *jidaimono* plays, and consists of a passage with *chobo* accompaniment in which the character bewails—for example— the fleeting nature of human life and happiness. The photograph shows a *kudoki* scene from the play *Hadesugata Onna Maiginu*, in which Osono laments her lot because her husband has acquired a mistress. The use of a lantern as the *onnagata* moves about during his speech is a convention of the *kudoki*. (*Osono*, Nakamura Utaemon)

171. *Shaberi*

One of the specialties of the *onnagata* actor, *shaberi* is a special technique of speaking very volubly in a somewhat humorous evocation of feminine talkativeness. Such passages create a *sewamono* type of atmosphere. The *shaberi* spoken by Yaegiri in *Komochi Yamamba* is one of the most famous of its kind. A woman peddling love-letters is summoned to the mansion of a young noblewoman, where she relates an amusing love story with mime. (*Yaegiri*, Nakamura Shikan)

Pl. 43. *Michiyuki in Jidaimono*
The *michiyuki*, a scene with a strongly stylized dance element in which two characters (most often a pair of lovers) are shown on a journey, is used in both *jidaimono* and *sewamono* to provide a touch of color and romantic emotion. The majority of *michiyuki* are accompanied by *jōruri* music, and it was formerly customary to insert one such scene as a miniature dance-drama in every day's performance. The eighth act of *Kanadehon Chūshingura* is a *michiyuki* known as "The Bride's Journey," and is a *shosagoto* showing a mother taking her daughter to be married. (*Konami the daughter*, Nakamura Tokizō; *Tonase the mother*, Sawamura Sōjūrō)

Pl. 44. *Michiyuki in Sewamono*
The most characteristic type of *michiyuki* in a *sewamono* piece is that in which two lovers are on their way to commit double suicide or trying to escape from the authorities. One of the most famous examples is the *michiyuki* performed by Umegawa and Chūbei in the play *Koibikyaku Yamato Ōrai*. The lovers wear matching kimono for the occasion. The man has a shawl draped over his head and tied under his chin, and the woman wears a similar shawl draped loosely around her head. They move along the *hanamichi*, hastening to reach the village where Chūbei's father lives. (*Umegawa*, Nakamura Utaemon; *Chūbei*, Nakamura Senjaku)

172. *Saya-ate* (Scabbard Brushing)

Two men become involved in a quarrel—in which they "brush scabbards"—over some subject such as a love triangle with a courtesan. It is a tradition that in the middle of the quarrel there should appear a male or female character (*tomeotoko* or *tomeonna*) whose sole task is to pacify the two. The play *Ukiyozuka Hiyoku no Inazuma* is an example of this idea used as the theme for an independent one-act play. (*Nagoya Sanza*, Ichikawa Jukai III; *tomeonna*, Nakamura Kanzaburō; *Fuwa Banzaemon*, Ichikawa En'ō)

173. *Zōriuchi* (Striking with a Sandal)

Zōriuchi as a scene in its own right came into existence in Genroku times. In it, one of the characters suffers in silence the indignity of being struck on the head with an adversary's straw sandal—which was considered to constitute the supreme insult. (*Onoe* in *Kagamiyama Kokyō no Nishiki-e*, Nakamura Utaemon; *Iwafuji*, Nakamura Ganjirō II)

174. *Ikenba* (Admonition Scene)

The "admonition" in most cases is administered to a character who is considering suicide. The same type of scene is sometimes referred to as *ikengoto*. In the play *Kagamiyama Kokyō no Nishiki-e*, the maid Ohatsu massages Onoe's shoulders for her. As she does so she seeks to dissuade her, with references to the *Chūshingura* story, from committing suicide. (*Onoe*, Nakamura Utaemon; *Ohatsu*, Onoe Baikō)

175. *Kamisuki (Hair Combing)–1*

A celebrated variant on the usual "hair-combing" is performed by Oiwa, the unfortunate heroine of the bloodcurdler *Tōkaidō Yotsuya Kaidan*. Oiwa has been given poison, and her face is terribly disfigured as a result. Thinking to go next door to unburden herself of her woes, she sets about tidying her hair, but cannot unfasten the paper cord holding it in place. The scene is played to heartrending *meriyasu* accompaniment. (*Oiwa*, Nakamura Utaemon)

177. *Kamisuki–3*

This *kata* is often used in scenes illustrating the love between a man and woman, or between a mother and her daughter. One of the two characters dresses the other's hair with a comb or ornamental hairpin, the action being combined with affectionate caresses. Such scenes are usually accompanied by the highly atmospheric type of music known as *meriyasu*. The courtesan Michitose is shown here using an ornamental hairpin to comb the hair of her lover Naozamurai, a shogunate vassal. (*Michitose* in *Kumo ni Magō Ueno no Hatsuhana*, Onoe Kikugorō; *Naozamurai*, Ichikawa Danjūrō)

176. *Kamisuki–2, print by Torii Kiyomasu*

This Edo period print depicts a "hair combing" scene with the actors Ichimura Takenojō and Ichimura Tamagashiwa of the Kyōhō era. The title of the play is unknown.

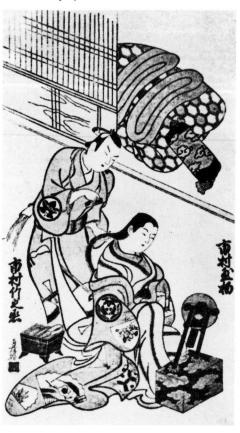

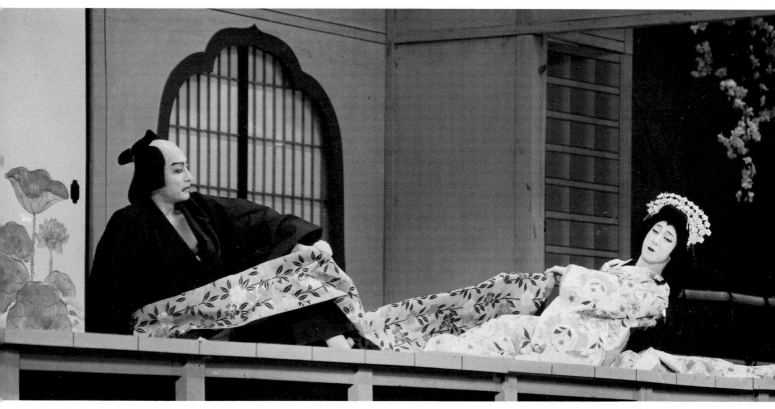

178. *Nureba*

This is a love scene between a well-born lady, Sakura-hime, and a man of humble origins, Tsurigane Gonsuke, set in the hermitage at Sakuradani. Tsurigane means "hanging bell" and refers to the tattoo of a hanging bell on Gonsuke's arm. This is a typical *nureba* ("moist scene") from a kabuki revival, *Sakura-hime Azuma Bunshō*. Although related to the *iro moyō*, it is more openly erotic and realistic. (*Gonsuke*, Kataoka Takao; *Sakura-hime*, Bandō Tamasaburō)

179. *Iro Moyō (Love Scene)*

Iro moyō is a particular type of tender love scene with a strongly stylized dance element. A typical example is the scene between Okaru and Kampei, the fugitive lovers in *Kanadehon Chūshingura*, who display their love in a typical *michiyuki* dance. (*Okaru*, Nakamura Kotarō; *Kampei*, Nakamura Kankurō)

180. *Yukizeme (Snow Torture)–1*
The *seme* passage is another common *kata* in kabuki plays. Not, strictly speaking, "torture," the term *seme* embraces all kinds of bullying and ill treatment. Other similar scenes that are not played nowadays included the "gridiron torture" and the "snake torture." In the "snow torture," one of the characters is beaten with split bamboo in the snow, and the scene is accompanied by profoundly melancholy music.

Hibariyama Hime Sutematsu is a *jidaimono* in which the heroine, Chūjō-hime, beaten by her stepmother Iwane Gozen on accont of a misdeed of which she is innocent, finally loses consciousness in the snow. (*Chūjō-hime*, Nakamura Utaemon; *Iwane Gozen*, Nakamura Tokizō III)

181. *Yukizeme–2*
Akegarasu Hana no Nure-ginu is a *sewamono*, in which Urazato is beaten with a bamboo broom when she tries secretly to meet with her lover and is discovered. (*Urazato*, Nakamura Tokizō III; *old woman*, Ichikawa Dannosuke)

182. *Yusuriba (Extortion Scene)–1*
The "extortion scene" became a regular feature of kabuki plays as the *shiranamimono* became popular in the latter part of the Edo period, and is one of the principal standbys of *kizewamono*. In the play *Aoto Zōshi Hana no Nishiki-e*, there is a scene where a petty thief disguised as a young girl extorts money from the owner of a cloth shop as compensation for a supposed slight to his honor. The point at which the young man—Benten Kozō—is exposed and proudly announces his true identity is the climax of the whole play. (*Benten Kozō*, Onoe Kikugorō)

183. *Yusuriba–2*
In the example shown here, the masseur Dōgen has come to a merchant house to practice a little extortion. (*Dōgen* in *Mekura Nagaya Ume ga Kagatobi*, Nakamura Kanzaburō)

184. *Enkiriba (Breaking off an Affair)*
The *enkiriba* (literally, "relation-severing scene") is an important ingredient in many *sewamono* plays. In it, one of a pair of lovers pretends to have tired of the other because he or she believes this course to be for the other's benefit, or in order to save the other's life. It is often accompanied by melancholy music played on the *kokyū*, a three-stringed bowed instrument that originated in China. In *Ise Ondo Koi no Netaba*, the courtesan Okon severs relations with Mitsugi. (*Fukuoka Mitsugi*, Ichikawa Danjūrō XI; *Okon*, Onoe Baikō)

185. *Koroshiba (Killing Scene)–1*
The *koroshiba* in the *sewamono* play is characterized by a greater degree of realism than in *jidaimono*. Yet even here—as in the scene from the play *Kagotsurube Sato no Eizame* shown here, in which Sano Jirōzaemon slashes with his sword at a woman who has broken off their relationship, and the woman does a "prawn" bend to avoid the weapon—the need for stylization is not forgotten. (*Sano Jirōzaemon*, Matsumoto Hakuō; *Yatsuhashi*, Nakamura Utaemon)

186. *Koroshiba–2*
In the play *Kasane*, Yoemon is driven by the jealousy of his ugly wife, Kasane, to kill her with a sickle on the outskirts of their village. The play makes much use of *kiyomoto* music. (*Kasane*, Onoe Baikō; *Yoemon*, Onoe Kikugorō)

187. *Koroshiba–3*

In this celebrated murder scene from a *sewamono* play, the young good-for-nothing Yohei kills the wife of a merchant, a dealer in oil. There is a good deal of slipping about in blood and spilt oil, but the scene, for all its bloodthirstiness, manages to convey a stylized beauty. (*Okichi* in *Onnagoroshi Abura no Jigoku*, Nakamura Shikan; *Yohei*, Kataoka Takao)

188. *Koroshiba–4*

The love suicide scene at the end of *Sonezaki Shinjū*. Ohatsu, holding a rosary in her hands, shows her readiness to die. After killing her, Tokubei takes his own life. (*Ohatsu*, Nakamura Senjaku, *Tokubei*, Nakamura Ganjirō II)

189. *Tachimawari–1*

Kabuki swordfights usually have several *mie* worked into them in order to accentuate their climactic moments. Shown here is one of the many well-known swordfight passages engaged in by the character Higuchi in the play *Hiragana Seisuiki*. He is surrounded by Yoshitsune's retainers, who are disguised as boatmen. In this fight, the group forms a pattern suggesting a boat. (*Higuchi no Jirō*, Matsumoto Hakuō)

190. *Tachimawari–2*

This is a *sewamono* fight from *Sannin Kichiza Kuruwa no Hatsugai*, a play about a band of thieves. The fights in *sewamono* are characterized by a greater realism than those in *jidaimono*, but even here attention is still paid to the stylized composition of the scene on the stage. (*Ojō Kichiza*, Nakamura Tokizō III; *Oshō Kichiza*, Ichikawa En'ō; *Obō Kichiza*, Matsumoto Hakuō)

191. *Tachimawari–3*

This is a fighting scene in *Suibodai Godō no Nozarashi* between Nozarashi Gosuke and Daiba no Nisaburō, using the scaffolding at a temple under construction. The throng of constables, carrying umbrellas, performs a revue-like group *tachimawari*. On the umbrellas is the family crest of the actor playing the role of Gosuke, his "shop name" (*yagō*), or the name of the street (Kioi) where he lives. For the clothing as well, cotton kimono bearing the fixed pattern of the actor's family are used. (*Nisaburō*, Kawarazaki Gonjūrō; *Gosuke*, Onoe Tatsunosuke)

Pls. 45–46. *Tachimawari–4*
This is the *tachimawari* of Keisei Yaegiri in *Komochi Yamamba*. After her effeminate husband commits *seppuku* and his spirit enters her,

Yaegiri is transformed from a gentle woman into a powerful one, and disperses the constables. This is a very old-fashioned, colorful *tachimawari* performed by an *onnagata*. (*Yaegiri*, Onoe Kikugorō)

Pl. 47. *Tachimawari–5*
The *tachimawari* between the *iro-yakko* (see Fig. 203) Tsumahei and several constables in the Kiyomizu scene of *Shin Usuyuki Monogatari* illustrates a stylized *tachimawari* using wooden buckets. The striking of a succession of different poses with the aid of props such as small wooden buckets or umbrellas, evoking a succession of changing images in the audience's mind, is characteristic of the swordfights in *jidai-mono* plays. This *tachimawari* imitates the practice long ago of sprinkling water from a bucket during wedding ceremonies.

YAKUGARA

193. *Tachiyaku-1*

An important type of *tachiyaku* is the role that specializes in *jitsugoto*, suggesting a character of manly bearing, ripe in both years and ability. The acting must give the impression of poise, judgment, and reserve. This type of role forms a central pivot around which the great heroic dramas revolve. (*Ōboshi Yuranosuke* in *Kanadehon Chūshingura*, Onoe Shōroku)

194. *Tachiyaku-2: Nimaime (Romantic Lead) in a Jidaimono*

Kajiwara Heizō is usually depicted in kabuki as a villain, but in *Kajiwara Heizō Homare no Ishikiri* he is a handsome, young samurai with a heart. Although on the side of the Genji forces in Kamakura, he sympathizes with the Heike, and buys the sword of a Heike warrior who has fallen on hard times. Holding paper between his teeth so as not to breathe on the sword, he tests it to see if it is genuine. (*Heizō*, Kataoka Takao)

195. *Tachiyaku-3: Shimbō tachiyaku*

Most sumo wrestler parts in kabuki are what are known as *shimbō tachiyaku*—"good" male characters who suffer some inner torment or misunderstanding in silence. Nuregami in *Futatsu Chōchō Kuruwa Nikki* is a wrestler who allows himself to be beaten by a younger man for the sake of his patron. (*Nuregami Chōgorō*, Bandō Mitsugorō VIII)

◁ **192. *Jitsuaku***

The *jitsuaku* role is the opposite of the *tachiyaku*, a collective term referring to the various "good" male roles. He is a dyed-in-the-wool villain preoccupied with power, and the actor who plays him must have an impressive bearing with a touch of the terrifying at the same time. Shown here is Nikki Danjō in *Meiboku Sendai Hagi* about to commit his final murder. (*Nikki Danjō*, Onoe Shōroku)

196. *Tachiyaku-4: Otokodate*

The *otokodate* role—the dashing, chivalrous commoner—was the most spectacular of all in the *sewamono* plays, and that of Chōbei is perhaps the finest of them all. (*Chōbei* in *Banzui Chōbei Shōjin Manaita*, Onoe Shōroku)

197. *Tachiyaku-5*

The *sewamono* character Sakura Sōgo can also be classified as a "silent sufferer." A leader in an impoverished country village, he becomes the chief plotter in a peasant uprising. Here, he is being pursued by constables, but has reached his home for a last farewell to his family. (*Sakura Sōgo* in *Sakura Giminden*, Matsumoto Hakuō)

Pl. 48. *Hime (Young Woman of Noble Birth)*
Of all the *hime* parts, Yaegaki-hime in *Honchō Nijūshi Kō*, Toki-hime in *Kamakura Sandaiki*, and Yuki-hime in *Gion Sairei Shinkōki*—collectively known as the "three *hime* roles"—are considered the three most exacting. Sakura-hime in *Sakura-hime Azuma Bunshō*, shown here, is another difficult role, since at a late stage in the play she becomes a prostitute in a wayside brothel. (*Sakura-hime*, Bandō Tamasaburō)

Pl. 49. *Musume: Merchant-class Girl*
There are two types of *musume* roles in the *sewamono* play—the town girl and the country girl. The part of Osome in *Osome Hisamatsu Ukina no Yomiuri* is that of a daughter of a prosperous merchant, a young woman of considerable grace and refinement; yet it is characteristic of the type of role that her passions are strong enough to make her leave home and follow Hisamatsu, the clerk with whom she is in love. (*Osome*, Nakamura Kotarō)

Pl. 50. *Tayū*
The *tayū* or high-ranking courtesan is one of the most important *tate-oyama* roles, so important in fact that a top-ranking *onnagata* was often referred to as *tayū*. Both the hairstyle and the clothing are of the utmost elaboration. (Nakamura Jakuemon)

Pl. 52. *Akuba (Desperate Woman)*
The *akuba* is a feminine version of the not entirely unattractive scoundrel who appears so often in kabuki. For example, Kirare Otomi (''Scarred Otomi'') in *Musume-gonomi Ukina no Yokogushi* is a feminine version of Kirare Yosa. She is driven by despair at the many wounds disfiguring her face to indulge in extortion, blackmail, and other socially unacceptable ways of gaining a livelihood. (*Kirare Otomi*, Kawarazaki Kunitarō)

Pl. 51. *Chaya no Nyōbō*
This role of a very chic (*iki*) wife of the proprietor of a teahouse is performed in an extremely stylish way, and the feeling is conveyed even in the hairdo and the way the kimono is worn. The black satin at the collar was customary of kimono worn among townsmen's wives. (Sawamura Sōjūrō)

198. *Katahazushi*

A type of role representing chiefly the women of a high-ranking samurai household is known as *katahazushi*, a name derived from the characteristic hairstyle worn by such women. A typical example is the nurse Masaoka in *Meiboku Sendai Hagi*. This role, that of a mature, strong-willed woman, requires an imposing presence that places it in the *tateoyama* category. A male role with which it might be compared is that of Yuranosuke in *Kanadehon Chūshingura*. (*Masaoka*, Nakamura Utaemon)

199. *Female Villain*

The female villain is the equivalent of the male *jitsuaku* role. Many "wicked woman" roles are played by actors normally specializing in male roles, including Yashio in *Meiboku Sendai Hagi*. (*Yashio*, Nakamura Kanzaburō)

200. *Female Fukeyaku*

The *fukeyaku* role is that of a man or woman who suffers some great misfortune in old age. Mimyō in *Ōmi Genji Senjin Yakata* is one of three celebrated parts known as the "Three Old Women." It is a difficult role, since Mimyō has to allow her beloved young grandson to commit *seppuku*, and the actor must convey the sorrow of a heart torn between the proud spirit of a samurai family and human love for her grandson. (*Mimyō*, Nakamura Ganjirō II)

201. *Koyaku (Child Role)*

This child attendant to a courtesan is called a "kamuro." A great courtesan has two *kamuro*; they wear kimono with trailing sleeves and have large ornamental combs in their hair. In principle, such parts are played by boys. They deliver their lines in a characteristic shrill monotone.

202. *Tachiyaku–6: Kugeyaku (Court Noble)*
The *kugeyaku* shown here is the character Ichijō Ōkura-kyō, the hero of *Kiichi Hōgen Sanryaku no Maki*. He is a court noble who feigns madness in order to escape persecution by the Taira family, and secretly gives his support to the Minamoto family, rival of the Taira in a struggle for control of the nation. The actor must present a brilliant exterior, yet suggest an undercurrent of isolation and a desire to shun the world. (*Ichijō Ōkura-kyō*, Nakamura Kanzaburō)

203. *Iro Yakko*
In the early stages of the kabuki, there was a type of part known as *yakkogata*, representing a foot-soldier in the service of a samurai. Later, it came to be known as *date* ("dashing," "dandy") *yakko*, and acquired a certain glamor. The *iro yakko* of today is a kind of subhero. (*Chienai* in *Kiichi Hōgen Sanryaku no Maki*, Onoe Shōroku)

204. *Iro Wakashu (Handsome Youth)*
A typical example of a youth with his front hair still unshaven is Torazō in *Kiichi Hōgen Sanryaku no Maki*. This type of role characteristically has an almost feminine grace, but that of Torazō also has the dignity and strength of a samurai. (*Torazō*, Ichikawa Danjūrō)

205. *Ara Wakashu (Strong Youth)*
Typical of the strong-charactered youth or *aragotoshi* of the *jidaimono* play is Soga no Gorō. As he appears in *Kotobuki Soga no Taimen*, he still has his front hair unshaven—a sign of immaturity—but this is offset by a stylized wig and a special type of red makeup known as *mukimi*. He throws his kimono off his shoulders, showing the fine style of his red underkimono as he sets about dealing with a wicked character. (*Soga no Gorō*, Onoe Tatsunosuke)

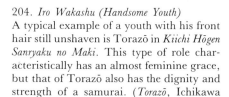

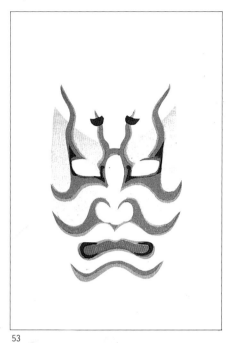

53

54

Pl. 53. *Aiguma*
Aiguma, the makeup for a wicked nobleman, is used for Shihei in the "Kuruma-biki Scene" of *Sugawara Denju Tenarai Kagami*.

Pl. 54. *Mukimiguma*
Mukimiguma is used for Sakuramaru in the "Kuruma-biki Scene" of *Sugawara Denju Tenarai Kagami*.

Pl. 55. *Ipponguma*
This type of makeup is used for Matsuōmaru in the "Kuruma-biki Scene" of *Sugawara Denju Tenarai Kagami*.

Pl. 56. *Sujiguma or Nihonguma*
This type of makeup is often used for the heroes of *aragoto* pieces. Umeōmaru uses it in the "Kuruma-biki Scene" of *Sugawara Denju Tenarai Kagami*.

55

56

Pl. 57. *Sugawara Denju Tenarai Kagami: The Kuruma-biki Scene*
This scene is often presented independently as a typical representative of the stylized acting and production of the *jidaimono*, and of the *aragoto* style of acting in particular. The villain Shihei is a *kugeaku* role. Of the three brothers (from left to right), Sakuramaru is a *wakashugata* role, Umeōmaru an *aragotoshi*, and Matsuōmaru a *tachiyaku*. Since they are brothers, they wear matching outer kimono, and their individual red undergarments have designs of cherry blossoms, plum blossoms, and pine trees, symbolizing the names Sakuramaru, Umeōmaru, and Matsuōmaru respectively. In the scene shown here, the checked outer kimono are thrown off the shoulders in preparation for a fight.

206. *Tachiyaku-7: Nimaime in a Sewamono*
Kamiya Jihei in the play *Shinjū Ten no Ami-jima* is a typical Osaka-style romantic lead part of a townsman, also known as *wagotoshi*. Torn between his wife and his mistress, a courtesan, he finally seeks a solution in suicide. The manner in which he walks vacantly down the *hanamichi*, his will to live gone, sums up the very essence of this type of role. (*Kamiya Jihei*, Nakamura Senjaku)

207. *Tachiyaku-8: Pintokona*
The odd name *pintokona* is applied chiefly to the hero of the play *Ise Ondo Koi no Netaba*. Mitsugi, formerly a samurai in the service of a Shinto shrine, is a rather soft character, with a touch of something effeminate, and it is this characteristic that is referred to in the term. The white summer kimono is traditional to the role and is appropriate for this play performed in the summer. (*Mitsugi*, Ichikawa Danjūrō)

208. *Tachiyaku-9: Tsukkorobashi (Pushover)*
This type of role, typified by the merchant Yogorō in *Futatsu Chōchō Kuruwa Nikki*, is a young man, well-bred but rather vapid and lacking in character. The role is held to be particularly difficult for the actor who approaches it in a modern, rationalistic spirit, and actors who are successful with it are highly valued. (*Yogorō*, Bandō Minosuke)

209. *Male Fukeyaku*
Shown here is a *fukeyaku* in a *sewamono* play. The unfortunate old man is Magoemon in *Koibikyaku Yamato Ōrai*. (*Magoemon*, Kataoka Nizaemon)

210. *Katakiyaku–1: Kugeaku (Wicked Nobleman)*
This kind of evil noble aims to usurp the state's power. With his great "prince wig," his dark makeup, and his gold headgear, he exudes malevolence. (Bandō Mitsugorō VIII)

211. *Katakiyaku–2*
The character Dōgen in the *sewamono* play *Mekura Nagaya Ume ga Kagatobi* is a masseur of the merchant class, a middle-aged man who pretends to be blind and engages in extortion. (*Dōgen*, Nakamura Kanzaburō)

212. *Katakiyaku–3*
This is the role of an aging villain (*fuke no katakiyaku*) in *jidaimono*. A very imposing and dignified warrior, he has white hair, wears a magnificent costume, and carries a staff with the figure of a dove carved on the handle. (*Kiichi* in *Kiichi Hōgen Sanryaku no Maki*, Kawarazaki Gonjūrō)

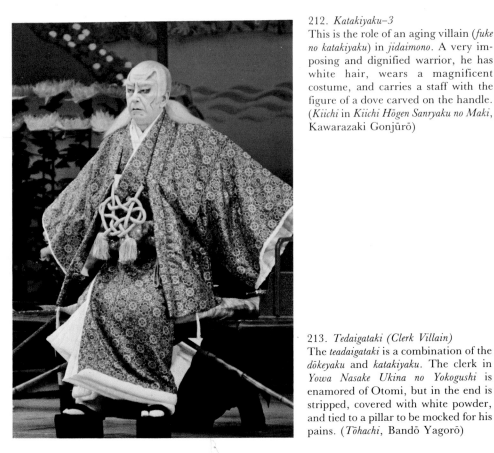

213. *Tedaigataki (Clerk Villain)*
The *teadaigataki* is a combination of the *dōkeyaku* and *katakiyaku*. The clerk in *Yowa Nasake Ukina no Yokogushi* is enamored of Otomi, but in the end is stripped, covered with white powder, and tied to a pillar to be mocked for his pains. (*Tōhachi*, Bandō Yagorō)

214. *Dōkeyaku*

This is an example of a comic role in a *shosagoto* (dance-drama). Hayami no Tōta in the *michiyuki* of *Yoshitsune Sembonzakura*, Sagisaka Bannai in the *michiyuki* of *Kanadehon Chūshingura*, and Ibuki no Tōta (shown here) in *Ōmi Genji Senjin Yakata* all belong to this category. The makeup is deliberately comical, the costume yellow and padded, and the actor carries a small fan. His role is to hamper the activities of the *tachiyaku*, or occasionally to serve as a kind of messenger. (*Ibuki no Tōta*, Nakamura Fukusuke)

215. *Shitatachiyaku–1*

In the "Palace Scene" in *Imoseyama Onna Teikin*, it is customary for the large number of ladies-in-waiting to be played by *shitatachiyaku* who usually play male roles, rather than by *onnagata*. The "ladies-in-waiting" here are a malicious group who torment the lovely heroine, Omiwa, and make themselves generally unpleasant. Their lines are spoken in normal male voices rather than in the "feminine" voices affected by true *onnagata*.

216. *Shitatachiyaku–2*

The *shitatachiyaku* known as *Takeda yakko* in the play *Yoshitsune Koshigoejō* all come from the *ōbeya* (the communal dressing room used for the lower-ranking actors). They perform in the manner of puppets at the old Takeda-za puppet theater (hence the name), and behave in a comic fashion.

217. *The Horse's Legs*
The two men who play the front and back legs respectively of kabuki horses are also drawn from the *shitatachiyaku* of the *ōbeya*. The man who plays the front legs is considered the senior of the two.

218. *Rats*
Kabuki rats are played by a child actor inside a cloth "skin." In *Meiboku Sendai Hagi*, there is a scene in which a magician turns himself into a rat and hides beneath the floor so as to steal a list of confederates. Discovered by the hero Otoko-nosuke, the rat disappears through a trapdoor in the *hanamichi* and reappears as the sorcerer Nikki Danjō.

219. *Wild Boar*
A boar appears on the stage in the fifth act of *Kanadehon Chūshingura*. A boy actor wears a prop "boar" over his head and shoulders, dangling his hands in front of him to represent the front legs. He runs out along the *hanamichi* and is "shot" by Kampei.

220. *Cats*
Imitating a woman, the cat in *Nomitori Otoko* dances with the valiant *wakashu*. As in the case with other animals, a special costume (*nuigurumi*) is worn.

222. *Onnagata Makeup*
The basic makeup for an *onnagata* is an overall white base with a little rouge at the outer corners of the eyes. Sometimes red is also used for the eyebrows.

223. *Wig-fitting*
The wig is the last thing to be put on, after makeup has been applied and the actor is in costume.

224. *Quick Change*
In the "Seven Osome Roles" a single actor must appear as seven different characters, male and female, in a short space of time. To achieve this a large number of people are put to work at the same time behind the scenes.

221. *Kumadori (overleaf)*
When an actor of male roles puts on *kumadori* or similar makeup, he strips to the waist. At the same time, he prepares the foundation for his wig. In the application of the makeup, he uses a flat brush, a line brush, and his fingertips.

225. *Kyōgenkata and Clappers*
Striking the wooden clappers is the role of the *kyōgenkata*. As well as serving as signals to actors in the dressing room, they also provide a kind of musical effect in their own right, and must always be struck so as to fit in with any music being played in the *geza*. There are different patterns to be followed depending on whether the play is a *jidaimono* or a *sewamono*, and the opening and closing of the main curtain are especially important moments. The beating of the clappers at the beginning of the Prologue to *Kanadehon Chūshingura* is particulary difficult: there are forty-seven strokes—symbolizing the forty-seven loyal retainers of the play—and they must be timed so that the last stroke falls just as the curtain, being pulled open by the stage hands, finally disappears into its box.

226. *The Curtain Man*
The man who opens and closes the curtain wears black garments and a kind of overskirt drawn in below the knees known as *tattsuke*. About one-third of his body is visible to the audience as he opens the curtain at a signal from the clappers, or closes it in time to the beating of the clappers. The task requires a thorough knowledge of the theater, and cannot be performed well without years of experience.

227. *Clappers*
Besides the type of clappers consisting of two blocks of wood held in the hands and struck against each other, there is another type that consists of a flat board placed on the floor and struck with two blocks of wood. This type is used to heighten the excitement in fight scenes, to mark the point at which an actor strikes a *mie* or breaks into a run, and so on. In the Kyoto-Osaka area it is the *kyōgenkata* who are responsible for these clappers, but elsewhere they are struck by the scene-shifters. They are known as *tsuke*, or in the Kyoto-Osaka area as *kage*.

228. Kōken-1

There are passages in *Kitsunebi* in which Yaegaki-hime acts in the stylized manner of a puppet. There are three "puppeteers" who go through the motions of "manipulating" the "doll." Of these, the chief puppeteer is known as *kōken* and wears the formal *kamishimo*, while the puppeteers managing the left arm and legs are played by *kurogo*.

229. Kōken-2

Tsura-akari ("face light"), also known as *sashidashi* ("thrusting out"), makes use of a candle fixed to a stand on the end of a long rod, and is sometimes used as a kind of spotlight when the leading actor appears on the *hanamichi* or rises through a trapdoor. The candles are held by *kōken*.

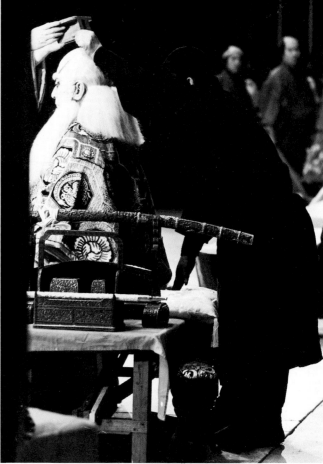

230–231. *Kurogo–1*

It is the duty of the *kurogo* to handle all kinds of props. In one scene in *Sukeroku*, the hero places a wooden clog on the head of the villain Ikyū in order to insult him. The clog does not in fact rest on his head, but is held just above it by a *kurogo* who lurks behind Ikyū's back. This technique illustrates the kabuki characteristic of creating beautiful poses rather than expressing literal realism.

232. *Kurogo–2*

Another of the *kurogo*'s tasks is to place a tall stool unobtrusively behind a leading character to provide support or to enable him to sit down while suggesting that he is standing quite still in a dignified pose.

233. *Inside the Toya*

In the *toya*, the small room next to the entrance to the *hanamichi* where an actor waits for his cue, black-robed attendants are ready to hand him his umbrella or any other prop he will carry, and to assist in any other ways necessary.

234. *Ōdōgukata–1*

The scene-shifters, known as *ōdōgukata*, perform such tasks as clearing away a "quick-drop" curtain.

235–236. *Ōdōgukata–2*

Another of the wide variety of tasks of the *ōdōgukata* is to lie in the "river" in the scene in the hills in *Imoseyama Onna Teikin* and to hand on, from one to another, props such as a *koto* and dolls for the Doll Festival that are supposed to be floated across from one side of the river to the other.

237–238. *Kagebayashi*

Kagebayashi, offstage musicians, play music in the special *geza* box on the left of the stage. The *geza* has a bamboo blind through which the musicians can observe the movements of the actors. This type of music produces a special atmosphere.

239. *Ōzatsuma*

The reciter who performs *ōzatsuma*, a type of *nagauta*, appears in front of the curtain at the beginning of a piece, wearing crested formal kimono and *hakama*, and chants a stirring piece to the accompaniment of the shamisen, which is played by a musician who stands with one foot on an *aibiki* (a stool), with the shamisen propped on his knee.

240. Nagauta Musicians
The musicians who appear on the stage in a dance-drama are those responsible for performing *nagauta*. They sit in rows on a tiered platform at the back of the stage. Typical is the arrangement shown here, in *Musume Dōjōji*. The upper row includes, on the left and right respectively, the singers and shamisen players. The lower row includes, from left to tight, the stick drums, the large hand drums, the small hand drums, and the flutes.

241. Yosogoto Jōruri
When *jōruri* music, either *tokiwazu* or *kiyomoto*, is performed onstage, the musicians are usually lined up on a *yamadai*, but in cases where the music is supposed to come from a neighboring house—when it is known as *yosogoto jōruri* ("other people's *jōruri*")—it is performed from within a stage house. The *kiyomoto* music in *Kumo ni Magō Ueno no Hatsuhana*, shown here, is not *yosogoto jōruri* in the strict sense, but the manner of performance is the same.

242. Degatari
In a piece where there is *degatari*—appearance of the musicians on the stage in a *jōruri* piece—an assistant in black robes with a red cord beats the clappers and announces the names of the reciter and shamisen players to the audience.

SETS, CEREMONIES, AND THEATERS

243. This print shows the mechanics of a revolving stage. From *Shibai Kimmō Zui*, 1830.

244. *Revolving Stage–1*

Shown here is the "Iriya Tambo ("Fields near the Yoshiwara Gay Quarters") Scene" from *Kumo ni Magō Ueno no Hatsuhana*, in which the revolving stage (*mawaru butai*) is half turned. The scene so far has been the interior of a noodle shop; now it changes to the snowy exterior in front of the shop. The stage is covered with a white "snow cloth."

245–247. *Revolving Stage–2*

When the curtain opens in the "Nozaki Village Scene" in *Shimpan Utazaimon*, the front of Kyūsaku's house is in view (245); as the play progresses the stage revolves half-way, revealing the back of the house and the path along the river bank (246). At curtain-fall, the stage revolves completely, and the surface of the stage becomes a river. Osome goes by boat with her mother down the regular *hanamichi*, while Hisamatsu goes by palanquin along the secondary *hanamichi* (247).

248. *Musicians' Dais*
The plays adapted from puppet theater libretti are accompanied by *jōruri* music for the *gidayū* reciter and shamisen. The music is performed on a high dais to the right of the stage, where the musicians can see the movements of the actors.

249–250. *Seridashi*
This method has an actor make a sudden appearance via a trapdoor (known as *suppon*, ''turtle'') in the *hanamichi*. In the dance *Shiokumi*, shown here, a supernatural piece, the actor uses *seridashi* for his first entrance.

251. *Snow Cloth*
Various cloths are spread on the stage to match different scenes. Thus there are cloths representing the bare earth, waves, and snow. The photograph shows scene-shifters laying the cloth for the snow scene in *Sannin Kichiza Kuruwa no Hatsugai* before the curtain goes up.

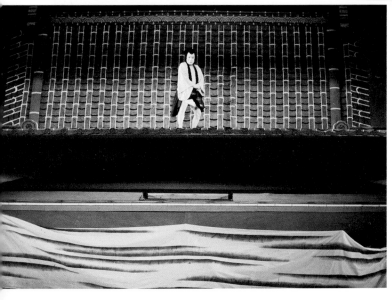

252–257. *Gandōgaeshi*
This spectacular method of changing scenes has a part of the stage flip over on a central pivot. In *Aoto Zōshi Hana no Nishiki-e*, Benten Kozō, surrounded by constables, commits suicide on top of the roof of a temple gateway. The roof tips backwards, and the action moves without a break into a confrontation scene between Nippon Daemon within the gate and Aoto Saemon, who rises up through the stage in front of it. The last scene of this play is a parody of the ''Gateway Scene'' in *Sammon Gosan no Kiri*. Note that the setting and the characters are almost exactly the same as those in Plate 58.

258. *Sakura-hime Azuma Bunshō, design of the stage for the Kaminari Gate Scene*
This kind of drawing (*dōgūchō*) of a set is made for each scene in a kabuki performance; the actual sets are constructed using it as a model.

259-260. Collapsing Building
This is a contrivance by which an apparently substantial building is made to disintegrate before the audience's eyes. At the end of the dance-drama *Masakado*, the disused Sōma Palace collapses, and Takiyasha appears on top of the roof standing on a toad.

261-262. Receding Scenery
In the scene before the main gate of Enya Hangan's mansion in *Kanadehon Chūshingura*, following Hangan's suicide, his faithful retainer Ōboshi Yuranosuke bids a sorrowful farewell to the home that he will see no more, and swears to avenge his master's death. At this point, the scenery representing the gate is gradually drawn backward to suggest the increasing distance separating it from Yuranosuke as he walks away.

263. *Presentation Curtain*
When the first piece, a *jidaimono*, is over and the second piece, the *sewamono*, is about to begin, a brightly dyed curtain presented to the actors by their supporters is customarily used. The curtain shown here bears, in separate sections, the crests of both Danjūrō and Kikugorō.

264. *Fence Curtain*
A fence is depicted on a curtain that is dropped to effect a change of scene. Music is played in the *geza* while this is being done.

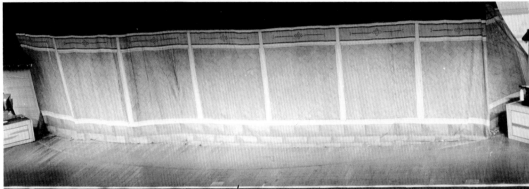

265. *Quick-drop Curtain*
Sometimes, when the main curtain is opened, another, light blue curtain is revealed behind it. After a short passage of *jōruri* music, the curtain is suddenly released from the pole on which it is suspended over the stage. It falls, and is instantly whisked away. The technique is used to enhance the effect of a spectacular, colorful set.

266. *Concealing Curtain*
A black curtain or blanket is used to allow a character who has been killed to effect his exit without having to "come to life" in full view of the audience.

191

267. *Seashore–1*
This is the Yaguchi Ford scene in *Shinrei Yaguchi no Watashi*. The house of Tombei the ferryman revolves to show the lookout tower projecting over the sea at the rear. Tombei, an evil character, is shot to death by a divine arrow as he is riding in a boat. Cloth painted with a pattern of waves is spread on the stage to represent the sea.

268. *Seashore–2*
Scenery can be divided, roughly speaking, into two types representing interior and exterior scenes. The scenery for *Heike Nyogo no Shima*, shown here, has some unusual features. The sea is shown in the distance, with rocky eminences on both sides of the stage, but later the stage revolves, and the rocks on the left come to the center of the stage, forming a platform on which Shunkan is standing as the curtain falls. Another interesting effect involves the boat, which is first seen small out at sea, then appears large as it is pushed out from the right of the stage. As the waves creep in up to the feet of the actors, a cloth representing water is drawn across the stage.

Pl. 58. *Sammon Gosan no Kiri: The Gateway Scene*
The scene at the great gate of the Nanzenji Temple in *Sammon Gosan no Kiri* is a classic example of a spectacular kabuki stage set. The highlight of the scene, which lasts only about three minutes, is the raising through the stage, amidst cherry blossoms, of the brilliantly colored gateway, with the bandit Ishikawa Goemon on top of it.

Pl. 59. *Hakata Kojorō Nami Makura: The Great Boat Scene*
The "Great Boat Scene" in this play is typical of many scenes showing a boat at sea. Here, the smugglers' boat has made a half-turn, just before Sōshichi is thrown into the water and Kezori strikes a *mie* in the prow.

Pl. 60. *Gion Sairei Shinkōki: The Kinkaku-ji Scene*
In this spectacular scene the Kinkakuji—the "Golden Pavilion" in Kyoto—is raised through the stage. On the left is a great waterfall, in which a stage "dragon" is visible. The scene conveys well the fantastic, romantic aspects of the great *jidaimono* plays.

Pl. 61. *Sannin Kichiza Kuruwa no Hatsugai: The Watchtower Scene*
The fire watchtower scene of this play, in which the three robbers around whom the play revolves are surrounded by constables, shows a typical snowy street scene in old Edo. The scene is a parody of a similar scene in *Date Musume Koi no Higanoko*.

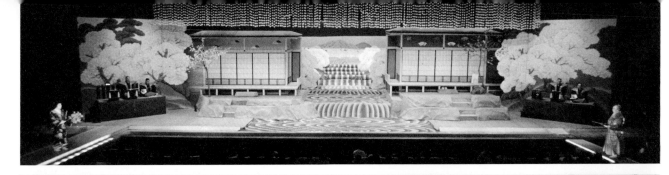

274. *Kōjō and Niramu*
The *kōjō*, an address made from the stage directly to the audience, is used principally in the ceremony at which an actor assumes the name of an illustrious predecessor. Where the acting family is powerful and the name a famous one, a special one-act piece is put on to celebrate the occasion. The dress for the ceremony, in accordance with long-standing tradition, is the formal *kamishimo*. At the ceremony in which an actor of the Ichikawa family assumes one of the family's traditional names, it is customary for him to announce to the audience, "Now I will glare (*niramu*) for you," and to strike a *mie* with one knee raised, holding in one hand a small wooden table on which a scroll rests. Shown here is the address at the name-assuming ceremony of the present Ichikawa Danjūrō.

◁ 269. *The River Scene in Imoseyama Onna Teikin*
Two hills, Imoyama and Seyama, are shown on either side of the stage, with the river Yoshino flowing between them. The twin *hanamichi* represent its two banks.

270. *Jinya*
The *jinya* is the battle headquarters of a high-ranking samurai. The raised floor is conventional to a general's residence. The whole structure is surrounded by curtains bearing his personal crest.

271. *Commoner's Dwelling in a Sewaba*
Mats spread on the stage and a framework "entrance" are conventional indications that the front of the stage is also within the house. The doorway with a curtain in the center, the closet to the right of it, and the shoji-surrounded room are also standard features.

272. *Riverbank*
Riverside scenes, with the Sumida River visible in the background, appear frequently in kabuki plays. For a dance-drama, the background is as cheerful and attractive as possible.

273. *Matsuhame*
Matsuhame is the wooden paneling with a picture of a venerable pine tree that forms the back of the stage in the Nō theater. The kabuki version is taken over directly from the Nō, but, as might be expected, is more lavishly decorative.

275. *Night View of the Kabuki-za, Tokyo*
The Kabuki-za was opened in 1925. The Momoyama period-style building is strikingly situated in the modern Ginza district.

Pl. 62. *The Minami-za, Kyoto*
This is the only theater still standing on the same site as in the early days of kabuki, although it was rebuilt in 1929. The actors' names are lined up by rank on placards with pointed "roofs" at the top.

Pl. 63. *The Nakamura-za Theater in Edo in the Early Genroku Era (1688–1704), screen painting by Hishikawa Moronobu, Tokyo National Museum*
Placards outside the theater proclaim the titles of the plays being per-formed. The dance in progress on the stage is doubtless one of them—*Taiheiraku Ō-odori* ("Grand Dance of Peace and Prosperity"), which enjoyed great popularity around the seventh year of Genroku (1694).

HISTORY

Pl. 64. *Okuni Kabuki, screen painting, painter unknown, Keichō era (1596–1614), Idemitsu Art Gallery*
The female lead, dressed as a male, and the proprietress of a teahouse, played by a man, engage in dalliance on the stage. The comic *saruwaka* (later, *dōke*) on the right acts as the procurer. The musicians seated on the carpet behind them play an accompaniment. *Shamisen* still cannot be seen. The roof covers the stage and the seats (*sajiki*) on the left and right; there is no roof over the spectators watching the performance on carpets spread on the ground. High-ranking spectators are watching the performance from the *sajiki* on either side. The theater as a whole is surrounded by a bamboo palisade and straw mats. To prevent spectators from watching the performances without paying, the entrance, called *nezumi kido* (''rat gate'') is made extremely small and has a high threshold. The lances and other weapons in the *yagura* (''tower'') over the gate are used to discourage disorderly behavior. A large drum was beaten in the tower to signal the beginning and end of a performance. The date of the performance and name of the female lead (*tayū*) are written on the board to the right of the entrance.

Pl. 65. *Yūjo Kabuki, a section from Screen Depicting Amusements on the Riverbed at Shijō, painter unknown, late Keichō to early Kan'ei, Seikadō Bunko*
This is a scene of a public performance of kabuki at Shijō in Kyoto by *yūjo* (''prostitutes'') imitating Okuni kabuki. The actresses dance in a circle around the star. She is seated in the center on a chair covered with an imported tiger skin and plays an imported *shamisen*. The women on the right side of the stage are also playing *shamisen*. The *shamisen* was first used in *yūjo kabuki*.

276. *Screen Painting of a Special Festival in the Hōkoku Shrine, seventeenth century*
At the festival held at the Hōkoku Shrine in Kyoto in the eighth month of 1604 to mark the seventh anniversary of the death of Toyotomi Hideyoshi, all the various districts of the capital put on their own *furyū odori*. These were, in fact, almost identical to what came to be known as *kabuki odori*, and the foundations on which the latter developed are clearly discernible.

277. *Painting of Ukon Genzaemon, Tokyo National Museum*
Referred to as a forebear of the modern *onnagata*, Ukon Genzaemon was celebrated as a master of the *komai*. He went to Edo from the Kyoto-Osaka area in 1652, winning a reputation with his performances of the dance *Kaidō-kudari*, and is said to have first thought up the *okitenugui*, a folded cotton towel placed on top of the head during the dance.

278. *Screen of Yarō Kabuki, ca. 1652*
This screen depicts *yarō kabuki* at an early point, and shows a dance performed by an ensemble extending from the *hashigakari* bridge to the main stage. At the left-hand edge of the *hashigakari*, a large stick drum, small hand drum, and flute provide a musical accompaniment. The actors' heads are probably covered in an attempt to hide the fact that the front has been shaved. The stage may have been converted directly from a Nō stage.

279. *Takayasugayoi, from Kokon Yakusha Monogatari, an illustrated kyōgenbon*
The *Kokon Yakusha Monogatari* (''Stories of Actors Past and Present''), which was published in Empō 6 (1678), sixteen years after the ban on *wakashu kabuki*, gives a good picture of the stage used at the time. The piece illustrated here, which is also known as *Kawachigayoi*, draws its theme from the *Tales of Ise*, and tells of a man of the Heian period who frequently visited his mistress in the country village of Takayasu in the province of Kawachi, and of the feelings of the man's wife. It was one of the most popular plays of the Kambun and Empō eras (1661–80), and was a favorite vehicle for the art of the actor Tamagawa Sennojō.

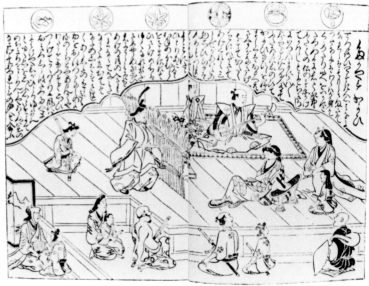

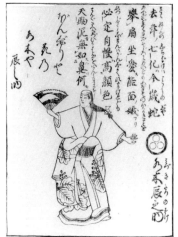

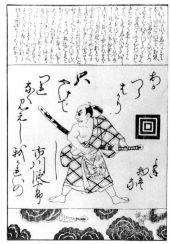

280. *Sakata Tōjūrō, from the book Ogakuzu*
One of the leading actors of the Kyoto-Osaka area during the Genroku era, Sakata Tōjūrō's performance as Izaemon in *Yūgiri Nagori no Shōgatsu* is said to have marked the beginning of true *yatsushi* (*wagoto*) acting, and his collaboration with the dramatist Chikamatsu Monzaemon marked the artistic peak of the plays centering on the gay quarters.

281. *Yoshizawa Ayame, from the book Yarō Sekizumō*
An *onnagata* of the Kyoto-Osaka area during the Genroku era, Yoshizawa Ayame was highly skilled. The record of his sayings, *Ayamegusa*, is a kind of "*onnagata*'s bible.''

282. *Mizuki Tatsunosuke, from the book Kiku no Masegaki*
This famous *onnagata* of the Genroku era was renowned for his dancing in *shosagoto* pieces. He made his reputation in *nanabake* pieces as well as in the ''spear dance,'' and with his miming as a cat. The modern Mizuki school of Japanese dance looks on him as its founder.

283. *Ichikawa Danjūrō I, from the book Shibai Hyakunin-shu*
One of the leading actors of male roles during the Genroku era in Edo, Danjūrō I was the founder of the *aragoto* style of acting. He often wrote plays under the pen name of Mimasuya Hyōgo.

284. *Nakamura Shichisaburō, from the book Musashi Abumi*
This actor was one of the most celebrated exponents of the *wagoto* type of male role in Edo during the Genroku era.

285. *Keisei Asamagadake, from an illustrated kyōgenbon*
Keisei Asamagadake was one of the most popular plays of the Genroku era (1688–1704). Its highlight is the appearance of the spirit of the courtesan Ōshū from the flames of an impassioned love letter written by Asama Tomoenojō. The first performance took place in the first month of the eleventh year of Genroku (1698) at the Sōun-za in Kyoto.

286. *Gempei Narukami Denki, from an illustrated kyōgenbon*
First performed in 1698 at the Nakamura-za in Edo, this play provided a good vehicle for stirring *aragoto* acting, with celebrated actor Ichikawa Danjūrō I as Saint Narukami, matching his art against that of Ogino Sawanojō as Kumo no Taema.

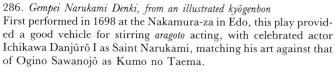

Pl. 66. *A Kabuki Stage in Edo at the End of the Empō Era (1673–81), print by Hishikawa Moronobu, Tokyo National Museum*
On the stage, Nakamura Denkurō and Kanzaki Ichiya are playing the man and woman respectively in the *Ninin* (''two-person'') *Saruwaka* dance, performed before an actor portraying a woman daimyo. On the left an early form of the *hanamichi* can be seen.

Pl. 67. *A Theater of the Kyōhō Era (1716–1736), screen painting by Oku-mura Masanobu, Idemitsu Art Gallery*
The scene shows the exterior and interior of the Nakamura-za in Edo at the New Year, 1731, when the play *Keisei Fukubiki Nagoya* was being performed. Outside, *kido-geisha* are standing on benches with outspread fans, doing imitations of the actors' voices in order to draw in more patrons. The title of the play being performed, *Fūryū Saya-ate*, can be found on the *daijin-bashira* (the column on the right front corner of the stage). On the *nadai-kamban* near the entrance is a list of actors; they include Sawamura Sōjurō, Ichikawa Danjūrō II, and Segawa Kikunojō.

287. *Segawa Kikunojō I (1693–1749), print by Torii Kiyomasu, Tokyo National Museum*
A celebrated *onnagata* of the Kyōhō era, Kikunojō was noted for his acting in plays such as *Dōjōji Nogami no Hanjo.*

288. *Nakamura Tomijūrō I (1719–86), print by Torii Kiyohiro, Tokyo National Museum*
Tomijūrō was a famous *onnagata* of the Kyoto-Osaka area during the Kyōhō era, the third son of Yoshizawa Ayame I. He was the first to perform many well-known pieces.

289. *Illustrated Kyōgenbon for Sanjikkoku Yobune no Hajimari*
This work was wrtten by Namiki Shōzō and first performed in the twelfth month of 1758 at the Nakayama-za in Osaka. The revolving stage was used for the first time in this performance.

290. *A theater stage, print by Okumura Masanobu (1686–1764), Tokyo National Museum*
This is a performance of *Momo Chidori Musume Dōjōji* at the Nakamura-za in the third month of 1744. A *shirabyōshi*, or female entertainer, played by Segawa Kikunojō I, performs a *michiyuki* on the *hanamichi.* On the stage are Mongaku, played by Ichikawa Ebizō II, and Benkei, played by Ōtani Hiroji I. As the costumes suggest, Mongaku and Benkei are well-known strong-willed priests. One of numerous Dōjōji pieces, this predates *Kyōganoko Musume Dōjōji* in the current repertoire.

292. *Nakamura Nakazō I in the Dressing Room*, print by Katsukawa Shunshō (1726–1792), Tokyo National Museum
In this print, Nakazō is dressed as Ōmi for one of the Soga plays. He is waiting for his cue. Standing behind him is either a hairdresser or a costumer.

291. *The Ichimura-za Theater in Edo in the Eleventh Month of Meiwa 1 (1764), woodblock print*
This *manaita-ban* print for a hanging scroll two feet wide and over three feet long shows the interior and the exterior of the Ichimura-za during the *kaomise* performance. On the stage, Onoe Kikugorō, Nakamura Nakazō, Yoshizawa Sakinosuke (playing the role of a flower vendor on the *hanamichi*), and Onoe Matsusuke are performing in *Wakagi no Hana Suma no Hatsuyuki*. The stage in this period still had a gable over it. Notice the spectators sitting in the section called *rakandai* in the upper left-hand corner.

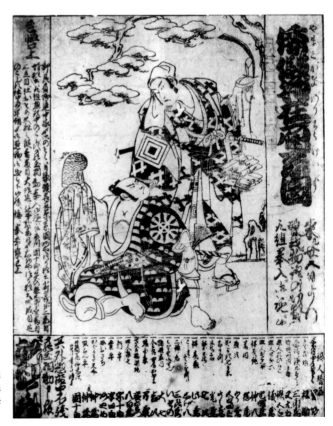

293. *Poster for the Nakamura-za Theater, Edo*
This poster (*tsuji-banzuke*) announces the opening, in the fifth month of 1781 at the Nakamura-za of *Yamatogana Ariwara Keizu*. Ichikawa Danjūrō V plays the role of the courier Chūji who, in reality, is Prince Koretaka, and Nakamura Nakazō I plays the role of Rampei.

294. *Onnagata Dressed for Paying New Year's Visits, print by Torii Kiyonaga (1752–1815)*
For going to pay his respects to patrons and others at the beginning of the year, the *onnagata* wore a long-sleeved kimono of the kind worn by women, with the *kamishimo* typical of men's formal wear on top of it, together with a type of head covering known as *yarōbōshi*. The two actors shown here are Segawa Kikunojō III (right) and Iwai Hanshirō IV (left).

295. *Tsuruya Namboku (1755–1829), from the libretto of Osome Hisamatsu Ukina no Yomiuri, Tsubouchi Memorial Theatre Museum*
Namboku was the leading playwright in the Bunka and Bunsei eras (1804–29). The fourth in line of the same name, he is often known as the "Great Namboku." It is he who was responsible for developing the ghost play and the *kizewamono* type of play. He wrote about 120 plays, most famous among them *Tenjiku Tokubei Ikokubanashi*, *Tōkaidō Yotsuya Kaidan*, and *Osome Hisamatsu Ukina no Yomiuri*. Namboku is shown in the dressing room of Iwai Hanshirō V during the performance of *Osome Hisamatsu Ukina no Yomiuri*. Kneeling below Namboku is the wigmaker Tomokurō.

296. *An Audience of the Bunka Era (1804–18), from the Kyakusha Hyōbanki*
Published in 1811 with text by Shikitei Samba and pictures by Utagawa Kunisada, the work humorously applies the drama criticism methods of the *yakusha hyōbanki* to the audiences themselves. Shown here are members of the audience in the *mukō sajiki*, some of the cheapest and most distant seats of all.

297. *Kawatake Mokuami (1816–93)*
Mokuami was the leading playwright of the closing years of the Edo period and the early Meiji era. He excelled at *kizewamono* pieces, and especially in *shiranamimono*.

298. *A Theater at the End of the Edo Period, print by Utagawa Toyokuni III (1786–1864), Tsubouchi Memorial Theatre Museum*
The stage juts forward into the auditorium, and the old gable over the stage has disappeared. The *geza* at the time was on the right of the stage, and the left of the stage—where the *geza* is located today—was occupied by cheap seats for the audience. On the stage, the "Bamboo Chamber Scene" of *Meiboku Sendai Hagi* is in progress.

299. *Nakamura Shikan IV (1829–99), lithograph*
Shikan IV was renowned for his dancing, and enjoyed great popularity from the end of the Edo period on into the Meiji era. Here he is shown as Sekibei in *Seki no To*.

300. *Ichikawa Danjūrō IX (1838–1903) as Banzuiin Chōbei*
Danjūrō IX was the leading actor of the Meiji era. He gave the first performance of *katsurekigeki*, the historical dramas based directly on fact, and did much to elevate the social status of actors.

301. *Onoe Kikugorō V (1844–1903), Off the Stage*
During the Meiji era, the fame of Kikugorō V rivaled that of Danjūrō IX. Where Danjūrō specialized in *jidaimono*, Kikugorō excelled in *sewamono*, and often acted in the *zangirimono* that portrayed manners and customs of the new post-Restoration era.

302. *The Hisamatsu-za Theater in Tokyo, triptych by Hiroshige III, Tsubouchi Memorial Theatre Museum*
This theater was the precursor of the existing Meiji-za. It was first built in the Hisamatsu district and named the Kishō-za, but was rebuilt and reopened in August, 1879, as the Hisamatsu-za. This print shows the opening ceremony of the rebuilt theater.

303. *Yatai Kabuki at Chichibu City, Saitama Prefecture*
During the late Edo period and early Meiji era, kabuki, under the name of *ji shibai* (“local theater”) or *ji kyōgen* (“local plays”), spread to farming and fishing communities throughout the country, where it took root and still persists in some cases to the present day. It retains aspects no longer to be found in the towns, and has a definitely archaic flavor.

Kabuki is performed on stages built onto festival floats which are exhibited every year from December 1 to 3 in Chichibu City. Some of the stages even revolve. The play being performed here is *Ehon Taikōki*.

APPENDICES

LIST OF PLAYS

Note: Short titles followed by "See . . ." are popular names for the plays. The numbers enclosed in parentheses refer to the plates. "Pl." indicates that it is a color plate; a number alone indicates that it is a black-and-white plate.

Abura Jigoku: See *Onnagoroshi Abura no Jigoku*
Aburaya: See *Ise Ondo Koi no Netaba*
Adasan: Act III of *Ōshū Adachigahara*
Aibara: See *Shin Usuyuki Monogatari*
Akegarasu Hano no Nureginu 明烏花濡衣 by Sakurada Jisuke III. *Sewamono.* The "Yamanaya Scene" is the most famous. 1851. (181)
Akoya no Kotozeme: See *Dannoura Kabuto Gunki.* (12, 147)
Ame no Gorō 雨の五郎 by Mimasuya Nisōji. *Nagauta* dance-drama. 1841. (Pl. 9; 131)
Aoto Zōshi Hana no Nishiki-e 青砥稿花紅彩画 by Kawatake Mokuami. *Jidai-sewa-mono.* The "Hamamatsuya Shop," "Inase River," and "Gokurakuji Temple" scenes are famous. 1862. (140, 182, 252–57)
Asagao Nikki: See *Shō-utsushi Asagao Banashi*
Asazuma Bune 浅妻船 by Sakurada Jisuke II. *Nagauta* dance-drama. 1820.
Ashiya Dōman Ōuchi Kagami 蘆屋道満大内鑑 by Takeda Izumo. *Jōruri jidaimono.* Five acts, of which the "Kuzu no Ha no Kowakare Scene" in Act IV is frequently performed. 1734.
Awa no Naruto: See *Keisei Awa no Naruto*
Ayatsuri Sambasō 操三番叟 Shinoda Sasuke. *Nagauta* dance-drama. 1853.

Badarai no Mitsuhide: See *Tokimo Kikyō Shusse no Ukejō*
Banchō Sarayashiki 番町皿屋敷 by Okamoto Kidō. New Kabuki. 1916.
Banzui Chōbei Shōjin Manaita 幡随長兵衛精進組板 by Sakurada Jisuke I. *Sewamono.* The "Suzugamori Scene" is very famous. 1803. (196)
Benkei Jōshi: See *Gosho-zakura Horikawa Youchi*
Benten Kozō: See *Aoto Zōshi Hana no Nishiki-e*

Chayaba ("Ichiriki Teahouse Scene"): Act VII of *Kanadehon Chūshingura.* (113–17)
Chijimiya Shinsuke: See *Hachiman Matsuri Yomiya no Nigiwai*
Chikagoro Kawara no Tatehiki 近頃河原の達引 by Tamekawa Sōsuke and others. *Jōruri sewamono.* Three acts, of which the "Horikawa Scene" is still staged. 1785.
Chūjō-hime: See *Hibariyama Hime Sutematsu*

Daianji: See *Kataki Uchi Tsuzure no Nishiki*
Dakki no Ohyaku: See *Zenaku Ryōmen Konotegashiwa*
Danjūrō Musume: See *Ōmi no Okane*
Dannoura Kabuto Gunki 壇浦兜軍記 by Bunkōdō and Hasegawa Senshi. *Jōruri jidaimono.* Five acts, of which only the "Akoya no Kotozeme Scene" in Act III is still performed. 1732. (12, 147)
Date Kurabe Okuni Kabuki 伊達競阿国戯場 by Sakurada Jisuke I. *Jidaimono.* The "Dobashi Scene" is still performed. 1778.

Date Musume Koi no Higanoko 伊達娘恋緋鹿子 by Suga Sensuke and others. *Jōruri sewamono.* Eight acts, of which only the "Yagura no Oshichi Scene" ("Oshichi on the Watchtower") is performed. 1773.
Dobashi: See *Date Kurabe Okuni Kabuki*
Dōjōji: See *Musume Dōjōji*
Domomata: See *Keisei Hangonkō*
Dōmyōji: See *Sugawara Denju Tenarai Kagami.* (Pl. 28; 36–39)
Dontsuku どんつく by Sakurada Jisuke III. *Tokiwazu* dance-drama. 1846.

Echigojishi 越後獅子 by Shinoda Kinji I. *Nagauta* dance-drama. 1811.
Edo Sodachi Omatsuri Sashichi 江戸育御祭佐七 by Kawatake Shinshichi III. *Kizewamono.* 1898. (21)
Ehon Taikōki 絵本太功記 by Chikamatsu Yanagi and others. *Jōruri jidaimono.* Thirteen acts, of which the "Amagasaki Scene" in Act X is the most famous. 1799.

Fūingiri: See *Koibikyaku Yamato Ōrai.* (Pl. 18)
Fuji Musume 藤娘 by Katsui Gempachi. *Nagauta* dance-drama. 1826. (Pl. 23)
Fujitomimasu Suehiro Soga 富治三升扇曾我 by Kawatake Mokuami. *Jidaimono.* 1866.
Funa Benkei 船弁慶 by Kawatake Mokuami. *Nagauta* dance-drama. 1885.
Fune e Uchikomu Hashima no Shiranami 船打込橋間白浪 by Kawatake Mokuami. *Sewamono.* 1866.
Futaomote 双面 by Kawatake Shinshichi I. *Tokiwazu* dance-drama. 1775. (27)
Futatsu Chōchō Kuruwa Nikki 双蝶々曲輪日記 by Takeda Izumo. *Jōruri sewamono.* Nine acts, of which the "Sumō Scene" in Act II and the "Hikimado (Skylight) Scene" in Act VIII are famous. 1749. (195, 208)

Ga no Iwai: See *Sugawara Denju Tenarai Kagami.* (Pl. 42–46)
Gappō: See *Sesshū Gappō ga Tsuji*
Gempei Nunobiki no Taki 源平布引滝 by Namiki Senryū and Miyoshi Shōraku. *Jōruri jidaimono.* Five acts, of which the scene at Kurōsuke's house in Act III is frequently performed. 1749.
Genta Kandō: See *Hiragana Seisuiki*
Gion Sairei Shinkōki 祇園祭礼信仰記 by Nakamura Akei and others. *Jōruri jidaimono.* Five acts, of which the "Kinkakuji Scene" in Act IV is famous and frequently performed. 1757. (Pl. 60; 146)
Go Taiheiki Shiraishi-banashi 碁太平記白石噺 by Utei Emba and others. *Jōruri jidai-sewa-mono.* Eleven acts, of which the "Shin Yoshiwara Ageya Scene" in Act VII is the most famous. 1780.
Godairiki Koi no Fūjime 五大力恋緘 by Namiki Gohei. *Sewamono.* 1795.
Gompachi 権八 by Fukumori Kyūsuke. *Kiyomoto* dance-drama. 1816.
Gosho no Gorozō: See *Soga Moyō Tateshi no Gosho-zome*
Gosho-zakura Horikawa Youchi 御所桜堀川夜討 by Bunkōdō and Miyoshi Shōraku. *Jōruri jidaimono.* Five acts, of which the "Benkei Jōshi Scene" in Act III and the "Tōyata Monogatari Scene" in Act VI are famous. 1737.

Goten: See *Imoseyama Onna Teikin*. (13)
Goten and *Yukashita:* See *Meiboku Sendai Hagi*. (14–15)
Gozabune: See *Hachijin Shugo no Honjō*

Hachijin Shugo no Honjō 八陣守護城 by Nakamura Gyogan and Sagawa Tōta. *Jōruri jidaimono.* Eleven acts, of which only the "Gozabune Scene" in Art IV and the "Masakiyo Honjō Scene" in Act VIII are performed. 1807.
Hachiman Matsuri Yomiya no Nigiwai 八幡祭小望月賑 by Kawatake Mokuami. *Sewamono.* 1860.
Hadesugata Onna Maiginu 艶容女舞衣 by Takemoto Saburōbei. *Jōruri sewamono.* Three acts, of which the "Sakaya Scene" in Act III is the most famous. 1772. (170)
Hakata Kojorō Nami Makura 博多小女郎浪枕 by Chikamatsu Monzaemon. *Jōruri sewamono.* Three acts, of which the "Great Boat Scene" and the "Okudaya Scene" in Act I and the "Shinseimachi Scene" in Act II are still performed. 1718. (Pl. 59; 128)
Hakone Reigen Izari no Adauchi 箱根霊験躄仇討 by Shiba Shisō. *Jōruri jidaimono.* Twelve acts, of which the "Amida Temple Scene" in Act II is most frequently performed. 1801.
Hamamatsu Kaze 浜松風. Author unknown. *Nagauta* dance-drama. 1808.
Hanabusa Shūjaku Jishi 英執着獅子. Author unknown. *Nagauta* dance-drama. 1754.
Hane no Kamuro 羽根の禿. Author unknown. *Nagauta* dance-drama. 1785.
Hangaku Mon Yaburi: See *Wada Kassen Onna Maizuru*
Heike Nyogo no Shima 平家女護島 by Chikamatsu Monzaemon. *Jōruri jidaimono.* Five acts, of which the "Kikai ga Shima Scene" in Act II is the most frequently performed. 1719. (Pls. 19–20)
Hibariyama Hime Sutematsu 鶸山姫捨松 by Namiki Sōsuke. *Jōruri jidaimono.* Five acts. The "Yukizeme Scene" in Act III is the most famous. 1740. (180)
Hidakagawa Iriai-zakura 日高川入相花王 by Chikamatsu Hanji and others. *Jōruri jidaimono.* Five acts, of which the "Hidakagawa Scene" in Act IV is frequently performed. 1759.
Higashiyama Sakura Sōshi 東山桜荘子. Another name for *Sakura Giminden.*
Hikosan Gongen Chikai no Sukedachi 彦山権現誓助剣 by Umeno Shitakaze and Chikamatsu Yasuzō. *Jōruri jidaimono.* Eleven acts, of which the "Keyamura Scene" in Act IX is the most famous. 1786.
Hiragana Seisuki ひらかな盛衰記 by Bunkōdō and others. *Jōruri jidaimono.* Five acts. The "Genta Kandō Scene" in Act II, the "Sakaro Scene" in Act III, and the "Muken no Kane Scene" in Act IV are the most famous. 1739. (189)
Hōjō Kudai Meika no Isaoshi 北条九代名家功 by Kawatake Mokuami. *Jidaimono.* One of the "New Eighteen Favorite Kabuki Plays." 1884.
Hōkaibō: See *Sumidagawa Gonichi no Omokage*
Honchō Nijūshi Kō 本朝廿四孝 by Chikamatsu Hanji and others. *Jōruri jidaimono.* Five acts, of which the scene at Kansuke's house in Act III and the "Jisshukō" and "Kitsunebi" scenes in Act IV are most frequently performed. 1766. (228)
Horikawa: See *Chikagoro Kawara no Tatehiki*

Ibaragi 茨木 by Kawatake Mokuami. *Nagauta* dance-drama. 1883. (130)
Ichijō Ōkura-kyō: See *Kiichi Hōgen Sanryaku no Maki*
Ichinotani Futaba Gunki 一谷嫩軍記 by Namiki Sōsuke and others. *Jōruri jidaimono.* Five acts, of which the "Jimmon" and "Kumiuchi" scenes in Act II and the "Kumagai Jinya Scene" in Act III are often performed. 1751. (Pls. 15–16; 132, 145, 153, 167–69)
Igagoe Dōchū Sugoroku 伊賀越道中双六 by Chikamatsu Hanji and Chikamatsu Kasaku. *Jōruri jidaimono.* Ten acts, of which the "Numazu Scene" in Act VI and the "Okazaki Scene" in Act VIII are frequently performed. 1783. (140)
Ikake Matsu: See *Fune e Uchikomu Hashima no Shiranami*
Imorizake: See *Karukaya Dōshin Tsukushi no Iezuto*
Imoseyama Onna Teikin 妹背山婦女庭訓 by Chikamatsu Hanji and

others. *Jōruri jidai (ōdai) mono.* Five acts, of which the "Yama no Dan" of "Yoshinogawa Scene" in Act III, and the "Sugisakaya," "Michiyuki Koi no Odamaki" and "Palace" scenes are especially famous. 1771. (13, 139, 215, 235–36, 269)
Ise Ondo Koi no Netaba 伊勢音頭恋寝刃 by Chikamatsu Tokuzō. *Sewamono.* The "Aburaya Scene" is the most famous. 1796. (184, 207)
Ishikawa Goemon: See *Sammon Gosan no Kiri*
Ishikiri Kajiwara: See *Kajiwara Heizō Homare no Ishikiri*
Iwakawa: See *Sekitori Senryō Nobori*
Izari Katsugorō: See *Hakone Reigen Izari no Adauchi*
Izayoi Seishin: See *Kosode Soga Azami no Ironui*

Jidai Dammari: During the Tempo era (1830–44), *jidai dammari* including Kurama, Miyajima, etc. performed for the first time. (Pl. 40; 9–10, 148)
Jishin Katō: See *Zōho Momoyama Monogatari*
Jisshukō: See *Honchō Nijūshi Kō*

Kagamijishi 鏡獅子 by Fukuchi Ōchi. *Nagauta* dance-drama. 1893. (25–26, 158)
Kagamiyama Gonichi no Iwafuji 鏡山再岩藤 by Kawatake Mokuami. *Jidaimono.* 1860. (143)
Kagamiyama Kokyō no Nishiki-e 鏡山旧錦絵 by Yō Yōdai. *Jōruri jidaimono.* Eleven acts. The "Zōri-uchi Scene" in Act VI and the "Nagatsubone" and "Okuniwa" ("Rear Garden") scenes are frequently performed. 1782. (173–74)
Kagatobi: See *Mekura Nagaya Ume ga Kagatobi*
Kagekiyo 景清. Author unknown. One of the "Eighteen Favorite Kabuki Plays." 1732. (8)
Kagotsurube Sato no Eizame 籠釣瓶花街酔醒 by Kawatake Shinshichi III. *Sewamono.* The "Shin Yoshiwara Nakanochō" and "Hyōgoya Brothel" scenes are the most famous. 1888. (Pl. 17; 21, 159, 185)
Kairaishi 傀儡師 by Sakurada Jisuke III. *Nagauta* dance-drama. 1824.
Kajiwara Heizō Homare no Ishikiri 梶原平三誉石切 by Bunkōdō and Hasegawa Senshi. *Jōruri jidaimono.* Five acts, of which the third act is performed. 1730. (194)
Kakubei 角兵衛 by Segawa Jokō. *Tokiwazu* dance-drama. 1828.
Kamagafuchi Futatsu Domoe. 釜淵双級巴 by Namiki Sōsuke. *Jōruri jidaimono.* Three acts, of which the "Mamako Ijime Scene" in Act II and the "Kamairi" of the last scene are famous. 1737. (144)
Kamakura Sandaiki 鎌倉三代記. Author unknown. *Jōruri jidaimono.* Ten acts, of which the "Kinugawa Mura Kankyo Scene" in Act VII is performed. 1781.
Kami no Megumi Wagō no Torikumi 神明恵和合取組 by Takeshiba Kisui. *Sewamono.* 1890.
Kamiji: See *Shinjū Ten no Amijima*
Kamiyui Shinza: See *Tsuyu Kosode Mukashi Hachijō*
Kamo-zutsumi: See *Sugawara Denju Tenarai Kagami.* (30)
Kanadehon Chūshingura 仮名手本忠臣蔵 by Takeda Izumo and others. *Jōruri jidaimono.* Eleven acts. With the exception of the second and tenth acts all are frequently performed. 1748. (Pls. 33–35, 42; 87–124, 179, 193, 219, 225, 261–62)
Kanda Matsuri 神田祭 by Mimasuya Nisōji. *Kiyomoto* dance-drama. 1839.
Kanjin Kammon Tekuda no Hajimari 韓人漢文手管始 by Namiki Gohei I. *Jidaimono.* 1789.
Kanjinchō 勧進帳 by Namiki Gohei III. *Nagauta* dance-drama. 1840. (Pl. 14; 3, 152)

Kanki Yakata: See *Kokusenya Kassen*
Karukaya Dōshin Tsukushi no Iezuto 苅菅桑門筑紫轢 by Namiki Sōsuke and others. *Jōruri jidaimono.* Five acts, of which the "Imorizake Scene" is still performed. 1735.
Kasane 累 by Matsui Kōzō. *Kiyomoto* dance-drama. 1823. (Pl. 21; 186)
Kasane: See *Date Kurabe Okuni Kabuki*
Kasuga no Tsubone 春日局 by Fukuchi Ōchi. *Jidaimono.* 1891.
Kataki Uchi Tengajaya Mura 敵討天下茶屋聚 by Nagawa Kamesuke and others. *Jidaimono.* 1816. (11)
Kataki Uchi Tsuzure no Nishiki 敵討襤褸錦 by Bunkōdō and Miyoshi

Shōraku. *Jōruri jidaimono.* Three acts. The "Daianji Scene" in Act III is the most famous. 1736.

Katsuragawa Renri no Shigarami 桂川連理柵 by Suga Sensuke. *Jōruri sewamono.* Two acts, of which the second act ("Rokkakudō," "Obiya," and *michiyuki*) are frequently performed. 1776.

Kawashō: See *Shinjū Ten no Amijima*

Kawazura Yakata: See *Yoshitsune Sembonzakura.* (79–84)

Keisei Awa no Naruto 傾城阿波の鳴渡 by Chikamatsu Hanji and others. *Jōruri jidaimono.* Ten acts, of which the "Jūrōbei Uchi Scene," also known as "Junreiuta," in Act VIII is especially famous. 1768.

Keisei Hangonkō 傾城反魂香 by Chikamatsu Monzaemon. *Jōruri jidaimono.* Three acts, of which the "Shōgen Kankyo" and "Domomata" scenes are performed. 1708.

Kenkaba: Act III of *Kanadehon Chūshingura.* (Pl. 35; 93–95)

Kenuki 毛抜 by Tsuuchi Hanjūrō. *Jidaimono.* One of the "Eighteen Favorite Kabuki Plays." 1742. (6)

Keyamura: See *Hikosan Gongen Chikai no Sukedachi*

Kezori: See *Hakata Kojorō Nami Makura*

Kiichi Hōgen Sanryaku no Maki 鬼一法眼三略巻 by Bunkōdō and Hasegawa Senshi. *Jōruri jidaimono.* Five acts, of which the "Kikubatake Scene" in Act III and the "Ichijō Ōkura-kyō scene" in Act IV are famous. 1731. (202, 203, 204, 212)

Kijin no Omatsu: See *Shimpan Koshi no Shiranami*

Kikubatake: See *Kiichi Hōgen Sanryaku no Maki*

Kinkakuji: See *Gion Sairei Shinkōki.* (Pl. 60)

Kioijishi 勢獅子 by Segawa Jokō. *Tokiwazu* dance-drama. 1851.

Kirare Otomi: See *Musume-gonomi Ukina no Yokogushi* (Pl. 52)

Kirare Yosa: See *Yowa Nasake Ukina no Yokogushi*

Kiri Hitoha 桐一葉 by Tsubouchi Shōyō. New Kabuki. 1907.

Kitsunebi: See *Honchō Nijūshi Kō* (228)

Kiwametsuki Banzui Chōbei 極付幡随長兵衛 by Kawatake Mokuami. *Sewamono.* 1881.

Kōchiyama: See *Kumo ni Magō Ueno no Hatsuhana*

Koharu Jihei: See *Shinjū Ten no Amijima* and *Shingure no Kotatsu*

Koi Musume Mukashi Hachijō 恋娘昔八丈 by Matsu Kanshi. *Jōruri sewamono.* Five acts. 1775.

Koi Bikyaku Yamato Ōrai 恋飛脚大和往来. An adaptation by Suga Sensuke and Wakatake Fuemi from *Meido no Hikyaku.* (Pls. 18, 44, 51; 157, 209)

Koi Nyōbō Somewake Tazuna 恋女房染分手綱 by Yoshida Kanshi and Miyoshi Shōraku. Thirteen acts. Only the "Shigenoi Kowakare Scene" is frequently performed. 1751.

Kokusenya Kassen 国姓爺合戦 by Chikamatsu Monzaemon. *Jōruri jidaimono.* Five acts, of which the "Shishigajō Scene" is the most famous. 1715.

Komochi Yamamba 嫗山姥 by Chikamatsu Monzaemon. *Jōruri jidaimono.* Five acts, of which only the scene at Kanefuyu's mansion in Act II is performed. 1712. (Pls. 45–46; 171)

Komori 子守 by Masuyama Kimpachi. *Kiyomoto* dance-drama. 1823.

Konomi: See *Yoshitsune Sembonzakura.* (64–67)

Kosode Soga Azami no Ironui 小袖曾我薊色縫 by Kawatake Mokuami. *Kizewamono.* 1863.

Kotobuki Soga no Taimen 寿曾我対面 by Kawatake Mokuami. *Jidaimono.* 1903. (1–2, 205)

Kotsuyose: See *Kagamiyama Gonichi no Iwafuji*

Kowakare: See *Sakura Giminden*

Kumagai Jinya: See *Ichinotani Futaba Gunki* (Pls. 15–16; 132, 167–69)

Kumo ni Magō Ueno no Hatsuhana 天衣紛上野初花 by Kawatake Mokuami. *Sewamono.* 1881. (Pl. 13; 155, 177, 241, 243)

Kumo no Hyōshimai 蜘蛛拍子舞 by Sakurada Jisuke. *Nagauta* dance-drama. 1781.

Kurama no Dammari: See *Jidai dammari.* (9–10)

Kuramajishi 鞍馬獅子 by Nakamura Jūsuke. *Nagauta* dance-drama. 1777.

Kuruma-biki: See *Sugawara Denju Tenarai Kagami.* (Pl. 57; 40–41, 148)

Kuruwa Bunshō 廓文章 by Chikamatsu Monzaemon. *Jōruri sewamono.* 1808. (Pl. 12)

Kusazuri-biki 草摺引. Author unknown. *Nagauta* dance-drama. 1814. (136)

Kutsukake Mura: See *Koi Nyōbō Somewake Tazuna*

Kuzu no Ha: See *Ashiya Dōman Ōuchi Kagami*

Kuzu no Ha no Kowakare: See *Ashiya Dōman Ōuchi Kagami*

Manaita no Chōbei: See *Banzui Chōbei Shōjin Manaita*

Manjū Musume: See *Igagoe Dōchū Sugoroku*

Masakado 将門 by Takarada Jusuke. *Tokiwazu* dance-drama. 1836. (22, 229, 259–60)

Masakiyo Honjō: see *Hachijin Shugo no Honjō*

Masaoka Chūgi: See *Meiboku Sendai Hagi*

Masu Otoshi: See *Meido no Hikyaku*

Matsukiri: Act II of *Kanadehon Chūshingura.* (90)

Megumi no Kenka: See *Kami no Megumi Wagō no Torikumi*

Meiboku Sendai Hagi 伽羅先代萩 by Matsu Kanshi and others. *Jōruri jidaimono.* Nine acts, of which the "Goten" and "Yukashita" scenes in Act VI and the "Taiketsu Scene" in Act IX are the most famous. 1785. (14–15, 154, 192, 198, 199, 218)

Meido no Hikyaku 冥土の飛脚 by Chikamatsu Monzaemon. *Jōruri sewamono.* Three acts, of which the "Fūingiri (Seal-breaking) Scene" in Act Two and "Ninokuchi Mura" of the last scene are most frequently performed. 1711.

Mekura Nagaya Ume ga Kagatobi 盲長屋梅加賀鳶 by Kawatake Mokuami. *Kizewamono.* 1886. (17–18, 183, 211)

Migawari Ondo: See *Ōtōnomiya Asahi no Yoroi*

Mitsumen Komori 三面子守 by Tsuuchi Jihei II. *Tokiwazu* dance-drama. 1829.

Miyagi Shinobu: See *Go Taiheiki Shiraishi-banashi*

Miyajima no Dammari: See *Jidai dammari.* (Pl. 40)

Modorikago 戻駕 by Sakurada Jisuke I. *Tokiwazu* dance-drama. 1788.

Momijigari 紅葉狩 by Fukuchi Ōchi. *Tokiwazu* dance-drama. 1887. (24)

Moritsuna Jinya: See *Ōmi Genji Senjin Yakata.* (160–166)

Motobune: See *Hakata Kojorō Nami Makura*

Muken no Kane: See *Hiragana Seisuiki*

Munekiyo 宗清 by Nagawa Motosuke. *Tokiwazu* dance-drama. 1828.

Musume Dōjōji 娘道成寺. Author unknown. *Nagauta* dance-drama. 1753. (Pls. 25–26, 38–39; 240)

Musume-gonomi Ukina no Yokogushi 処女翫浮名横櫛 by Kawatake Mokuami. *Kizewamono.* 1864. (Pl. 52)

Nagamachi Onna no Harakiri 長町女腹切 by Chikamatsu Monzaemon. *Jōruri sewamono.* Three acts. 1712.

Naozamurai: See *Kumo ni Magō Ueno no Hatsuhana*

Narukami 鳴神 by Tsuuchi Hanjūrō. *Jidaimono.* One of the "Eighteen Favorite Kabuki Plays." 1742. (Pl. 11; 7, 127, 129)

Narukami Fudō Kitayama-zakura 鳴神不動北山桜 by Tsuuchi Hanjūro and others. Includes *Kenuki, Narukami,* and *Fudō* of the "Eighteen Favorite Kabuki Plays." 1742. (126)

Natorigusa Heike Monogatari 牡丹平家譚 by Kawatake Mokuami. *Jidaimono.* 1876.

Natsumatsuri Naniwa Kagami 夏祭浪花鑑 by Namiki Senryū and others. *Jōruri sewamono.* Nine acts, of which the scene "Sumiyoshi Shrine" in Act III, the scene at Sabu's home in Act VI, and the "Side Street off Nagamachi Scene" in Act VII are frequently performed. 1745. (138)

Nebiki no Kadomatsu 寿門松 by Chikamatsu Monzaemon. *Jōruri sewamono.* Three acts. 1718.

Nezumi Komon Haru no Shingata 鼠小紋東君新形 by Kawatake Mokuami. *Sewamono.* 1857.

Nezumi Kozō: See *Nezumi Komon Haru no Shingata*

Nijūshi Kō: See *Honchō Nijūshi Kō*

Ninjō: Act III of *Kanadehon Chūshingura;* see also *Meiboku Sendai Hagi.* (Pl. 35; 93–95)

Ninokuchi Mura: See *Koibikyaku Yamato Ōrai.* (Pl. 43; 209)

Nomitori Otoko 蚤取男 by Kimura Tomiko. *Nagauta* dance-drama. 1929. One of Eno's ten favorite plays. (220)

Noriai-bune 乗合船 by Sakurada Jisuke III. *Tokiwazu* dance-drama. 1843.

Nozaki Mura: See *Shimpan Utazaimon.* (142, 245–47)

Nozarashi Gosuke: See *Suibodai Godō no Nozarashi*

Numazu: See *Igagoe Dōchū Sugoroku.* (141)

Ōakinai Hiru ga Kojima 大商蛭小島 by Sakurada Jisuke I and Masuyama Kimpachi. *Jidai-sewa-mono.* 1784.

Obiya: See *Katsuragawa Renri no Shigarami*

Ochiyo Hambei: See *Shinjū Yoi Gōshin*

Ochūdo: Michiyuki of *Kanadehon Chūshingura.* (101–5)

Ofune Tōmbei: See *Shinrei Yaguchi no Watashi*

Ohan Chōemon: See *Katsuragawa Renri no Shigarami*

Oharame 小原女 by Segawa Jokō. *Nagauta* dance-drama. 1810.

Ohatsu Tokubei: See *Sonezaki Shinjū*

Ōgiya Kumagai: See *Suma no Miyako Gempei Tsutsuji*

Oigawa: See *Shō-utsushi Asagao Banashi*

Oiwa: See *Tōkaidō Yotsuya Kaidan*

Okazaki: See *Igagoe Dōchū Sugoroku*

Okoma Saiza: See *Koi Musume Mukashi Hachijō*

Okudaya: See *Hakata Kojorō Nami Makura*

Omatsuri Sashichi: See *Edo Sodachi Omatsuri Sashichi*

Ōmi Genji Senjin Yakata 近江源氏先陣館 by Chikamatsu Hanji and others. *Jōruri jidaimono.* Nine acts, of which the "Moritsuna Jinya Scene" alone is staged. 1769. (160–66, 200, 214)

Ōmi no Okane 近江のお兼 by Sakurada Jisuke II. *Nagauta* dance-drama. 1813. (28) Also called *Danjūrō Musume,* or *Sarashime.*

Ōmori Hikoshichi 大森彦七 by Fukuchi Ōchi. *Tokiwazu* dance-drama. 1897.

Oni Azami: See *Kosode Soga Azami no Ironui*

Onna-goroshi Abura no Jigoku 女殺油地獄 by Chikamatsu Monzaemon. *Jōruri sewamono.* Three acts. 1721. (187)

Ōshū Adachigahara 奥州安達原 by Chikamatsu Hanji and others. *Jōruri jidaimono.* Five acts, of which the "Sodehagi Saimon Scene" is especially famous. 1762. (16)

Osome お染 by Tsuruya Namboku IV. *Kiyomoto* dance-drama. 1825.

Osome Hisamatsu: See *Shimpan Utazaimon* and *Some Moyō Imose no Kadomatsu*

Osome Hisamatsu Ukina no Yomiuri 於染久松色読販 by Tsuruya Namboku IV. *Sewamono.* 1813. (Pl. 49; 224, 295)

Osome no Nanayaku: See *Osome Hisamatsu Ukina no Yomiuri.*

Ōtōnomiya Asahi no Yoroi 大塔宮曦鎧 by Takeda Izumo. *Jōruri jidaimono.* Five acts, of which the "Migawari Ondo Scene" is the most famous. 1723.

Ōtsu-e 大津絵 by Kawatake Mokuami. *Tokiwazu-kiyomoto* dance-drama. 1871.

Otsuma Hachirōbei: See *Sakuratsuba Urami no Samezaya*

Rampei Monogurui: See *Yamato-gana Ariwara Keizu*

Renjishi 連獅子 by Kawatake Mokuami. *Nagauta* dance-drama. 1861.

Rokkasen Sugata no Irodori 六歌仙容彩 by Matsumoto Kōji. *Kiyomoto* dance-drama. 1831.

Rōmon: See *Kokusenya Kassen*

Sagi Musume 鷺娘 by Horikoshi Nisōji. *Nagauta* dance-drama. 1762. (Pl. 23)

Sakaro: See *Hiragana Seisuiki.* (191)

Sakaya: See *Hadesugata Onna Maiginu.* (170)

Sakura Giminden 佐倉義民伝 by Segawa Jokō III. *Sewamono.* 1851. (197)

Sakura-hime Azuma Bunshō 桜姫東文章 by Tsuruya Namboku and others. *Jidai-sewa-mono.* 1817. (Pl. 48: 178, 258)

Sakura Sōgo: See *Sakura Giminden*

Sakuratsuba Urami no Samezaya 桜鍔恨鮫鞘. Author unknown. *Jōruri sewamono.* The number of acts is unknown. Only the "Unagidani Scene" is performed. 1773.

Sammon Gosan no Kiri 楼門五三桐 by Namiki Gohei. *Jidaimono.* Only the spectacular "Sammon Scene" is staged. 1778. (Pl. 58)

Sanemori Monogatari: See *Gempei Nunobiki no Taki*

Sanja Matsuri 三社祭 by Segawa Jokō II. *Kiyomoto* dance-drama. 1832.

Sanjikkoku Yobune no Hajimari 三十石䑓始 by Namiki Shōzō. *Jidaimono.* 1758. (289)

Sanjūsangendō Munagi no Yurai 三十三間堂棟木由来 by Wakatake Fuemi and others. *Jōruri jidaimono.* Five acts. 1760.

Sankatsu Hanshichi: See *Hadesugata Onna Maiginu*

Sannin Kichiza Kuruwa no Hatsugai 三人吉三廓初買 by Kawatake Mokuami. *Sewamono.* 1860. (Pl. 61; 190, 251)

Sarashime: See *Ōmi no Okane*

Sarumawashi: See *Chikagoro Kawara no Tatehiki*

Sasaki Takatsuna 佐々木高綱 by Okamoto Kidō. New Kabuki. 1913.

Satomi Hakkenden 里見八犬伝 by Sakurada Jisuke III. *Jidaimono.* 1852.

Saya-ate: See *Ukiyozuka Hiyoku no Inazuma*

Seki no To 関の扉 by Takarada Jurai. *Tokiwazu* dance-drama. 1784. (Pls. 22, 36–37; 23, 135)

Sekitori Senryō Nobori 関取千両幟 by Chikamatsu Hanji and others. *Jōruri sewamono.* Nine acts, of which the scene at Iwakawa's house and the "Sumō Scene" in Act II are performed. 1767.

Sembonzakura: See *Yoshitsune Sembonzakura*

Sendai Hagi: See *Meiboku Sendai Hagi*

Senryō Nobori: See *Sekitori Senryō Nobori*

Sesshū Gappō ga Tsuji 摂州合邦辻 by Suga Sensuke and Wakatake Fuemi. *Jōruri jidaimono.* Three acts, of which the scene at Gappō's house is frequently performed. 1773.

Shaberi: See *Komochi Yamamba.* (171)

Shibaraku 暫 by Ichikawa Danjūrō I. *Jidaimono.* One of the "Eighteen Favorite Kabuki Plays." 1697. (125)

Shichimise: See *Some Moyō Imose no Kadomatsu*

Shigemori Kangen: See *Natorigusa Heike Monogatari*

Shigenoi Kowakare: See *Koi Nyōbō Somewake Tazuna*

Shigure no Kotatsu 時雨の炬燵. The most famous adaptation from *Shinjū Ten no Amijima.*

Shimpan Koshi no Shiranami 新版越白浪 by Sakurada Jisuke III. *Sewamono.* 1851.

Shimpan Utazaimon 新版歌祭文 by Chikamatsu Hanji. *Jōruri sewamono.* Two acts. The "Nozaki Mura Scene" is the most famous. 1780. (142, 245–47)

Shin Usuyuki Monogatari 新薄雪物語 by Bunkōdō and others. *Jōruri jidaimono.* Three acts. The "Kiyomizu Scene" in Act I, the "Sannin Warai Scene" in Act II, and the "Masamune Uchi Scene" in Act III are frequently performed. 1741. (Pl. 47)

Shin Yoshiwara Ageya: See *Go Taiheiki Shiraishi-banashi*

Shinjū Ten no Amijima 心中天網島 by Chikamatsu Monzaemon. *Jōruri sewamono.* Three acts, all commonly performed. 1720. (206)

Shinjū Yoi Gōshin 心中宵庚申 by Chikamatsu Monzaemon. *Jōruri sewamono.* 1722.

Shinodazuma 信田妻. Included in *Ashiya Dōman Ōuchi Kagami.*

Shinrei Yaguchi no Watashi 神霊矢口渡 by Fukuuchi Kigai and others. *Jōruri jidaimono.* Five acts, of which the "Tombei Sumika Scene" in Act IV is frequently performed. 1770. (150, 267)

Shinseimachi: See *Hakata Kojorō Nami Makura*

Shinshū Kawanakajima Kassen 信州川中島合戦 by Chikamatsu Monzaemon. *Jōruri jidaimono.* Five acts. Only the "Terutora Haizen Scene" in Act IV is performed. 1721.

Shiokumi 汐汲 by Sakurada Jisuke II. *Nagauta* dance-drama. 1811. (249–50)

Shiraishi-banashi: See *Go Taiheiki Shiraishi-banashi*

Shiranami Gonin Otoko: See *Aoto Zōshi Hana no Nishiki-e*

Shirokiya: See *Koi Musume Mukashi Hachijō*

Shisenryō Koban no Umenoha 四千両小判梅葉 by Sakurada Jisuke III. *Sewamono.* 1851.

Shishigajō: See *Kokusenya Kassen*

Shitadashi Sambasō 舌出三番叟 by Sakurada Jisuke II. *Nagauta-kiyomoto* dance-drama. This play is also known as *Tanemaki Sambasō* or *Shigayama Sambasō.* 1832.

Shō-utsushi Asagao Banashi 生写朝顔話 by Yamada Kakashi. *Jōruri jidaimono.* Five acts. 1832.

Shunkan: See *Heike Nyogo no Shima*

Shuzenji Monogatari 修禅寺物語 by Okamoto Kidō. New Kabuki. 1909.

Sodehagi Saimon: See *Ōshū Adachigahara.* (16)

Soga Moyō Tateshi no Gosho-zome 曾我綉侠御所染 by Kawatake Mokuami. *Jidai-sewa-mono.* 1864. (156)

Soga no Taimen: See *Kotobuki Soga no Taimen*

Some Moyō Imose no Kadomatsu 染模様妹背門松 by Suga Sensuke. *Jōruri sewamono.* Two acts. The "Aburaya Scene" in Act I and the "Shichiya Scene" in Act II are especially famous. 1767.

Sonezaki Shinjū 曾根崎心中 by Chikamatsu Monzaemon. *Jōruri sewamono.* Three acts. 1703. (19, 188)

Suda no Haru Geisha Katagi 隅田春妓女容性 by Namiki Gohei. *Sewamono.* 1796.

Sugawara Denju Tenarai Kagami 菅原伝授手習鑑 by Takeda Izumo and others. *Jōruri jidaimono*. Five acts, of which the "Dō-myōji Scene" in Act II, the "Kuruma-biki" and 'Ga no Iwai' scenes in Act III, and the "Terakoya Scene" in Act IV are commonly performed. 1746. (Pls. 26–28, 57; 29–54, 149)

Sugisakaya: See *Imoseyama Onna Teikin*

Suibodai Godō no Nozarashi 酔菩提悟道野晒 by Kawatake Mokuami. *Sewamono*. Two acts. 1865. (191)

Sukeroku Yukari no Edo-zakura 助六由縁江戸桜 by Tsuuchi Jihei. *Jidai-mono*. One of the "Eighteen Favorite Kabuki Plays." 1713. (Pls. 1–9; 230–31)

Suma no Miyako Gempei Tsutsuji 須磨都源平躑躅 by Bunkōdō and Hasegawa Senshi. *Jōruri jidaimono*. Five acts, of which only the "Ōgiya Kumagai Scene" in Act II is performed. 1730.

Suma no Ura: See *Ichinotani Futaba Gunki*. (145)

Sumidagawa Gonichi no Omokage 隅田川続俤 by Nagawa Shimesuke. *Sewamono*. 1784.

Sumōba: See *Futatsu Chōchō Kuruwa Nikki*

Sushiya: See *Yoshitsune Sembonzakura* (68–75)

Suzugamori: See *Banzui Chōbei Shōjin Manaita* and *Koi Musume Mukashi Hachijō*

Taiju: Act X of *Ehon Taikōki*

Taiketsu: See *Date Kurabe Okuni Kabuki*

Taikōki: See *Ehon Taikōki*

Taimen: See *Kotobuki Soga no Taimen*

Takatoki: See *Hōjō Kudai Meika no Isaoshi*

Takenoko-hori: See *Honchō Nijūshi Kō*

Takenoma: See *Meiboku Sendai Hagi*

Tamamo no Mae Asahi no Tamoto 玉藻前曦袂 by Namioka Kippei. *Jōruri jidaimono*. Five acts, of which, the "Dōshun's Mansion Scene" in Act III is still performed. 1751.

Tempaizan: See *Sugawara Denju Tenarai Kagami*. (47)

Tempō Rokkasen: See *Kumo ni Magō Ueno no Hatsuhana*

Tenaraiko 手習子 by Masuyama Kimpachi. *Nagauta* dance-drama. 1792.

Tenjiku Tokubei Ikoku-banashi 天竺徳兵衛韓噺 by Tsuruya Namboku IV. *Jidaimono*. 1804.

Terakoya: See *Sugawara Denju Tenarai Kagami*. (Pl. 26; 48–54)

Terutora Haizen: See *Shinshū Kawanakajima Kassen*

Toba-e 鳥羽絵 by Sakurada Jisuke II. *Kiyomoto* dance-drama. 1819.

Tōjin-goroshi: See *Kanjin Kammon Tekuda no Hajimari*

Tōkaidō Yotsuya Kaidan 東海道四谷怪談 by Tsuruya Namboku IV, *Sewamono*. 1825. (Pl. 42; 175)

Tokaiya: See *Yoshitsune Sembonzakura*. (59–60)

Tokimo Kikyō Shusse no Ukejō 時桔梗出世請状 by Tsuruya Namboku IV. *Jidaimono*. 1808.

Toribeyama Shinjū 鳥辺山心中 by Okamoto Kidō. New Kabuki. 1915.

Tōyata Monogatari: See *Gosho-zakura Horikawa Youchi*

Tsubosaka Reigenki 壺坂霊験記 by Kako Chika. *Jōruri sewamono*. 1887.

Tsuchigumo 土蜘 by Kawatake Mokuami. *Nagauta* dance-drama. 1881.

Tsuyu Kosode Mukashi Hachijō 梅雨小袖昔八丈 by Kawatake Moku-ami. *Kizewamono*. 1873.

Ukare Bōzu 浮かれ坊主 by Sakurada Jisuke II. *Kiyomoto* dance-drama. 1811.

Ukiyozuka Hiyoku no Inazuma 浮世柄比翼稲妻 by Tsuruya Namboku IV. *Jidaimono*. 1823. (134, 172)

Ume no Yoshibei: See *Suda no Haru Geisha Katagi*

Umegawa Chūbei: See *Meido no Hikyaku*

Unagidani: See *Sakuratsuba Urami no Samezaya*

Utsubozaru うつぼ猿 by Nakamura Jūsuke. *Tokiwazu* dance-drama. 1838.

Uwabami Oyoshi Uwasa no Adauchi 蟒於由曙評仇討 by Segawa Jokō III. *Kizewamono*. 1866.

Wada Kassen Onna Maizuru 和田合戦女舞鶴 by Namiki Sōsuke. *Jōruri jidaimono*. Five acts, of which the "Hangaku Mon Yaburi Scene" in Act II is the most famous. 1736.

Ya no Ne 矢の根 by Fujimoto Tobun. *Jidaimono*. One of the "Eighteen Favorite Kabuki Plays." 1740. (4–5)

Yadonashi Danshichi Shigure no Karakasa 宿無団七時雨傘 by Namiki Shōzō. *Sewamono*. 1768.

Yadoya: See *Shō-utsushi Asagao Nikki*

Yaegiri Kuruwa-banashi: See *Komochi Yamamba*

Yaguchi no Watashi: See *Shinrei Yaguchi no Watashi*

Yagura no Oshichi: See *Date Musume Koi no Higanoko*

Yamamba 山姥 by Mimasuya Nisōji. *Tokiwazu* dance-drama. 1848.

Yamashina Kankyo: See *Kanadehon Chūshingura*

Yamato-gana Ariwara Keizu 倭仮名在原系図 by Asada Itchō and others. *Jōruri jidaimono*. Five acts, of which the "Rampei Monogurui Scene" in Act IV is most frequently performed. 1752.

Yamazaki Kaidō: See *Kanadehon Chūshingura*. (106–7)

Yaoya Hambei: See *Shinjū Yoi Gōshin*

Yaoya Oshichi: See *Date Musume Koi no Higanoko*

Yasuna 保名 by Shinoda Kinji I. *Kiyomoto* dance-drama. 1818. (Pl. 39)

Yoshidaya: See *Kuruwa Bunshō*. (Pl. 12)

Yoshinogawa: See *Imoseyama Onna Teikin*

Yoshitsune Koshigoejō 義経腰越状 by Namiki Sōsuke. *Jōruri jidaimono*. Five acts. 1754. (216)

Yoshitsune Sembonzakura 義経千本桜 by Takeda Izumo and others. *Jōruri jidaimono*. Five acts. With the exception of Act I and II, all are commonly performed. 1747. (Pls. 29–32; 55–86, 151)

Yoshiwara Suzume 吉原雀 by Sakurada Jisuke I. *Nagauta* dance-drama. 1768.

Yotsuya Kaidan: See *Tōkaidō Yotsuya Kaidan*

Yowa Nasake Ukina no Yokogushi 与話情浮名横櫛 by Segawa Jokō III. *Kizewamono*. 1853. (137, 213)

Yudono no Chōbei: See *Kiwametsuki Banzui Chōbei*

Yūgiri Izaemon: See *Kuruwa Bunshō*

Zenaku Ryōmen Konotegashiwa 善悪両面児手柏 by Kawatake Mokuami. *Sewamono*. 1867.

Zōho Futatsu Domoe 増補双級巴 by Kimura Enji. *Jidaimono*. 1861. (144)

Zōho Momoyama Monogatari 増補桃山譚 by Kawatake Mokuami. *Katsurekigeki*. Four acts. 1869.

Zōri-uchi: See *Kagamiyama Kokyō no Nishiki-e*. (172)

GENERAL CHRONOLOGY

1558–69 (Eiroku era)	The musical instrument called the *jabisen* is introduced to Japan about this time from the Ryūkyū Islands. It first appears in the town of Sakai, near Osaka, is developed into the present shamisen, and thereafter becomes popular throughout the country.
1571 (Genki 2)	During *Bon* (the Buddhist Festival of the Dead), a great *furyū* is performed in the city of Kyoto. *Furyū* dances become very popular from the Tembun (1532–1555) through the Keichō eras.
1582 (Tenshō 10)	The three lords of Ōmura, Arima, and Ōtomo send emissaries to the Pope in Rome.
1583 (Tenshō 11)	Toyotomi Hideyoshi completes construction of Osaka Castle.
1587 (Tenshō 15)	Toyotomi Hideyoshi issues an edict against Christianity; it is not actively enforced.
1588 (Tenshō 16)	2nd month: Maidens in the service of the Izumo Taisha (Grand Shrine of Izumo) arrive in Kyoto and perform dances to the accompaniment of *kamiuta* (songs of the gods) and *kouta* (at that time meaning popular songs).
1590 (Tenshō 18)	The emissaries to Rome return.
1596 (Keichō 1)	Christians crucified.
1600 (Keichō 5)	Nyōgo Konoe (an imperial lady-in-waiting) requests the performance of *yayako odori* by the female dancers Kiku and Kuni.
	Tokugawa Ieyasu establishes himself in Edo Castle. Ieyasu defeats Ishida Mitsunari and Konishi Yukinaga at the Battle of Sekigahara.
1603 (Keichō 8)	*Nembutsu odori* and *kabuki odori* performed in Kyoto by Okuni of Izumo. *Onna kabuki* and *yūjo kabuki* troupes travel throughout the provinces. *Wakashu kabuki* also performed. Daigashira Kashiwagi and Kasaya Sankatsu, *kusemai* dancers, make their debut. Tokugawa Ieyasu becomes shogun.
1604 (Keichō 9)	In Kyoto, *furyū* dances are performed on a large scale during the special festival of the Hōkoku Shrine, and at the Kitano Shrine *onna kabuki* and *onna sarugaku* are performed.
1607 (Keichō 12)	Okuni of Izumo performs in Edo.
1610 (Keichō 15)	*Onna kabuki* staged to celebrate the completion of Nagoya Castle. Around this time Katō Kiyomasa orders *onna kabuki* to be staged in Kumamoto, Kyushu.
1612 (Keichō 17)	Christianity actively proscribed.
1615 (Genna 1)	Osaka Castle destroyed and Toyotomi family annihilated.
1624 (Ken'ei 1)	Saruwaka Kanzaburō opens the Saruwaka-za, the forerunner of the Nakamura-za. *Sekkyō* (this term referring to the didactic stories and parables used in Buddhist *sekkyō*, "sermons") *jōruri* becomes popular.
1629 (Kan'ei 15)	*Onna kabuki* and female participation in similar entertainments proscribed.
1632 (Kan'ei 9)	The Nakamura-za, puppet theaters, other entertainments forced to move from Nakanohashi to Negimachi by governmental edict.
1634 (Kan'ei 11)	The Murayama-za, the forerunner of the Ichimura-za, founded by Murayama Matasaburō at Sakaimachi.
1636 (Kan'ei 13)	Saruwaka Kanzaburō punished for the extravagance of his troupe's kabuki costumes. Travel abroad prohibited.
1639 (Kan'ei 16)	National isolation edict proclaimed; door closed to foreigners except Chinese and Dutch traders (at Nagasaki).
1648 (Keian 1)	Use of silk for kabuki costumes proscribed.
1651 (Keian 4)	Nakamura-za and other theaters ordered to move from Negimachi to Kami Sakaimachi. Shogun Iemitsu invites the Saruwaka *wakashu kabuki* troupe to Edo Castle three times.
1652 (Shō-ō 1)	*Wakashu kabuki* prohibited. Murayama-za becomes Ichimura-za.
1653 (Shō-ō 2)	*Wakashu kabuki* becomes known as *yarō kabuki*; official name of the drama changed to *monomane kyōgen zukushi*. Tamagawa Sennojō performs in the play *Takayasugayoi* at the Ichimura-za in Edo; achieves great popularity.
1657 (Meireki 3)	The great fire of Edo practically destroys the city; three kabuki theaters recover from the disaster. Puppet drama activity moves from Edo to Osaka.
1658 (Manji 1)	Nakamura Kanzaburō I dies.
1660 (Manji 3)	The Morita-za founded at Kobikichō in Edo.
1661 (Kambun 1)	Tamagawa Sennojō performs in *Takayasugayoi* at the Nakamura-za in a three year run.
1664 (Kambun 4)	Plays divided into many acts first appear both in Edo and Osaka. Wigs for female roles prohibited in Edo. Drawn curtain first used about this time.

1673 (Empō 1)	Ichikawa Danjūrō I performs in the play *Shitennō Osanadachi*, said to be the first instance of the *aragoto* acting style.		Miyako Itchū, the originator of *itchū bushi* music, dies.
1678 (Empō 6)	Sakata Tōjurō performs in *Yūgiri Nagori no Shōgatsu*. The book *Kokon Yakusha Monogatari* published.	1725 (Kyōhō 10)	Masumi Katō, the originator of *katō bushi* music, dies.
1680 (Empō 8)	Tominaga Heibei announces that he is a *kyōgen* playwright: the first instance of known *kyōgen* authorship.	1729 (Kyōhō 14)	The *onnagata* Yoshizawa Ayame dies. Danjūrō II performs in *Ya no Ne*. *Ōzatsuma* music played on stage.
1685 (Jōkyō 2)	Takemoto Gidayū establishes the Takemoto-za pupet theater at Dōtombori, Osaka.	1731 (Kyōhō 16)	Kikunojō's *Muken no Kane* enjoys huge success; this play was the first to use *meriyasu* music. *Hikinuki* costume change invented by Ōtani Hiroji.
1686 (Jōkyō 3)	Chikamatsu's *Shusse Kagekiyo* is performed at the Takemoto-za. From this time on, puppet plays are referred to as *shin jōruri*.	1732 (Kyōhō 17)	The *bungo bushi* chanter Miyakoji Bungo no Jō comes to Edo from Kyoto. *Bungo bushi* achieves great popularity in Edo.
1693 (Genroku 6)	Chikamatsu's kabuki play *Butsumo Mayasan Kaichō* is performed at the Mandayū-za in Kyoto.	1734 (Kyōhō 19)	Segawa Kikunojō's *Aioi Jishi* and *Yūgiri Asamagadake* performed at Edo's Nakamura-za. *Ashiya Dōman Ōuchi Kagami* performed for the first time at the Takemoto-za. Three men-operated puppets used for the first time in this play.
	Daimyo and samurai forbidden to go to the gay quarters.		
1694 (Genroku 7)	The *ukiyo-e* artist Hishikawa Moronobu dies.		
1697 (Genroku 10)	Ichikawa Danjūrō I performs in *Daifukuchō Sankai Nagoya* at the Nakamura-za; the play contains the *Shibaraku* sequence.	1735 (Kyōhō 20)	*Hikae yagura* (substitute performance rights) system adopted. The Kawaraki-za and Morita-za permitted to use *hikae yagura*. *Sonohachi bushi* music originated.
1698 (Genroku 11)	Nakamura Shichisaburō performs in *Keisei Asamagadaka*.		
1699 (Genroku 12)	Chikamatsu's *Keisei Hotoke no Hara* performed by Sakata Tōjūrō in Kyoto. *Yakusha Kuchi Jamisen*, a book on the popularity of actors, is published.	1739 (Gembun 4)	*Bungo bushi* proscribed. *Tokiwazu* and *Tomimoto* arise from *bungo bushi* and develop as theater music.
		1740 (Gembun 5)	Miyakoji Bungo no Jō dies in Kyoto.
1701 (Genroku 14)	The daimyo Asano Naganori attacks Kira Yoshinaka with a sword inside Edo Castle, resulting in the penalty of Asano's suicide.	1744 (Enkyō 1)	*Momochidori Musume Dōjōji* by Segawa Kikunojō I first performed.
1702 (Genroku 15)	The former retainers of Lord Asano, led by Ōishi Kuranosuke, slay Kira Yoshinaka and avenge their former lord's death. Later this story of revenge becomes the subject of numerous plays, *ukiyo-e* prints, and books.	1745 (Enkyō 2)	*Natsumatsuri Naniwa Kagami* by Namiki Senryū, Miyoshi Shōraku, and Takeda Koizumo performed for the first time at the Takemoto-za; this puppet play adapted for kabuki.
		1746 (Enkyō 3)	*Sugawara Denju Tenarai Kagami* by Takeda Izumo, Namiki Senryū, and Miyoshi Shōraku performed for the first time at the Takemoto-za.
1703 (Genroku 16)	Chikamatsu Monzaemon moves to Osaka from Kyoto. His first *sewamono jōruri* entitled *Sonezaki Shinjū* is performed at Osaka's Takemoto-za. Toyotake Wakatayū opens the Toyotake-za pupper theater at Dōtombori in Osaka.	1747 (Enkyō 4)	*Yoshitsune Sembonzakura* by Takeda Izumo, Namiki Senryū, and Miyoshi Shōraku performed for the first time at the Takemoto-za.
1704 (Hōei 1)	The actor Ichikawa Danjūrō I dies. The word *nagauta* first appears in a *banzuke* (program).	1748 (Kanen 1)	*Kanadehon Chūshingura* by Takeda Izumo, Namiki Senryū, and Miyoshi Shōraku first performed at the Takemoto-za. In the same year, this play performed by kabuki actors. *Shinnai bushi* originated.
1708 (Hōei 5)	The actor Nakamura Shichisaburō dies.		
1709 (Hōei 6)	The actor Sakata Tōjūrō dies.	1749 (Kanen 2)	The actor Segawa Kikunojō I dies.
1711 (Shōtoku 1)	The *jōruri* reciter Uji Kaganojō dies.	1751 (Hōreki 1)	Namiki Sōsuke (Senryū), *jōruri* playwright, dies.
1713 (Shōtoku 3)	Danjūrō II performs in *Hanayakata Aigo no Sakura* (which contains *Sukeroku*) at the Yamamura-za.	1753 (Hōreki 3)	Nakamura Tomijūrō's *nagauta* work *Kyōganoko Musume Dōjōji* first performed at the Nakamura-za. Namiki Shōzō invents *seridashi* technique.
1714 (Shōtoku 4)	The Yamamura-za closes due to the "Ejima-Ikushima affair," leaving only three theaters in Edo. Takemoto Gidayū, *jōruri* recitor and the originator of *gidayū bushi*, dies.	1756 (Hōreki 6)	The actor Sawamura Sōjūrō I dies. Takeda Izumo II (*jōruri* playwright) dies.
		1758 (Hōreki 8)	Revolving stage invented by Namiki Shōzō during production of *Sanjikkoku Yobune no Hajimari*.
1715 (Shōtoku 5)	Chikamatsu's *Kokusenya Kassen* first performed at the Takemoto-za. The play has a record run of seventeen months, and is performed at kabuki theaters in three cities.	1759 (Hōreki 9)	The actor Ichikawa Danjūrō II dies. Ōzatsuma Shuzendayū, the originator of *ōzatsuma* music, dies.
1720 (Kyōhō 5)	In Osaka the Sasase *renjū* is formed.	1762 (Hōreki 12)	The *nagauta* dance-drama *Sagi Musume* first performed at the Nakamura-za. Revolving stage first used in Edo.
1723 (Kyōhō 8)	Kabuki and *jōruri* plays with love-suicides are proscribed.		
1724 (Kyōhō 9)	Chikamatsu Monzaemon dies. Roofed, "permanent" theater construction begins.	1765 (Meiwa 2)	The polychrome wood-block print is developed by Suzuki Harunobu and others.

1766 (Meiwa 3)	Nakamura Nakazō presents a new interpretation of the character Sadakurō in *Chūshingura*.
1769 (Meiwa 6)	Fujima Kambei I, the founder of the Fujima school of dance, dies.
1770 (Meiwa 7)	Actor-portrait picture book *Ehon Butai Ōgi* by Ippitsusai Bunchō and Katsukawa Shunshō published.
1771 (Meiwa 8)	*Imoseyama Onna Teikin* by Chikamatsu Hanji performed for the first time at the Takemoto-za.
1773 (Anei 2)	Namiki Shōzō I (playwright) dies.
1776 (Anei 5)	*Yakusha Rongo* (*"Actors' Analects"*) published.
1777 (Anei 6)	*Meiboku Sendai Hagi* first performed at the Naka no Shibai Theater in Osaka.
1778 (Anei 7)	Namiki Gohei's *Kimmon Gosan no Kiri* first performed at the Naka no Shibai Theater in Osaka. *Date Kurabe Okuni Kabuki* performed for the first time at the Nakamura-za in Edo.
1781 (Temmei 1)	Tokiwazu Mojidayū I (originator of *tokiwazu* music) dies. *Kataki Uchi Tengajaya Mura* by Nagawa Kamesuke and others first performed at the Kado no Shibai Theater in Osaka.
1783 (Temmei 3)	The actor Onoe Kikugorō I dies. Chikamatsu Hanji I (*jōruri* playwright) dies.
1784 (Temmei 4)	The *tokiwazu* dance-drama *Seki no To* first performed at the Kiri-za in Edo.
1790 (Kansei 2)	The actor Nakamura Nakazō I dies.
1791 (Kansei 3)	The actor Nakamura Utaemon I dies.
from ca. 1792 (Kansei 4)	Various foreign powers petition the shogunate to open the country.
1794 (Kansei 6)	Segawa Jokō (playwright) dies.
1795 (Kansei 7)	*Godairiki Koi no Fūjime* first performed at the Miyako-za in Edo.
1796 (Kansei 8)	*Suda no Haru Geisha Katagi* and *Ise Ondo Koi no Netaba* first performed at Edo's Kiri-za and Osaka's Kado no Shibai theaters.
1801 (Kyōwa 1)	*Kezairoku* (a book on dramaturgy) by Namiki Shōzō II published. The actor Sawamura Sōjūrō III dies.
1804 (Bunka 1)	*Tenjiku Tokubei Ikokubanashi* first performed at the Kawarazaki-za in Edo.
1806 (Bunka 3)	The actors Ichikawa Danjūrō V and the playwright Sakurada Jisuke I die.
1808 (Bunka 5)	Namiki Gohei dies.
1810 (Bunka 7)	The actor Segawa Kikunojō III dies.
1811 (Bunka 8)	*Kabuki Nendaiki* (a record of kabuki performances) published.
1813 (Bunka 10)	*Osome Hisamatsu Ukina Yomiuri* by Tsuruya Namboku IV first performed at the Morita-za in Edo.
1814 (Bunka 11)	Kiyomoto Enjudayū creates *kiyomoto* music.
1818 (Bunsei 1)	*Yasuna* (*kiyomoto* dance-drama) first performed at the Miyako-za in Edo.
1823 (Bunsei 6)	The *kiyomoto* dance-drama *Kasane* first performed at the Morita-za.
1825 (Bunsei 8)	*Tōkaidō Yotsuya Kaidan* by Tsuruya Namboku IV first performed at the Nakamura-za. Kiyomoto Enjudayū I dies.
1829 (Bunsei 12)	The playwrights Tsuruya Namboku IV and Sakurada Jisuke II die.
1831 (Tempō 2)	The *kiyomoto-nagauta* dance-drama *Rokkasen* first performed at the Nakamura-za. The actor Bandō Mitsugorō III dies.
1836 (Tempō 7)	The *tokiwazu* dance-drama *Masakado* performed for the first time at the Ichimura-za.
1837 (Tempō 9)	The *tokiwazu* dance-drama *Utsubozaru* performed for the first time at the Ichimura-za. The actors Nakamura Utaemon III and Matsumoto Kōshirō V die.
1840 (Tempō 11)	Ichikawa Danjūrō VII performs in the play *Kanjinchō* at the Kawarazaki-za for the first time.
1842 (Tempō 13)	As a result of the Tempō Reforms, the theaters are moved to Saruwaka-chō. Performances within the precincts of temples and shrines proscribed. Actor prints proscribed. The actor Danjūrō VII exiled for reasons of extravagance.
1845 (Kōka 4)	The actor Iwai Hanshirō V dies. *Seikyoku Ruisan* (an encyclopedia of Japanese music) published.
1848 (Kaei 1)	*Sakusha Nenjū Gyōji* by Mimasuya Nisōji completed.
1849 (Kaei 2)	The actor Onoe Kikugorō III dies. Danjūrō VII is pardoned and returns to Edo.
1851 (Kaei 4)	*Higashiyama Sakura Sōshi* performed for the first time at the Nakamura-za.
1852 (Kaei 5)	The actor Nakamura Utaemon IV dies.
1853 (Kaei 6)	*Yo wa Nasake Ukina no Yokogushi* performed for the first time at Nakamura-za. Sawamura Sōjūrō V dies.
1854 (Ansei 1)	United States–Japan treaty signed as a result of Commodore Perry's visit. Subsequently treaties signed with other powers.
1859 (Ansei 6)	*Kosode Soga Azami no Ironui* first performed at the Ichimura-za. The actor Ichikawa Danjūrō VII dies.
1860 (Manen 1)	*Sannin Kichiza Kuruwa no Hatsugai* and *Hachiman Matsuri Yomiya no Nigiwai* first performed at the Nakamura-za.
1862 (Bunkyū 2)	*Aoto Zōshi Hana no Nishiki-e* first performed at the Nakamura-za.
1864 (Bunkyū 4)	*Soga Moyō Tateshi no Gosho-zome* first performed at the Ichimura-za.
1866 (Keiō 2)	The actor Ichikawa Kodanji IV dies.
1867 (Keiō 3)	The Edo period ends with the fall of the shogunate and the restoration of the emperor to administrative power.
1869 (Meiji 2)	The play *Zōho Momoyama Monogatari* is the first instance of *katsurekigeki*.
1872 (Meiji 5)	The *ningyō jōruri* (puppet drama) becomes known as Bunraku. The Morita-za moves from Saruwaka-chō to Shintomi-chō. The first of the *zangirimono* plays, *Kutsunaoshi Warabe no Oshie* (adaptation from Smiles' *Self-Help*) and *Sono-irodori Toki no Kōeki* are performed in the Minami no Shibai and Kita no Shibai theaters in Kyoto.
1873 (Meiji 6)	*Zangirimono* play entitled *Tokyo Nichinichi Shimbun* first performed at the Morita-za in Tokyo.
1875 (Meiji 8)	The Morita-za changes its name to the Shintomi-za and becomes a joint stock corporation.
1878 (Meiji 11)	New building of the Shintomi-za completed. Western-style "picture-frame" stage is used for the first time in Japan. Gaslights installed in a theater for the first time, and the opening ceremony of the theater is conducted in Western style.

1879 (Meiji 12)	*Ningen Banji Kane no Yononaka*, an adaptation of Robert Lytton's *Money*, performed at the Shintomi-za. The *Kabuki Shimpō*, the first magazine about kabuki, is published.
1881 (Meiji 14)	*Kumo ni Magō Ueno no Hatsuhana* and *Tsuchigumo* first performed at the Shintomi-za.
1882 (Meiji 15)	An edict limiting the number of kabuki theaters issued.
1886 (Meiji 19)	A society for improving the theater, called the Engeki Kairyō Kai, is formed under the leadership of Suematsu Kenchō. Toyama Shōichi publishes his critique *Engeki Kairyō Shikō;* Suematsu Kenchō publishes a similar critique, *Engeki Kairyō Iken.* The actor Nakamura Nakazō III dies.
1887 (Meiji 20)	The Emperor Meiji views kabuki for the first time.
1888 (Meiji 21)	*Sōshi shibai* (the forerunner of *Shimpa*) is originated by Sudō Sadanori.
1889 (Meiji 22)	The Kabuki-za opened. Fukuchi Ōchi attempts to introduce greater realism into kabuki. An actor's union is formed. The actor Nakamura Sōjūrō I dies.
1890 (Meiji 23)	*Kami no Megumi Wagō no Torikumi* is first performed at the Shintomi-za. The Danjo Engeki Kairyō Kai ("Association for Male-Female Theater") is founded under the leadership of Yoda Gakkai.
1893 (Meiji 26)	Kawatake Mokuami (playwright) dies. The *nagauta* dance-drama *Kagamijishi* performed for the first time at the Kabuki-za.
1894 (Meiji 27)	Tsubouchi Shōyō's play *Kiri Hitoha* (New Kabuki) is completed.
1895 (Meiji 28)	The actor Kataoka Nizaemon X dies.
1897 (Meiji 30)	The actor Morita Kanya XII dies. Tsubouchi Shōyō completes *Hototogisu Kojō no Rakugetsu* (New Kabuki).
1902 (Meiji 25)	The brothers Shirai Matsujirō and Ōtani Takejirō establish the Shōchiku company.
1903 (Meiji 36)	Hanayagi Jusuke I (the founder of the Hanayagi school of dance), the actors Onoe Kikugorō V and Ichikawa Danjūrō IX die. *Kiri Hitoha* is performed by Nakamura Shikan (Utaemon V) at the Tokyo-za for the first time. Tsubouchi Shōyō produces *Shinkyoku Urashima*, incorporating new concepts of dance. Ihara Toshirō's *Nihon Engekishi*, a history of Japanese theater, published. Kiyomoto Enjudayū V and the actor Ichikawa Sadanji I die.
1904 (Meiji 37)	Russo-Japanese War.
1906 (Meiji 39)	Fukuchi Ōchi (playwright and critic), Tokiwazu Rinchū (musician), and Fujinami Yohei I (properties man) die. Ichikawa Sadanji II goes to Europe.
1909 (Meiji 42)	Bungei Kyōkai (actors' troupe) founded by Tsubouchi Shōyō. Jiyū Gekijō (a Shingeki troupe) founded by Osanai Kaoru. Ichikawa Sadanji II performs *Narukami* at the Meiji-za in commemoration of the theater's opening.
1911 (Meiji 44)	Teikoku Gekijō (Imperial Theater) opened. *Shuzenji Monogatari* first performed.
1923 (Taishō 12)	The great Kantō Earthquake occurs. Ichikawa Ennosuke II (later En'ō) founds Shunjū-za.
1925 (Taishō 14)	Kabuki-za theater newly rebuilt and opened. Shimbashi Embujō opened.
1928 (Shōwa 3)	Ichikawa Sadanji II and his troupe tour the Soviet Union.
1930 (Shōwa 5)	Onoe Kikugorō VI establishes the Nihon Haiyū Gakkō ("Japan Actors' School").
1931 (Shōwa 6)	Zenshin-za troupe formed.
1932 (Shōwa 7)	The actor Morita Kanya XIII dies. Ichimura-za destroyed by fire.
1934 (Shōwa 9)	The actors Kataoka Nizaemon XI and Onoe Baikō VI die. *Genroku Chūshingura* by Mayama Seika first performed.
1935 (Shōwa 10)	The actor Nakamura Ganjirō I, Tsubouchi Shōyō (playwright) die.
1936 (Shōwa 11)	The actors Sawamura Gannosuke IV, Ichikawa Chūsha VII die.
1940 (Shōwa 15)	The actors Ichikawa Sandanji II and Nakamura Utaemon V die.
1943 (Shōwa 18)	Kiyomoto Enjudayū V (musician) and the actor Ōtani Tomoemon VI die.
1944 (Shōwa 19)	The Kabuki-za and all large theaters in Japan are ordered by the government to close. Plays can be performed only two and one-half hours a day.
1945 (Shōwa 20)	The Bunraku-za (Osaka), Kabuki-za, Shimbashi Embujō are bombed and destroyed by fire. The actor Ichimura Uzaemon V dies. Performance of *Terakoya* prohibited and a list of proscribed plays compiled.
1946 (Shōwa 21)	Bunraku-za reconstructed. The actor Kataoka Nizaemon XII dies.
1948 (Shōwa 23)	The actor Nakamura Baigyoku III dies. Shimbashi Embujō rebuilt.
1949 (Shōwa 24)	The actors Matsumoto Kōshirō VII, Sawamura Sōjūrō VII, Onoe Kikugorō VI die. All sixty-nine members of the Zenshin-za troupe become members of the Japan Communist Party.
1951 (Shōwa 26)	Kabuki-za reconstructed and opened. The actor Jitsukawa Enjaku II dies.
1954 (Shōwa 29)	The actor Nakamura Kichiemon I dies.
1958 (Shōwa 33)	Osaka Shin Kabuki-za is newly constructed and opened.
1960 (Shōwa 35)	Kabuki troupe including Nakamura Utaemon, Nakamura Kanzaburō, Onoe Shōroku, etc. present the first performance in the U.S. after the war.
1961 (Shōwa 36)	Matsumoto Kōshirō VII, Ichikawa Chūsha, and others leave Shōchiku and conclude exclusive contracts with Tōhō. Ichikawa Ennosuke II, Nakamura Utaemon, and others tour the Soviet Union and stage kabuki performances. Tōhō Gekidan's first kabuki performance.
1963 (Shōwa 38)	Ichikawa En'ō dies.
1966 (Shōwa 41)	The actors Bandō Mitsugorō VII and Ichikawa Danjūrō XI die. National Theater opened.
1969 (Shōwa 44)	Ichikawa Sadanji III dies.
1971 (Shōwa 46)	Ichikawa Jukai III dies.
1972 (Shōwa 47)	Contract between Matsumoto Kōshirō VII (Hakuō) and Tōhō company is dissolved.
1975 (Shōwa 50)	Morita Kanya XIV dies.
1981 (Shōwa 56)	Kawarazaki Chōjūrō II dies.
1982 (Shōwa 57)	Nakamura Kan'emon III dies. Matsumoto Hakuō dies. Old Shimbashi Embujō Theater is torn down and new building constructed.
1983 (Shōwa 58)	Nakamura Ganjirō II dies.
1985 (Shōwa 60)	Ichikawa Ebizō X succeeds to the name Danjūrō XII.

BIBLIOGRAPHY

PUBLICATIONS IN ENGLISH AND GERMAN

ARNOTT, PETER D. *The Theatres of Japan*. New York: St. Martin's Press, 1969.

BOWERS, FAUBION. *Japanese Theatre*. New York: Hermitage House, 1962.

BRANDON, JAMES R., with TAMAKO NIWA. *Kabuki Plays: Kanjinchō and the Zen Substitute*. New York: Samuel French, 1966.

———. *Traditional Asian Plays*. New York: Hill and Wang, 1972.

BRANDON, JAMES R., WILLIAM P. MALM, and DONALD SHIVELY. *Studies in Kabuki*. A Culture Learning Institute Monograph. East-West Center. Honolulu: The University Press of Hawaii, 1978.

DUNN, CHARLES J. and BUNZO TORIGOE (tr./ed.). *The Actors' Analects: Yakusha Rongo*. New York: Columbia University Press, 1969.

ERNST, EARLE. *The Kabuki Theatre*. Rev. ed. Honolulu: The University Press of Hawaii, 1974.

———. *Three Japanese Plays*. New York: Oxford University Press, 1959.

GUNJI, MASAKATSU. *Buyō: The Classical Japanese Dance*. Tr. by Don Kenny. New York: Walker/Weatherhill, 1971.

HAAR, FRANCIS and EARLE ERNST. *Japanese Theatre in Highlight*. Tokyo: Charles E. Tuttle, 1952.

HALFORD, AUBREY S. and GIOVANNA M. HALFORD. *The Kabuki Handbook*. Tokyo: Charles E. Tuttle, 1956.

HAMAMURA, YONEZO et al. *Kabuki*. Tokyo: Kenyūsha, 1956.

JONES, STANLEIGH H. (tr./ed.). *Sugawara and the Secrets of Calligraphy*. New York: Columbia University Press, 1985.

Kabuki: The Program Book of Japan's Grand Kabuki on its 1982 Tour. New York: Theatre Arts, 1982.

KAWATAKE, MOKUAMI. *The Love of Izayoi and Seishin*. Trans. by FRANK T. MOTOFUJI. Tokyo: Charles E. Tuttle, 1966.

KAWATAKE, SHIGETOSHI. *Kabuki: Japanese Drama*. Tokyo: Foreign Affairs Association of Japan, 1958.

KAWATAKE, TOSHIO. *A History of Japanese Theater, II: Bunraku and Kabuki*. Tokyo: Kokusai Bunka Shinkokai, 1971.

KEENE, DONALD. *Chūshingura: The Treasury of Loyal Retainers*. New York: Columbia University Press, 1971.

———. *Major Plays of Chikamatsu*. New York: Columbia University Press, 1961.

KINCAID, ZOE. *Kabuki: The Popular Stage of Japan*. New York: Macmillan, 1925.

KOMIYA, TOYOTAKA (ed.). *Japanese Music and Drama in the Meiji Era*. Tr. and adapted by Donald Keene and Edward G. Seidensticker. Tokyo: Ōbunsha, 1956.

LEITER, SAMUEL (tr.). *The Art of Kabuki*. Berkeley: University of California Press, 1979.

———. *Kabuki Encyclopedia, an English-language Adaptation of Kabuki Jiten*. Westport, Conn.: Greenwood Press, 1979.

MALM, WILLIAM P. *Nagauta: The Heart of Kabuki Music*. Tokyo: Charles E. Tuttle, 1964.

MIYAKE, SHŪTARŌ. *Kabuki Drama*. Tokyo: Japan Travel Bureau, 1949.

———. *Kabuki: Japanisches Theater*. Berlin: Safari-Verlag, 1965.

ORTOLANI, BENITO. *Das Kabuki Theater: Kulturgeschichte der Anfange*. Monumenta Nipponica Monographs, No. 19. Tokyo: Sophia University Press, 1964.

RICHIE, DONALD and MIYOKO WATANABE (tr.). *Six Kabuki Plays*. Hokuseido Press, 1963.

SCOTT, ADOLPHE CLARENCE. *The Kabuki Theatre of Japan*. London: George Allen and Unwin, 1955.

——— (tr.). *Kanjinchō: A Japanese Kabuki Play*. Tokyo: Hokuseido, 1953.

SEGAWA, JOKO. *Genyadana: A Japanese Kabuki Play*. Tr. by A. C. Scott. Tokyo: Hokuseido, 1953.

SENZOKU, TAKAYASU. *Kabuki*. Tokyo: Japanisch-Deutsche Gesellschaft e. V., 1964.

SHAVER, RUTH M. *Kabuki Costumes*. Tokyo: Charles E. Tuttle, 1966.

SHIOYA, SAKAE. *Chūshingura: An Exposition*. 2nd ed. Tokyo: Hokuseido Press, 1956.

SHIVELY, DONALD H. *The Love Suicide at Amijima*. Cambridge, Mass.: Harvard University Press.

TATEISHI, RYŪICHI. *Classic Dancing in Japan*. Tr. by Hideo Aoki and Tatsuo Shibata. Tokyo: Tokyo Shobo, 1969.

THORNBURY, BARBARA E. *Sukeroku's Double Identity: The Dramatic Structure of Edo Kabuki*. Michigan Papers in Japanese Studies, No. 6. Ann Arbor: University of Michigan, 1982.

TOITA, YASUJI (ed.). *Kabuki: The Popular Theatre*. Tr. by Don Kenny. New York: Walker/Weatherhill, 1970.

TSUBOUCHI, SHŌYŌ and JIRO YAMAMOTO (eds.). *History and Characteristics of Kabuki, the Japanese Classical Drama*. Tr. by Ryōzo Matsumoto. Yokohama: Yamagata Printing Co., 1960.

UNESCO, Japanese National Commission (compiler). *Theatre in Japan*. Tokyo: Tokyo Government Printing Bureau, 1963.

YOSHIDA, CHIAKI. *Kabuki: The Resplendent Japanese Theatre*. Tokyo: The Japan Times, Ltd., 1977.

PUBLICATIONS IN JAPANESE

GENERAL

ATSUMI, SEITARŌ (渥美清太郎). *Kabuki Taizen* (歌舞伎大全). Shin Taishūsha, 1943. Later revised edition entitled *Kabuki Nyūmon* (歌舞伎入門). Tōkai Shobō, 1949. A comprehensive introduction to kabuki.

DŌMOTO, MASAKI (堂本正樹). *Dentō Engeki to Gendai* (伝統演劇と現代). Sanichi Shobō, 1971. Classical theater today.

GOTŌ, KEIJI (後藤慶二). *Nihon Gekijōshi* (日本劇場史). Iwanami Shoten, 1925. A history of theaters.

HACHIMONJIYA, JISHŌ (八丈舎自笑). *Shibai Ichiran* (劇場一覧). 1795.

Each phase of kabuki production individually described—stage settings, machinery, properties, wigs, musical instruments, etc.

—— (ed.). *Yakusha Zensho* (役者全書). 5 vols. 1774. General discussion of actors, playwrights, plays, etc. Also known as *Shinkoku Yakusha Zensho* (新刻役者全書).

IIZUKA, TOMOICHIRŌ (飯塚友一郎). *Kabuki Gairon* (歌舞伎概論). Hakubunkan, 1928. The first complete and systematic study of every aspect of the production and development of kabuki.

KAWATAKE, SHIGETOSHI (河竹繁俊). *Kabuki Kōwa* (歌舞伎講話). Ōkōchi Shoten, 1947. Brief study of kabuki from many aspects.

KISHIDA, RYŪSEI (岸田劉生). *Engeki Biron* (演劇美論). Tōei Shoin, 1930. A unique introduction to kabuki by a famous painter written intuitively from an aesthetic point of view. Revised edition entitled *Kabuki Biron* (歌舞伎美論).

KŌBUNSHA, SEISHI (好文舎青氏). *Shibai Setsuyōshū* (劇場節用集). 1801. A dictionary of kabuki, based mainly on Osaka kabuki, covering all aspects.

MIMASUYA, NISŌJI (三升屋二三治). *Gakuya Suzume* (賀久屋寿々免). 5 vols. 1845. Exact description of the birth of Edo kabuki, events of the year, stage settings, performances, playwrights, actors, etc. Also known as *Kabuki Shinasadame* (歌舞伎品定).

——. *Kamikuzukago* (紙屑籠). 1843. Practices and customs of Edo theaters and episodes dealing with playwrights and actors.

——. *Mimasuya Nisōji Shibai Kakitome* (三升屋二三治戯場書留). 2 vols. 1840. Vol. I: Practices of theaters, plays, and actors. Vol. II: A short chronology of kabuki in the Edo period.

MOKUMOKU, GYOIN (黙々漁隠) (text) and UTAGAWA KUNISADA (歌川国貞) (illustrations). *Gekijō Ikkan Mushimegane* (戯場一観顕微鏡). 2 vols. 1829. Details of roles, programs, plays, theater practices, etc. Also known as *Shibai Manroku* (戯場漫録).

NAKAMURA, JŪSUKE (中村重助). *Shibai Noriaibanashi* (芝居乗合咄). 1799. A collection of episodes dealing with playwrights and actors. Description of the development of kabuki in the Edo period, events of the year, theaters, etc.

NIIZEKI, RYŌZŌ (新関良三). *Nihon Engekiron* (日本演劇論), Unebi Shobō, 1942. A study of Japanese theater, mainly kabuki.

NOGUCHI, TATSUJI (野口達二) and YOSHIDA, CHIAKI (吉田千秋). *Kabuki Saiken* (歌舞伎再見). Iwanami Shoten, 1983. Full-colored guidebook to kabuki plays.

TAKAMURA, CHIKURI (篁竹里) (text) and UTAGAWA TOYOKUNI (歌川豊国) (illustrations). *Ehon Shibai Nenjū Kagami* (絵本戯場年中鑑). 3 vols. 1803. Valuable explanations of theaters, performances, production, actors, plays, and development of kabuki.

TAMENAGA, ITCHŌ (為永一蝶). *Kabuki Kotohajime* (歌舞伎事始). 5 vols. 1762. General discussion of history, theaters, stage settings, actors, plays, music, etc.

TSUBOUCHI, SHŌYŌ (坪内逍遙). *Kabuki Gashōshiwa* (歌舞伎画証史話). Tokyodō, 1931. Changes and development of early kabuki and kabuki theaters, comparing theaters in foreign countries.

WATANABE, TAMOTSU (渡辺保). *Oyama no Unmei* (女形の運命). Kinokuniya Shoten, 1974. About Nakamura Utaemon VI.

Yakusha Meibutsu Sode-nikki (役者名物袖日記). 5 vols. 1769. History of Edo kabuki, production, actors, and playwrights. Also known as *Yakusha Meibutsu Taizen* (役者名物大全).

YAMAGUCHI, KŌICHI (山口廣一). *Nishi to Higashi no Kabuki* (西と東の歌舞伎). Engeki Shuppansha, 1980. Comparative studies between kabuki in Tokyo and in Osaka.

YAMAMOTO, KATSUTARŌ (山本勝太郎). *Kabukigeki no Keizaishiteki Kōsatsu* (歌舞伎劇の経済史的考察). Hōbunkan, 1927. Kabuki studied from financial affairs appearing in plays.

HISTORY

AKIBA, TARŌ (秋庭太郎). *Meiji no Engeki* (明治の演劇). Nakanishi Shobō, 1937. Kabuki in the Meiji era.

AKIBA, YOSHIMI (秋葉芳美) and SHUZUI, KENJI (守随憲治). *Kabuki Zusetsu* (歌舞伎図説). Manyōkaku, 1931. Detailed explanations to valuable illustrations for the study of kabuki.

DŌMOTO, KANSEI (堂本寒星). *Kamigata Engekishi* (上方演劇史). Shunyōdō, 1934. Description of the development of kabuki from the sixteenth century to the Taishō era in the Kyoto-Osaka area.

Edo Shibai Nendaiki (江戸芝居年代記). Yoneyamadō, 1928. A record of kabuki performances from 1624 to 1819.

HAINO, SHŌHEI (灰野庄平). *Dai-Nippon Engekishi* (大日本演劇史). Dai-ichi Shobō, 1932. From the birth of entertainments in the seventh century to kabuki of the Genroku era (1688-1704).

HAMAMATSU, UTAKUNI (浜松歌国) et al. *Ōkabuki Gedai Nenkan* (大歌舞伎外題年鑑). Naniwa Sōsho Kankōkai, 1927. A record of kabuki performances in Osaka from 1801 to 1853.

HARADA, KYŌICHI (原田亨一). *Kinsei Nihon Engeki no Genryū* (近世日本演劇の原流). Shibundō, 1928. Detailed discussion of Okuni kabuki and its development.

HAYASHIYA, TATSUSABURŌ (林屋辰三郎). *Kabuki no Seiritsu* (歌舞伎の成立). Suiko Shoin, 1949. Examination of the entertainments preceding kabuki and their development into kabuki in its present form.

HŌKAISHI (豊芥子). *Zoku Kabuki Nendaiki* (続歌舞伎年代記). Kokusho Kankōkai, 1907. A record of kabuki performances from 1809 to 1859.

IHARA, TOSHIRŌ (伊原敏郎). *Dangiku Igo* (団菊以後). Sagami Shobō, 1937. Kabuki after the death of Danjūrō IX and Kikugorō V.

——. *Zoku Dangiku Igo* (続団菊以後). Sagami Shobō, 1937. Sequel to *Dangiku Igo*.

—— (ed.). *Keihan Kabuki Nendaiki* (京阪歌舞伎年代記). A record of performances of kabuki in the Kyoto–Osaka area.

——. *Kinsei Nihon Engekishi* (近世日本演劇史). Waseda University Press, 1913. A history of kabuki from the Kansei era (1789-1801) to the Kaei era (1848-1854).

——. *Meiji Engekishi* (明治演劇史). Waseda University Press, 1933. A history of theater during the Meiji era.

——. *Nihon Engekishi* (日本演劇史). Waseda University Press, 1904. A history of kabuki from its beginning in the sixteenth century to the Hōreki era (1751-1764).

Kabuki Remmen Kagami (歌舞伎連綿鑑). A chronology of two theaters in Osaka from 1772 to 1833.

KAWATAKE, SHIGETOSHI (河竹繁俊). *Kabuki no Kenkyū* (歌舞伎の研究). Tokyodō, 1943. A systematic history of kabuki and general study of kabuki after the Edo period.

KODERA, YŪKICHI (小寺融吉). *Nihon Kinsei Buyōshi* (日本近世舞踊史). Yūzankaku, 1931. A history of Japanese dance.

MONDA, SŌRŌBEI (門田候兵衛) (ed.). *Yakusha Meiseichō* (役者名声牒). A history of actors from 1716 to 1770.

MORIYA, TAKESHI (守屋毅). *Kabuki no Jidai* (「かぶき」の時代), Kadokawa Shoten, 1976. A study about the formation of early kabuki.

OGASAWARA, KYŌKO (小笠原恭子). *Kabuki no Tanjō* (かぶきの誕生). Meiji Shoin, 1972. About Okuni Kabuki.

SEKINE, MOKUAN (関根黙庵). *Meiji Gekidan Gojūnenshi* (明治劇壇五十年史). Gembunsha, 1918. A history of kabuki during the Meiji era.

SEKINE, SHISEI (関根只誠) (ed.). *Gijō Nempyō* (戯場年表). A record of performances in Edo during the Edo period, including some articles on performances.

—— (ed.). *Tōto Gekijō Enkakushi* (東都劇場沿革史). Chinsho Kankōkai, 1917. Collection of materials for study of kabuki from the beginning of the Edo period to the end.

SUWA, HARUO (訪諏春雄). *Kabuki Kaika* (歌舞伎開花). Kadokawa Shoten, 1970. A collection of Edo-period paintings on Kabuki.

TAKANO, TATSUYUKI (高野辰之). *Nihon Engekishi* (日本演劇史). 3 vols. Tokyodō, 1947-49. Excellent, comprehensive study of the history of Japanese theater. Vol. I: From the entertainments in the sixth century to Nō and Kyōgen in the sixteenth century. Vol. II: Early kabuki. Vol. III: Chikamatsu Monzaemon.

TAMURA, NARIYOSHI (田村成義) (ed.). *Zokuzoku Kabuki Nendaiki* (続々歌舞伎年代記). Kokusho Kankōkai, 1922. A record of kabuki performances from 1859 to 1903.

TATEKAWA, EMBA (立川焉馬) (ed.). *Hana no Miyako Kabuki Nendaiki* (花江都歌舞伎年代記). Kabuki Shuppanbu, 1926. A record of kabuki performances from 1624 to 1804.

TOKYO DAIGAKU ENGEKISHI GAKKAI (東京大学演劇史学会) (ed.). *Engekishi Kenkyū* (演劇史研究). 3 vols. Dai-ichi Shobō, 1932. A compilation of various studies of the history of Japanese theater.

TOKYO DAIGAKU ENGEKISHI KENKYŪKAI (東京大学演劇研究会) (ed.). *Genroku Gekihen* (元禄劇篇). Kōgeisha, 1936. Studies of kabuki of the Genroku era.

WAKATSUKI, YASUJI (若月保治). *Kinsei Shoki Kokugeki no Kenkyū* (近世初期国劇の研究). Seijisha, 1944. A study of early kabuki, including *Yamato no Kami Nikki* (大和守日記), a very important diary by a daimyo of the sixteenth century recording early kabuki.

BIOGRAPHIES OF PLAYWRIGHTS

KAWATAKE, SHIGETOSHI (河竹繁俊). *Kabuki Sakusha no Kenkyū* (歌舞伎作者の研究). Kaizōsha, 1940. Biographies of important authors of kabuki and *jōruri*, their way of writing plays, and their everyday life,

KIMURA, MOKURŌ (木村黙老). *Kyōsetsu Gesakusha Kō* (京摂戯作者考). Short biographies of kabuki and *jōruri* authors in the Kyoto-Osaka area.

MIMASUYA, NISŌJI (三升屋二三治). *Sakusha Meimoku* (作者名目). 1844. Short biographies of playwrights in Edo.

———. *Sakusha Tanaoroshi* (作者店卸). 1843. Short biographies of playwrights.

BIOGRAPHIES OF ACTORS

HACHIMONJIYA, KISHŌ (八文舎其笑) and HACHIMONJIYA, ZUISHO (瑞笑). *Shinsen Kokon Yakusha Taizen* (新撰古今役者大全). 6. vols. 1750. Short biographies and critical articles on celebrated actors until 1750.

HINO, TATSUO, (ed.) (日野龍夫). *Gosei Ichikawa Danjūrō Shū* (五世市川団十郎集). Yumani Shobō, 1975. Biography of Ichikawa Danjūrō V.

HAIYŪDŌ, MUYŪ (俳優堂夢遊). *Santo Yakusha Yoyo no Tsugiki* (三都役者世々接木). 5 vols. Short biographies and critical articles on famous actors at the end of the Edo period.

KATAOKA, NIZAEMON (片岡仁左衛門). *Yakusha Shichijūnen* (役者七十年). Asahi Shimbunsha, 1976. Autobiography.

KAWARAZAKI, KUNITARŌ (河原崎国太郎). *Oyama no Michi Hitosuji* (女形ひとすじ). Yomiuri Shimbunsha, 1979. Autobiography.

NAKAMURA, GANJIRŌ (中村鴈治郎). *Yakusha Baka* (役者馬鹿). Nihon Keizai Shimbunsha, 1973. Autobiography.

NAKAMURA, KANEMON (中村翫右衛門). *Engi Jiden* (演技自伝). Miraisha, 1973. Autobiography.

NAKAMURA, KANZABURŌ (中村勘三郎). *Jiden Yappari Yakusha* (自伝・やっぱり役者). Bungei Shunjū, 1976. Autobiography.

ONOE, SHŌROKU (尾上松緑). *Yakusha no Ko wa Yakusha* (役者の子は役者), Nihon Keizai Shimbunsha, 1976. Autobiography.

SANTŌ, KYŌDEN (山東京伝). *Yakusha Ōkeizu* (役者大系図). Bunka era. Genealogy of actors in the three theaters in Edo.

PLAYS

IIZUKA, TOMOICHIRŌ (飯塚友一郎). *Kabuki Saiken* (歌舞伎細見). Daiichi Shobō, 1926. Short explanations of kabuki plays; very useful for plot outlines of each play.

NYŪGATEI, GANYŪ (入我宰我入). *Kezairoku* (戯財録). 1801. Discussion of technique and practices of writing plays.

NAKAMURA, KICHIZŌ (中村吉蔵). *Nihon Gikyoku Gikōron* (日本戯曲技巧論). Chūō Kōronsha, 1942. A study of the organization of kabuki and *jōruri* plays.

SHUZUI, KENJI (守随憲二). *Kabukigeki Gikyoku Kōzō no Kenkyū* (歌舞伎劇戯曲構造の研究). Hokuryūkan, 1947. Theoretical analysis of kabuki plays.

———. *Kinsei Gikyoku Kenkyū* (近世戯曲研究). Chūkōsha, 1927. Essential qualities and history of kabuki plays.

PROVINCIAL THEATERS

FUKUDA, SHŌEN (福田松園). *Kanazawa no Kabuki* (金沢の歌舞伎). Ōmi Shobō, 1943. A history of kabuki in Kanazawa City in northern Japan.

MATSUZAKI, SHIGERU (松崎茂). *Nihon Nōson Butai no Kenkyū* (日本農村舞台の研究). Matsuzaki Shigeru Kōgaku Hakase Rombun Kankōkai, 1971. Studies about provincial theaters in Japan.

SHIHŌDŌ, CHŪBEI (指峰堂忠兵衛) (ed.). *Biyō Shibai Kotohajime* (尾陽戯場事始). Yoneyamadō, 1927. A record of kabuki performances in Nagoya from the Keichō era (1596–1615) to the Gembun era (1736–1741).

TAKEUCHI, YOSHITARŌ (竹内芳太郎). *No no Butai* (野の舞台). Domesu Shuppan, 1981. Provincial theaters in Japan.

TSUNODA, ICHIRŌ (角田一郎) (ed.). *Nōson Butai no Sōgōteki Kenkyū* (農村舞台の綜合的研究). Ōhūsha, 1971. Comprehensive study of provincial theaters.

YOSHIDA, TERUJI (吉田暎二) (ed.). *Ise Kabuki Nendaiki* (伊勢歌舞伎年代記). Hōkabō Sho-oku, 1933. A record of kabuki performances in the Ise area from 1690 to the end of the Edo period.

DICTIONARIES

ATSUMI, SEITARŌ. *Nihon Engeki Dai-Jiten* (日本演劇大辞典). Shin Taishūsha, 1939. Mainly about kabuki.

THE TSUBOUCHI MEMORIAL THEATER MUSEUM (演劇博物館) (ed.). *Engeki Hyakka Dai-Jiten* (演劇百科大辞典). 6 vols. Heibonsha, 1961.

———. *Geinō Jiten* (芸能辞典), Tokyodō, 1942.

PRODUCTION

BANDŌ, MITSUGORŌ (坂東三津五郎). *Kabuki—Kyo to Jitsu* (歌舞伎—虚と実). Tamagawa Daigaku Shuppanbu, 1973. About kabuki performance.

BANDŌ, MITSUGORŌ (坂東三津五郎) and Morita, Toshirō (森田拾史郎). *Kumadori—Kabuki no Meikuappu* (限取り—歌舞伎のメークアップ). Haga Shoten, 1969. Kabuki makeup.

BANDŌ, YAENOSUKE (坂東八重之助), and GUNJI, MASAKATSU (郡司正勝). *Kabuki no Tate* (歌舞伎のタテ). Kodansha, 1984. Comprehensive studies on the fighting techniques in kabuki, also including practical techniques with illustrations.

FUJINAMI, YOHEI (藤浪与兵衛). *Shibai no Kodōgu—Sōi to Denshō* (芝居の小道具—創意と伝承). Nippon Hōsō Shuppan Kyōkai, 1974. Traditional and new stage properties.

KATAOKA, NIZAEMON (片岡仁左衛門). *Sugawara to Chūshingura* (菅原と忠臣蔵). Kōyō Shobō, 1981. About actors' performances of *Sugawara* and *Chūshingura*.

KIMURA, YŪNOSUKE (木村雄之助). *Keshō* (化粧), Nihon Bunka Kōryūkai, 1978. Kabuki makeup.

KOKURITSU GEKIJŌ (国立劇場) (ed.). *Kabuki no Ishō* (歌舞伎の衣裳). Fujin Gahōsha, 1974. Kabuki costumes.

MOCHIZUKI, TAINOSUKE (望月太意之助), *Kabuki Geza Ongaku* (歌舞伎下座音楽). Engeki Shuppansha, 1975. Kabuki music.

NAKAMURA, KANEMON (中村翫右衛門), *Kabuki no Engi* (歌舞伎の演技). Miraisha, 1974. About kabuki actors' performances.

ONOE, BAIKŌ (尾上梅幸). *Ume to Kiku* (梅と菊). Nihon Keizai Shimbunsha, 1979. Essays by a leading *onnagata* actor.

SANTEI, SHUMBA (三亭春馬) (text) and UTAGAWA, KUNISADA (歌川国貞) (illustrations). *Okyōgen Gakuya no Honzetsu* (御狂言楽屋本説). 3 vols. 1859. Discussion of stages, settings, machinery, properties, musical instruments, etc.

SANUKI, YURITO (佐貫百合人) (ed.). *Jūshichidai Ichimura Uzaemon Kikigaki* (十七代市村羽左衛門聞書). Nippon Hōsō Shuppan Kyokai, 1983. Recollections of performances and productions by Ichimura Uzaemon XVII.

SHIKITEI, SAMBA (式亭三馬) (text) and UTAGAWA, KUNISADA (歌川国貞) (illustrations). *Shibai Kimmō Zui* (戯場訓蒙図彙). 8 vols. 1803. Theaters, settings, costumes, events of the year, etc.

TANAKA, DENZAEMON (田中伝左衛門) and IMAO, TETSUYA (今尾哲也). *Hayashi* (囃子). Tamagawa Daigaku Shuppanbu, 1982. Kabuki music.

TŌYŌ Ongaku Gakkai (東洋音楽学会) (ed.). *Kabuki Ongaku* (歌舞伎音楽). Ongaku no Tomo Sha, 1980. Kabuki music.

INDICES

GENERAL INDEX

INDEX OF PLAYS

INDEX OF CHARACTERS